A CULINARY VOYAGE THROUGH GERMANY

FOR THE ENGLISH-LANGUAGE EDITION

Translator: Karen Green for First Edition Translations Ltd., U.K.
U.S. Adaptation: Norma Macmillan for First Edition
   Translations Ltd., U.K.
Editor: Sarah Key
Adaptation of interior typographic design: Barbara Sturman
Jacket design: Patricia Fabricant

FOR THE ORIGINAL EDITION

Project editor: Jutta Vogel
Recipe review: Centrale Marketinggesellschaft der deutschen
   Agrarwirtschaft, Bonn
Text editors: Christina Kempe, Monika Kellermann, Gertrud Köhn
Designer: Berndt Fischbeck, Reinbek
Production manager: Peter Karg-Cordes

The cooking times for meat are approximations only. Always use a
meat thermometer to ensure that meat and poultry are cooked
through, according to the information provided in the table below.
Author and publisher accept no liability with regard to use of
recipes in this book.

APPROXIMATE COOKING TIMES AT 350°F

Beef	15–35 minutes per pound, depending on cut
Pork	20–45 minutes per pound, depending on cut
Whole turkey or chicken	15–25 minutes per pound

Library of Congress Cataloging-in-Publication Data
Kulinarische Reise durch deutsche Lande.   English.
   A culinary voyage through Germany / Hannelore Kohl, general
editor ; commentary by Helmut Kohl.
      p.   cm.
   Translation of: Kulinarische Reise durch deutsche Lande.
   Includes index.
   ISBN 0-7892-0321-9
   1. Cookery, German.   I. Kohl, Hannelore.   II. Kohl, Helmut,
1930- .   III. Title.
TX721.K936 1997
641.5943—dc21   96-49951

HANNELORE KOHL, General Editor

A CULINARY VOYAGE THROUGH GERMANY

COMMENTARY BY

CHANCELLOR HELMUT KOHL

ABBEVILLE PRESS PUBLISHERS

NEW YORK LONDON PARIS

Dear Reader,

I t's exciting to think that right now you are leafing through my recipe book! Let the beautiful photographs whet your appetite for these well-loved dishes from all over Germany.

Master chef Alfons Schuhbeck has given me his valuable assistance, and my husband has also made his contribution, writing the introduction to each culinary region from his own personal viewpoint. On our many trips throughout Germany, both he and I have learned to appreciate traditional dishes as part of our culture and as one of the greatest pleasures in life.

In buying this cookbook—whether for

yourself or as a gift—you will be able to enjoy the delicious recipes and useful tips, and you will be supporting people in need of your help, because a percentage of the proceeds from each book goes toward the Hannelore Kohl Foundation.

This foundation provides long-term financial support for research into the rehabilitation of brain-damaged people. There is still a lot to be done in this field: problems relating to regeneration of the central nervous system, transplant possibilities, and psychological techniques to improve patients' quality of life—to name just a few. The foundation depends upon donations like the one it will receive when you buy this book.

With its know-how and expertise, the C.M.A. (Centrale Marketinggesellschaft der deutschen Agrarwirtschaft), guarantor for the quality and goodness of German produce, has given us continuous support in this project.

Relax over a convivial meal with friends and family and let this book provide you with ideas. Many of these delightful recipes have been handed down for generations.

Have fun cooking! Good luck and enjoy your meal!

Yours

Hannelore Kohl

5

CONTENTS

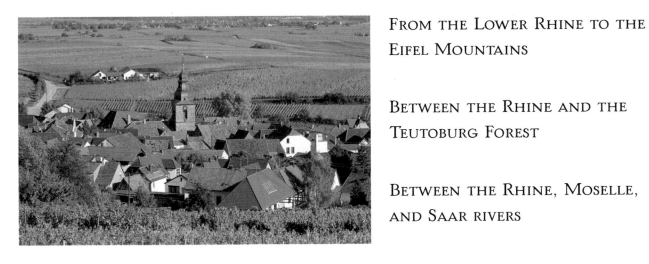

ON THE WATERFRONT

By Helmut Kohl

The tradition-rich
Hanseatic cities on the
North Sea and Baltic coasts
with their merchants' houses
and warehouses remain
Germany's gateway to the
world and the world's
gateway to Germany.
Lübeck, Rostock, Hamburg,
or Bremen, are reminders
of the importance of
the Hanseatic League cities,
as well as of the justified
pride their citizens take in
their independence and eco-
nomic success. Thomas
Mann portrayed them
lovingly but ironically.

▶

ON THE WATERFRONT

In Hamburg and Bremen, hordes of German emigrants waited for passage to North America. Who nowadays remembers that, in the seventh and eighth decades of the previous century, up to 120,000 people a year, the population of a large town, emigrated to the United States? These people took their way of life with them to the New World, and the culinary arts were no doubt part of it.

If I'm in Hamburg, I occasionally try to take a walk in the cemetery at Ohlsdorf. There I visit the grave of former mayor Weichmann, who was my mentor in the *Bundesrat* (Federal Parliament) when I was a young minister and President of Rhineland-Palatinate. I also visit the grave of a favorite author, Wolfgang Borchert. His play, *Draußen vor der Tür (The Man Outside),* greatly moved us as young people soon after the war.

Nature and culture both come into their own, here in the North, and there are beautiful contrasts. If you leave the big cities behind, you find reed-thatched houses, which look as though they have ducked down behind the sand dunes in the face of the approaching storm, windswept moorland bushes, and beaches that seem wrapped in pea-soup fog. This is how the weather may have been when Theodor Storm wrote his novella *Der Schimmelreiter (The Ghost Rider).* On days like these, I like to sit in front of an open fire with a plate of smoked sausage and a glass of aquavit or indulge in Friesian waffles with a cup of tea.

In the summer, this countryside is inviting for walks along the mudflats. The sea makes you hungry, sharpening your appetite for freshly caught and dressed crabs or red-berry compôte with vanilla sauce. Among other places on my North Sea travels, I have visited Sankt Peter-Ording, Nebel auf Amrum, Wyk auf Föhr, Förland auf Föhr, Westerland, and List auf Sylt, and I was impressed by the superb scenery.

Although fast transport and modern refrigeration and preservation techniques make it possible to eat any dish anywhere at any time, happily we are taking regional tradition and local specialties into consideration more and more. At one time, almost every farmhouse in Friesland had its own flour mill. A buckwheat crêpe is a typical snack that is worth trying, whether sweet or savory. And a visit to Hamburg would not be completely enjoyable to me without a meal of *Labskaus,* a hash made of meat, fish, and mashed potato.

We are also returning to the notion that some pleasures are seasonal, such as green cabbage with *Pinkel* (a smoked coarse sausage with oats). In the fall, those who love this traditional dish wait longingly for the first frost to touch the green cabbage, because only then does it taste right. In northern Germany, cabbage has a great agricultural and culinary tradition. The silty ground of the Dith marshes forms the largest cabbage-growing area in the whole of Germany. Every year, a girl is crowned "Cabbage Queen" in a big folk festival. A popular and true local saying is: "Cabbage may cause wind, but it also nourishes man." I like this saying, and it's very true!

A picture-postcard lighthouse at Westerhever, between Husum and Sankt Peter-Ording. It is flanked by two neat lighthouse-keepers' cottages. From its position on the bank, it is reflected in the water of the flooded meadow. Seagulls circle the slender tower and then beat toward the mudflats.

STUFFED HEAD OF CABBAGE

Gefüllter Kohlkopf

INGREDIENTS (Serves 4)

1 large head savoy or white cabbage
1¹/₂ pounds ground slab bacon or salt pork
Pinch of pickling spices
1 bay leaf
1 onion, peeled and halved
¹/₄ cup clarified butter
¹/₃ cup flour
Pinch sugar
Salt, pepper, and ground nutmeg to taste
1 cup sour cream

METHOD

1. Remove the cabbage stem. Bring plenty of salted water to a boil, add the head of cabbage, reduce heat, and and simmer for 10 minutes. Remove and leave to drain.

2. Cut the cabbage head in half and remove the heart from each half, reserving the hearts. Stuff the cavities with ground bacon or pork. Put the halves back together and tie them with kitchen string.

3. Put the cabbage in a pan with water to cover, the pickling spices, bay leaf, onion, and reserved cabbage hearts. Cook on a low heat for 1¹/₂ to 2 hours, until tender.

4. In another pan, melt the clarified butter, add the flour, and cook until brown. Using a whisk and stirring all the time, add enough stock from the cabbage to form a thick, smooth sauce. Season with the sugar, salt, pepper, and nutmeg and simmer gently for 10 minutes. Finally, stir in the sour cream.

5. Let the head of cabbage drain, remove the string, and arrange the cabbage on a serving dish. Pour the sauce over the cabbage. Serve with boiled potatoes and the cabbage hearts.

Braised Pork "Jardinière"

Schweinebraten "Gärtnerinnen Art"

INGREDIENTS (Serves 4)

4 tablespoons vegetable oil
1/2 cup herb vinegar
1/2 cup white wine
Salt, pepper, and sugar to taste
1 onion, finely chopped
1/4 teaspoon dried tarragon
Bunch each of fresh parsley, dill, and chives, minced
1 1/2 pounds boneless pork shoulder butt
1/4 cup clarified butter
4 leeks
1 tablespoon flour
1/2 cup sour cream

METHOD

1. Mix the oil, vinegar, wine, salt, pepper, and sugar to form a marinade. Stir in the onion and herbs.
2. Put the meat in a dish, pour the marinade over, and leave to marinate in the refrigerator for about 12 hours.
3. Remove the meat from the marinade and pat dry. Heat the clarified butter in a flameproof casserole and then brown the meat all over in it.
4. Deglaze the pan with a little marinade. Cover and leave to braise for about 1 1/4 hours, basting with the marinade now and again.
5. Clean the leeks thoroughly and cut in thin slices. Add to the meat 20 minutes before the end of cooking.
6. Remove the meat and keep warm. Mix the flour and sour cream together and use to thicken the juices.

Pork Cutlets with Marjoram

Schweinefilet mit Majoran

INGREDIENTS (Serves 4)

1 1/4 pounds boned pork loin
Salt and pepper to taste
German mustard
1 large onion
1 large apple
3 tablespoons clarified butter
2 tablespoons butter
1 tablespoon dried rubbed marjoram

METHOD

1. Cut the loin of pork into 1 1/4-inch thick slices. Gently flatten the slices with your hand, season with salt and pepper, and spread them with mustard.
2. Peel and slice the onion. Peel the apple, quarter, core, and cut into eighths. Melt the clarified butter in a frying pan and sweat the onion and apple in it. When everything is soft, remove and keep warm.
3. Add the butter to the pan. Brown the pork slices on both sides. Reduce the heat and cover the pan with a lid. After about 3 minutes sprinkle with the marjoram.
4. Add the onion and apple slices and cook everything together for 2 minutes longer. Arrange on a serving dish. Serve with boiled potatoes and a salad.

BRAISED PORK WITH PRUNES

Schweinebraten mit Pflaumen (photo below)

INGREDIENTS (Serves 4)

1 pound boneless pork loin roast
6 pitted prunes, soaked in brandy
1 teaspoon ground coriander
Salt and pepper to taste
Angostura bitters
1/4 cup clarified butter
1/2 cup white wine
1/2 cup meat stock
2 tablespoons crumbled Lebkuchen, gingerbread, or pumpernickel bread

METHOD

1. Make two deep incisions lengthwise in the pork loin but don't cut right through. Fill the incisions with the prunes. Roll the meat up and tie it with kitchen string. Rub with coriander, salt, pepper, and a couple of drops of Angostura bitters.

2. Heat the clarified butter in a casserole. Brown the roast on all sides over high heat. Reduce the heat. Gradually add the wine and stock. Cover and leave to braise over medium heat for about an hour.

3. Remove the pork and take off the string. Add the *Lebkuchen*, gingerbread, or pumpernickel to the pan juices. Over high heat, stir until a thick, creamy sauce forms. Season to taste. Serve with apple slices poached in white wine and boiled potatoes.

FRIESIAN SMOKED LOIN OF PORK WITH PEARS

Friesischer Kasseler Birnentopf

INGREDIENTS (Serves 4)

1 3/4 pounds boneless, smoked loin of pork (Canadian bacon)
3 onions
1 pound young carrots
1 pound potatoes
3/4 pound pears
2 tablespoons clarified butter
1 cup diced bacon
5 white peppercorns
1 bay leaf
2 cups meat stock

METHOD

1. Preheat the oven to 400°F. Cut the smoked pork loin in slices. Wash and peel the vegetables. Cut the onions in quarters and the carrots in half; slice the potatoes in 3/4-inch thick slices. Cut the pears in quarters, remove cores, and cut each quarter in two.

2. Melt the clarified butter in a roasting pan. Brown the bacon and onions in the butter. Layer the carrots, potatoes, and pears on top. Add the peppercorns and bay leaf and pour the meat stock over.

3. Place the slices of pork on top, cover with foil, and braise in the oven for about 45 minutes.

ROAST BEEF WITH HERB SAUCE

Roastbeef mit Kräutersauce

INGREDIENTS (Serves 4)

1¼ pounds boneless beef sirloin
    roast
Salt and pepper to taste
1½ tablespoons clarified butter
Bunch of mixed fresh herbs,
    e.g., parsley, chives, and basil
½ pickled gherkin
1¼ cups plain yogurt
Pinch of paprika

METHOD

1. Preheat the oven to 425°F.
Rub salt and pepper into the
sirloin and seal it in the hot
clarified butter. Transfer to
the oven and roast for about
30 minutes. Keep warm.
2. Wash the herbs, pat dry,
and mince. Cut the pickled
gherkin. Mix the yogurt with
the herbs and diced gherkin.
Season the sauce with salt,
pepper, and paprika.
3. Slice the roast beef and
serve it with the sauce.
Accompany with potato
nests filled with kohlrabi or
sautéed potatoes.

BEEF TENDERLOIN WITH BEETS

Rinderfilet mit roter Bete (photo right)

INGREDIENTS (Serves 4)

1¾ pounds beef tenderloin roast
Salt and pepper to taste
2 onions
1 carrot
1 leek
2 tablespoons juniper berries
    (optional)
¼ pound lean bacon
½ cup beef stock
2 tablespoons red currant jelly
¼ cup crème fraîche

FOR THE BEETS

3 apples
3 beets
6 tablespoons beet juice
A little cornstarch
1½ tablespoons red currant jelly
1 teaspoon sugar
1 teaspoon slivered almonds

METHOD

1. Season the beef with salt
and pepper. Peel the onions
and mince them. Peel the
carrot and wash the leek; cut
both in strips. Crush the
juniper berries in a mortar
with a pestle.
2. Dice the bacon and fry it to
render the fat. Brown the beef
quickly in the fat. Add the
onions and pour in the beef
stock.
3. Add the juniper berries,
carrot, and leek to the stock.
Simmer over medium heat for
20 to 25 minutes. Baste the
beef frequently with the stock.
4. To prepare the beets, peel
and slice the apples and beets.
Simmer both in the beet juice
over medium heat for 7 to 8
minutes. Mix the cornstarch
with a little cold water and
use it to thicken the liquid.
Stir in 1½ tablespoons red
currant jelly and sugar, and
transfer to a serving dish.
Garnish with the slivered
almonds.
5. Remove the meat from the
gravy. Strain the gravy, season
to taste, and thicken it with
red currant jelly and crème
fraîche. Slice the meat and
serve it with the gravy and
beets. Accompany with potato
croquettes.

HANNELORE KOHL

"We can buy beets all year round here. In May, the
new crop replaces the winter stock. You can now get
beets complete with the green part, which is full of
vitamins and can be prepared like spinach."

FISH SOUP WITH SHRIMP

Fischsuppe mit Krabben

INGREDIENTS (Serves 4)

³/₄ pound flounder
Juice of 1 lemon
Salt and pepper to taste
1 onion
2 tablespoons unsalted butter
2 leeks
2 carrots
1¹/₂ cups dry white wine
¹/₂ cup cooked, peeled small
  shrimp

METHOD

1. Dice the fish fillet and sprinkle with lemon juice. Season with salt, cover, and refrigerate.
2. Peel and mince the onion. Melt the butter in a pan and soften the onion in the butter.
3. Wash the leeks and slice thinly. Peel the carrots and cut in matchsticks.
4. Add the vegetables to the onion and sweat briefly. Deglaze with the wine and add 2 cups water. Season with salt and pepper. Leave to simmer over low heat for 20 minutes.
5. Add the diced fish to the stock and simmer for 10 minutes over low heat. Add the shrimp and just heat them through, until they lose their translucence.

PANFRIED SOLE WITH BACON

Gebratene Scholle mit Speck

INGREDIENTS (Serves 4)

4 sole or flounder, cleaned
Flour
2 tablespoons unsalted butter
1 cup diced Canadian bacon
Salt and pepper to taste
1 tablespoon lemon juice

METHOD

1. Wash the fish thoroughly in cold running water, pat dry, and coat in flour.
2. Melt the butter in a pan and fry the bacon for 2 to 3 minutes. Add the fish and fry until the bacon is crisp and brown, turning the fish once.
3. Remove the fish, season with salt and pepper, and arrange on plates. Sprinkle with lemon juice and with the cooked bacon.

HANNELORE KOHL

"Add a fine julienne of orange peel to the pan at the end of cooking. Then sprinkle the fish with orange juice instead of lemon juice."

PEARS, BEANS, AND BACON

Birnen, Bohnen und Speck (photo above)

INGREDIENTS (Serves 4)

1 pound slab bacon
2 cups water
1¹/₂ pounds green beans
Sprigs of fresh savory
1 pound small pears
Salt and pepper to taste
2 tablespoons chopped fresh
  parsley

METHOD

1. Cook the bacon in the water in a covered pan over low heat for about 50 minutes until tender.
2. Meanwhile, wash the beans; if necessary, remove any strings and cut the beans in half. After 20 minutes, add the beans to the bacon with the savory.
3. Wash the pears, halve, and core. Add to the beans about 20 minutes before the end of cooking time.
4. Remove the bacon and slice it. Season the beans to taste with salt and pepper, sprinkle with parsley, and arrange on plates with the pears and bacon.

MEAT PATTIES

Frikadellen

INGREDIENTS (Serves 4)

2 rolls
1/2 pound ground round
1/4 pound ground sirloin
1/4 pound ground pork
1 onion
1 egg
Minced fresh parsley
Salt and pepper to taste
2 tablespoons clarified butter
1 tomato

METHOD

1. Soak the rolls in water to soften them. Squeeze out the excess water and mix the bread with the ground meats.
2. Peel and mince the onion. Add to the meat mixture with the egg and parsley. Season with salt and pepper.
3. Dampen your hands and form 8 to 10 balls of equal size from the meat mixture. Press gently to flatten. Slowly fry the patties in the hot clarified butter over medium heat until crisp.
4. Slice the tomato, add to the pan shortly before serving, and let it soften slightly.

BRAISED BEEF, BREMEN-STYLE

Bremer Rinderbraten vom falschen Filet

INGREDIENTS (Serves 4)

2 pounds boneless beef rump
    roast
Salt and pepper to taste
3 tablespoons clarified butter
1 carrot
1/2 fennel bulb
1 Spanish onion
1 leek
1/2 cup dry red wine
2 cups meat stock
2 bay leaves
3 to 4 cloves
5 juniper berries (optional)

METHOD

1. Preheat the oven to 450°F.
Rub the meat with salt and
pepper. Heat the clarified
butter in a roasting pan
until foaming. On the stovetop brown the meat on
all sides.
2. Peel or trim the carrot,
fennel, onion, and leek;
chop the vegetables
coarsely. Add to the pan
and brown for 2 minutes.
3. Deglaze with the wine
and add the stock, bay
leaves, and spices. Cover
the pan and braise in the
oven for 1½ hours.
4. Remove the meat, wrap it
in foil, and keep warm.
Strain the meat juices;
reserve the vegetables.
Bring the juices to a boil,
season with salt and pepper,
and serve with the roast
and vegetables.

MARINATED BEEF SLICES

Saure Ochsenfleischschnitten

INGREDIENTS (Serves 6)

2 teaspoons salt
1 teaspoon pepper
1 teaspoon onion powder
1/2 teaspoon grated nutmeg
3½ pounds ox or beef flank
    steak
1 cup vinegar
1 bay leaf
3 juniper berries, crushed
    (optional)
1 teaspoon black peppercorns
Clarified butter
Unsalted butter

METHOD

1. Rub the salt, pepper, onion
powder, and nutmeg into the
beef. Roll up the meat and
secure it with kitchen string.
2. Using a saucepan into
which the meat fits snugly,
bring some water to a boil
and add the meat. Cover and
simmer for 2½ hours on
low heat.
3. Drain off the stock and
reduce to 1 cup. Add the
vinegar, bay leaf, crushed
juniper berries, and
peppercorns, and bring to a
boil. Pour the stock over the
meat to cover. Cover and
leave to marinate in the
refrigerator for 8 to 14 days.
4. Cut the meat into 3/4-inch
thick slices and fry until
golden brown on both sides in
hot clarified butter. Finally,
allow a little butter to melt
over the meat. Serve with
béchamel potatoes and beets.

SHOULDER OF LAMB WITH ROSEMARY

Lammkeule mit Rosmarin

INGREDIENTS (Serves 4)

2 garlic cloves

2 tomatoes

2 carrots

1/4 fennel bulb

1 rosemary sprig

Salt and pepper to taste

1 shoulder of lamb, weighing about 7 pounds

3 tablespoons clarified butter

1/2 cup red wine

1 cup meat stock

2 tablespoons ice-cold butter, cubed

3 tablespoons chopped fresh herbs, e.g., chervil, basil, and parsley

METHOD

1. Preheat the oven to 400°F. Peel the garlic cloves and cut them in quarters. Quarter the tomatoes also. Peel the carrots and trim the fennel; dice them coarsely. Chop the rosemary needles.

2. Rub salt, pepper, and rosemary into the lamb. Heat the clarified butter in a roasting pan and seal the meat all over on the stovetop. Add the garlic, tomatoes, carrots, and fennel and brown them briefly with the meat.

3. Roast the meat for about 2 hours, turning several times. When cooked, remove and keep warm.

4. Skim excess fat from the meat juices, deglaze with the red wine, add the meat stock, and leave to reduce. Season to taste with salt and pepper. Remove from the heat and whisk in the butter a cube at a time. Season with the herbs. Serve with steamed beans and tomatoes.

SADDLE OF LAMB WITH CREAM SAUCE

Heidschnuckenrücken in Sahne

INGREDIENTS (Serves 4)

2 pounds saddle of lamb
  (double loin roast)
Salt to taste
$1/2$ cup butter
Sprigs of fresh rosemary and
  thyme
1 bay leaf
1 clove
Juniper berries (optional)
1 cup meat stock
$1/2$ cup red wine
2 tablespoons heavy cream
Pinch of sugar

METHOD

1. Preheat the oven to 425°F. Remove the fat from the saddle of lamb and rub the meat with salt. Melt the butter in a roasting pan and brown the meat on all sides on the stovetop.

2. Meanwhile, chop the herbs. Add to the meat with the bay leaf, clove, and a few juniper berries. Pour in the meat stock. Roast the meat for about 1 hour. Baste it often with the juices.

3. Remove the meat and keep it warm on a pre-warmed serving platter. To make the sauce, deglaze the roasting juices with red wine, strain, thicken with the cream, and season with sugar. Serve the sauce in a sauceboat, and accompany with red cabbage and potato dumplings.

LEG OF LAMB WITH ROSEMARY

Heidschnuckenkeule mit Rosmarin

INGREDIENTS (Serves 6)

4 garlic cloves
Sprigs of fresh rosemary
Juice of 1 lemon
Pepper to taste
5 pounds leg of lamb
1 onion
1 slice of bulb fennel
1 small carrot
1 tablespoon oil
2 bunches of fresh parsley
$1^1/4$ cups breadcrumbs
Salt to taste

METHOD

1. Peel the garlic cloves and mince the rosemary. Crush 1 garlic clove and mix it with the lemon juice, some of the rosemary, and pepper. Spike the leg of lamb with slivers of the remaining cloves of garlic and brush with the lemon mixture. Leave to marinate overnight.

2. Preheat the oven to 400°F. Peel the onion and carrot and trim the fennel; dice them. Heat the oil in a roasting pan, add the leg of lamb, and roast for $1^1/4$ to $1^1/2$ hours. Baste the roast frequently with the juices.

3. Mince the parsley and mix with the remaining rosemary, the breadcrumbs, and salt. Coat the leg of lamb with this mixture and roast for 5 minutes longer. Serve with beans and potatoes baked in bouillon.

STUFFED LAMB SHANKS

Gefüllte Heidschnuckenhaxen

INGREDIENTS (Serves 4)

*4 lamb shanks, weighing about
 ³/₄ pound each*

Salt and pepper to taste

1 garlic clove

¹/₄ cup vegetable oil

1 carrot

¹/₄ fennel bulb

2 onions

¹/₂ leek

2¹/₂ tablespoons tomato paste

1 quart lamb stock

1 cup red wine

8 to 10 juniper berries (optional)

1 teaspoon chopped fresh thyme

1 bay leaf

1 clove

Peppercorns

1 head of savoy cabbage

Pork fat (caul)

¹/₃ cup diced cooked ham

*³/₄ pound sausage, casing
 removed*

¹/₄ cup chopped mixed fresh herbs

Chopped fresh chervil and chives

METHOD

1. Preheat the oven to 375°F. Season the lamb shanks with salt and pepper. Peel the garlic, crush it, and rub it into the lamb.

2. Heat the oil in a roasting pan and seal the shanks all over on the stovetop. Place in oven and roast for 15 minutes.

3. Peel or trim the carrot, fennel, onions, and leek and chop them coarsely. Add the vegetables to the lamb.

4. Stir in the tomato paste and add the lamb stock and red wine. Add the spices and cook the lamb for an hour.

5. Meanwhile, remove the cabbage stem and separate the leaves. Wash 12 to 16 pale green leaves and cut out the core. Blanch the leaves in boiling salted water for about 1 minute. Refresh in ice water and pat dry.

6. Soak the pork fat. After an hour take the lamb shanks out of the oven and leave to cool. Press the cooking liquid through a sieve, and set the gravy aside. Remove the meat from the lamb bones and shorten the bones.

7. Mix together the ham, sausage meat and chopped herbs. Spread a little of the stuffing over the cabbage leaves. Stuff the lamb shanks with the remaining stuffing and reshape them. Wrap the cabbage leaves around the lamb shanks. Drain the pork fat and cut it into four equal pieces. Wrap the caul around the lamb shanks.

8. Insert the shortened bones into the lamb shanks the wrong way around and wrap the ends in foil. Put the lamb in the roasting pan again and roast for about 20 to 25 minutes in the hot oven. Baste with the gravy a few times.

9. Remove the lamb shanks from the oven. Remove the foil. Serve with the gravy and glazed zucchini, carrots, shallots, and baby turnips, as well as mashed potato.

WESERBERGLAND MEAT STEW

Weserbergländischer Fleischtopf (photo below)

INGREDIENTS (Serves 4–6)

1¹/₄ *pounds boned pork shoulder*
1¹/₄ *pounds beef for stew (chuck)*
¹/₂ *pound Canadian bacon*
1 to 2 pig's feet (get your butcher
to chop them in pieces)
3 tablespoons pork drippings
Bunch of fresh parsley, chopped
Flour

FOR THE MARINADE
2 onions
¹/₂ *fennel bulb*
2 garlic cloves
2 bay leaves
4 sprigs of fresh thyme
3 cups dry white wine
Salt, pepper, and ground nutmeg
to taste

FOR THE VEGETABLES
³/₄ *pound onions*
1 pound leeks
2 carrots
2 pounds potatoes
Salt and pepper to taste

METHOD

1. A day in advance, cut the meat in bite-size pieces and the bacon in small dice. Put in a bowl with the chopped pig's feet. Peel or trim the vegetables for the marinade and cut them in small pieces. Add to the meat with the seasonings and wine.
2. The next day, preheat the oven to 350°F. Peel or trim the vegetables and slice them. Grease a *Schlemmertopf* (clay cooking pot) with the drippings. Remove the meat from the marinade and layer it alternately with the vegetables and bacon, in the pot. Season each layer with salt and pepper and sprinkle with parsley.
3. Pour on the marinade until everything is covered. Cover with the lid. Make a thick flour-and-water paste and use to seal the lid. Cook the meat stew for about 2¹/₂ hours. Serve straight from the pot.

CABBAGE PUDDING

Kohlpudding

INGREDIENTS (Serves 4)

1 head of savoy or white cabbage
2 rolls
1 onion
¹/₂ *pound ground round*
¹/₂ *pound ground sirloin*
¹/₂ *pound ground pork*
2 eggs
Salt and pepper to taste
Paprika to taste
1 tablespoon butter

METHOD

1. Wash the cabbage, remove the leaves, and blanch them for 2 to 3 minutes in boiling salted water. Cut out the core.
2. Soften the rolls in water and then squeeze them thoroughly. Peel and chop the onion. Mix the ground meats with the bread, eggs, onion, salt, pepper, and paprika, to form a stuffing.
3. Grease a pudding basin or other deep heatproof bowl or mold with the butter. Layer the cabbage leaves alternately with the meat mixture in the basin, pressing down firmly. Cover the pudding basin and steam for about 1¹/₂ hours in a pan of boiling water.

Meat, Fish, and Mashed Potato Hash

Labskaus

INGREDIENTS (Serves 4–6)

1 to 1¹/₄ pounds corned beef
¹/₂ small bay leaf
1 clove
3 peppercorns
¹/₃ to ²/₃ cup pickled beets
1 Matjes herring
1 pound onions
1 to 2 pickled gherkins
6 tablespoons pork drippings
3¹/₂ cups hot mashed potatoes
5 to 10 tablespoons liquid
   from the pickled gherkins
   or meat stock
¹/₂ garlic clove, minced
Salt to taste

METHOD

1. Add the meat, bay leaf, and spices to 2 cups boiling water, bring back to a boil, and cook over low heat until done.
2. Remove the meat and put it through a meat grinder or food processor with the drained beets, herring, peeled onions, and pickled gherkins.
3. Melt the pork drippings and fry the mixture in it for 5 minutes. Moisten with some of the meat stock and cook until well absorbed. Stir in the mashed potato. Season to taste with salt, pickling liquid or stock, and garlic.
4. Serve *Labskaus* with your choice of fried eggs, beets, pickled gherkins, and pickled herrings.

DUCK WITH SAVOY CABBAGE

Ente in Wirsing

INGREDIENTS (Serves 4)

*1 head of savoy cabbage,
   weighing about 2 pounds*
1 onion
3 tablespoons clarified butter
1 cup meat stock
1/2 cup white wine
2 duck legs
2 duck breast halves
Salt and pepper to taste

METHOD

1. Wash the savoy cabbage, cut in quarters, remove the stem, and cut the quartered cabbage in strips.
2. Peel and dice the onion, then fry until translucent in 1 tablespoon of the clarified butter. Add the savoy cabbage, pour in the stock and wine, cover, and leave to simmer for 30 minutes.
3. Heat the remaining clarified butter in a pan and seal the duck legs and breasts on all sides. Season with salt and pepper, cover, and leave to fry gently over low heat (duck breasts take 20 minutes, legs 30 minutes).
4. Add the duck legs and breasts to the cabbage and cook together for 5 minutes. To serve, make a bed of cabbage and arrange the duck portions on top of the cabbage. Serve with boiled potatoes.

EEL WITH DILL-CREAM SAUCE

Plöner See-Aal

INGREDIENTS (Serves 4)

*21/2 pounds eel, middle section,
   cleaned*
1 onion
2 cups water
1/2 cup white wine
2 bay leaves
2 bunches of fresh dill
1/2 cup butter
1 to 2 tablespoons flour
Salt and pepper to taste
1 cup cream
2 egg yolks

METHOD

1. Wash the skinned eel and cut it in portions. Peel and quarter the onion. Put the eel, onion, water, white wine, bay leaves, salt, and dill (reserve a few sprigs) in a pan, bring to a boil, and cook over low heat for 25 minutes or until done.
2. Remove the eel, cover, and keep warm. Strain the cooking liquid and reserve.
3. Melt half of the butter in a saucepan, stir in the flour to form a roux and cook for 2 minutes. Stirring constantly, pour the cooking liquid little by little into the roux. Cook until it forms a thick, smooth sauce.
4. Enrich the sauce with a mixture of the cream and egg yolks and season to taste with salt and pepper. Stir in the remaining butter. Mince the remaining dill and stir into the sauce. Serve the sauce with the eel, accompanied by cucumber salad and parsley potatoes.

CHRISTMAS HAM

Weihnachtsschinken (photo below)

INGREDIENTS (Serves 8–10)

7 *pounds lightly smoked,*
  uncooked ham, fat and rind
  removed
2 *bay leaves*
15 *white peppercorns*
1 *egg white*
2 *tablespoons German mustard*
1 *tablespoon sugar*
1/2 cup breadcrumbs
8 *to 10 apples, baked*
16 *to 20 pitted prunes, stewed in*
  red wine

METHOD

1. Put the ham in a pan and just cover with water; bring to a boil. Add the bay leaves and peppercorns and boil for about 2½ hours.
2. Remove the ham from the stock and drain. Mix together the egg white, mustard, and sugar and brush onto the ham. Coat thickly with the bread-crumbs.
3. Preheat the oven to 350 to 375°F. Bake the ham for about 30 minutes until golden brown.
4. Arrange on a serving dish with baked apples and prunes stewed in red wine. Serve with potato salad and a crisp lettuce and celery salad.

GREEN CABBAGE PLATTER

Grünkohlplatte

INGREDIENTS (Serves 4)

5½ pounds head of green
  cabbage
2 *onions*
6 *tablespoons pork drippings*
2 *bay leaves*
5 *allspice berries*
1 *tablespoon sugar*
5 *ounces slab bacon*
1 *pound smoked pork picnic*
  shoulder (smoked butt or
  tenderloin)
2 *to 3 cups stock*
1/4 cup rolled oats
1 *tablespoon German mustard*
4 *Kochwürste sausages, each*
  weighing 3 ounces
4 *Pinkel sausages, each weighing*
  3 ounces
Salt and pepper to taste

METHOD

1. Wash the cabbage and remove the stem.
2. Blanch the leaves in boiling salted water for about 2 minutes. Refresh them and cut in small pieces. Peel and slice the onions. Melt the drippings and fry the onions, bay leaves, allspice berries, and sugar until the onions are translucent.
3. Add the green cabbage, bacon, and smoked pork. Pour the stock over and simmer for 45 minutes.
4. Add the oats, mustard, and sausages and cook, covered, for 20 minutes longer. Season with salt and pepper. Serve with small sautéed potatoes.

NOTE

Kochwürste sausages contain precooked meat and some-times liver or blood. *Pinkel* contain bacon, onion, and oats and are eaten with cabbage in winter.

DRIED BEANS WITH SAUSAGE

Updrögt-Bohnen

INGREDIENTS (Serves 4)

*1 pound very fresh green beans,
   as free of string as possible*
1¹/₂ pounds slab bacon
1 onion
Salt and pepper to taste
1 pound potatoes
2 lean pork or beef link sausages

METHOD

1. Thread the beans onto a
thin string. Hang up in a
suitable place and leave to
dry for 1 to 2 weeks. Store the
dried beans in cheesecloth
bags.
2. Wash the dried beans well,
break in pieces, and soak
overnight in water.

3. Pour off the soaking liquid,
put the beans in a pan with
fresh cold water, bring to a
boil and cook over medium
heat for about 30 minutes.
Drain off the water.
4. Cut the bacon in slices, peel
and mince the onion. Simmer
the beans with the bacon and
onion in 2 cups water, for
about 1¹/₂ hours. Season to
taste with salt and pepper.
5. Peel and dice the potatoes.
Cook the potatoes and
sausages with the beans for
the last 30 minutes.

HARZ POTATO SALAD

Harzer Kartoffelsalat

INGREDIENTS (Serves 4)

2 pounds potatoes
1 cup yogurt-based mayonnaise
1 teaspoon German mustard
2 tablespoons milk
*2 tablespoons liquid from pickled
   gherkins*
Salt and pepper to taste
4 hard-boiled eggs
2 onions
4 pickled gherkins
³/₄ pound Jagdwurst (*smoked
   ham sausage*)
*1 tablespoon chopped fresh
   parsley*

METHOD

1. Boil the potatoes, refresh
in cold water, peel, and
leave to cool completely.
2. Mix the mayonnaise with
the mustard, milk, and
pickling liquid.
3. Shell the eggs and cut in
wedges. Slice the potatoes.
Peel the onions and dice;
dice the gherkins too. Cut
the sausage in strips.
4. Mix all the prepared
ingredients with the
mayonnaise and leave for
the flavors to develop and
combine.
5. Before serving, stir
2 tablespoons hot water
into the salad and sprinkle
with parsley.

FRUIT LOAF

Bremer Klaben (photo below)

INGREDIENTS (Makes 1 loaf)

5 cups golden raisins
1/2 cup diced candied lemon peel
1/2 cup diced candied orange
    peel
1/2 cup chopped almonds
2 tablespoons rum
1 1/4 cups lukewarm milk
4 3/4 cakes (0.6 ounce each)
    fresh compressed yeast or
    4 3/4 envelopes active dry yeast
6 1/2 tablespoons sugar
8 cups all-purpose flour
1 3/4 cups unsalted butter, at
    room temperature
1/2 teaspoon salt
Grated zest and juice of 1 lemon
1/2 teaspoon ground cardamom
3/4 cup confectioners' sugar
    for dusting

METHOD

1. Wash the raisins and leave to drain well. Mix the raisins, diced candied peel, and almonds in a small bowl, sprinkle with rum, and leave to soak overnight.
2. Mix together the milk, yeast, 1 teaspoon sugar, and 2 cups flour to form a dough. Leave to proof in a warm place for about 30 minutes.
3. Mix the dough with the remaining sugar and flour, then work in the butter, salt, lemon zest and juice, and cardamom. Knead to form a smooth dough. Work the rum-flavored fruits into the dough.
4. Place the dough in a well-buttered loaf pan. Cover and leave to rise in a warm place for an hour.
5. Preheat the oven to 350°F and bake for about an hour on the lowest shelf. Dust the *Bremer Klaben* with confectioners' sugar.

BUTTER CAKE

Butterkuchen

INGREDIENTS (Makes 1 cake)

FOR THE DOUGH

4 cups all-purpose flour
2 1/2 cakes (0.6 ounce each)
    fresh compressed yeast or
    2 1/2 envelopes active dry yeast
5 tablespoons sugar
1 cup lukewarm milk
1/2 cup butter
3/4 teaspoon salt
1 egg
Grated zest of 1 lemon
2/3 cup raisins

FOR THE TOPPING

14 tablespoons butter
1/2 cup slivered almonds
1 teaspoon ground cinnamon
2 cups sugar

METHOD

1. Sift the flour into a large bowl and make a well in the center. Crumble the yeast, dissolve with a little sugar in half of the milk, and pour into the well. Mix with a little flour. Cover and leave in a warm place to proof.
2. In a small saucepan melt the butter in the remaining milk; leave to cool a little. Add to the yeast mixture with the salt, egg, lemon zest, remaining sugar, and raisins. Knead to form a smooth dough. Leave to rise in a warm place.
3. Preheat the oven to 400°F. Using a little flour, roll out the dough to 3/4 inch thick, place on a buttered baking sheet, and form a border. Using fingertips, make little indentations in the dough.
4. For the topping, dot the butter over the surface of the dough. Scatter the slivered almonds on top and sprinkle liberally with a mixture of cinnamon and sugar. Bake for 20 to 30 minutes until golden brown.

STEAMED FRUIT PUDDING

Großer Hans (photo below)

INGREDIENTS (Serves 4)

9 tablespoons butter
6 egg yolks
1 1/2 cups milk
4 3/4 cups all-purpose flour
1 teaspoon baking powder
Grated zest of 1 lemon
6 egg whites
1/2 cup prunes
2/3 cup raisins
6 tablespoons unsalted butter,
  melted
6 tablespoons sugar

METHOD

1. In a large bowl beat the butter, egg yolks, and milk together. In a small bowl mix the flour with the baking powder and grated lemon zest. Mix with the egg and milk mixture until smooth.
2. In a medium bowl beat the egg whites until stiff and fold into the batter. Place a dampened cotton cloth or kitchen towel on the table. Cut the prunes in small pieces and pile them on top of the cloth with the raisins. Spread the batter over the fruit and tie the cloth up in a knot.
3. Bring some water to a boil in a large, deep pot. Using a slotted spoon, position the pudding so water comes halfway up it. Cook the pudding in the boiling water for about 2 hours, until done.
4. Remove the pudding and let the steam evaporate. Using a wire cheese cutter, cut it into slices. Arrange each slice of pudding on a plate, dot with melted butter, and sprinkle with sugar. Serve with fruit compôte.

DOUGHNUTS WITH APPLES

Prilleken mit Äpfeln

INGREDIENTS

FOR THE DOUGHNUTS

4 cups all-purpose flour
2 cakes (0.6 ounce each)
  fresh compressed yeast or
  2 envelopes active dry yeast
1/2 cup sugar
1 cup lukewarm milk
6 tablespoons unsalted butter, at
  room temperature
Pinch of salt
Grated zest of 1 lemon
Clarified butter
Sugar to dredge doughnuts

FOR THE APPLE SLICES

2 pounds firm, tart apples
1 cup water
1 cup dry white wine
3/4 cup sugar
1 cinnamon stick
Grated zest from 1/2 lemon

METHOD

1. Sift the flour into a large bowl and make a well in the center. Crumble the yeast and mix it with 2 teaspoons sugar and 2 teaspoons lukewarm milk. Pour into the well, mix with a little of the flour, cover, and leave to proof in a warm place.
2. When the yeast mixture is frothy, add the butter, remaining milk and sugar, salt, and lemon zest. Knead to form a smooth dough, incorporating all the flour.
3. Make little balls out of the dough, flatten them slightly, and leave to rise on a floured surface.
4. Heat a pan of clarified butter until it is hot enough so that bubbles form when a wooden spoon handle is dipped in. Fry the balls of dough in the butter until golden brown. Drain on paper towels and dredge immediately with lots of sugar.
5. Peel the apples, core, and cut in wedges. Poach in the water, wine, sugar, cinnamon, and lemon zest. The apples should be tender but not mushy. Serve lukewarm with the hot doughnuts.

GUELPH PUDDING

Welfenpudding

INGREDIENTS (Serves 4–6)

2 cups milk
¹/₂ cup plus 2 tablespoons sugar
1 teaspoon vanilla-flavored sugar
Pinch of salt
6 tablespoons cornstarch
4 eggs, separated
1 tablespoon lemon juice
1 cup white wine

METHOD

1. Reserve about 2 to 3 tablespoons milk; bring the rest to a boil in a medium saucepan with 3 tablespoons sugar, the vanilla sugar, and salt.
2. Mix 5 tablespoons cornstarch with the remaining milk and add to the hot milk. Bring to a boil, stirring all the time, and then remove from the heat. In a medium bowl beat the egg whites until stiff and fold into mixture. Spoon the custard into molds and refrigerate.
3. To make a sabayon sauce, in a medium pan thoroughly mix the egg yolks, remaining sugar, lemon juice, wine, and remaining cornstarch mixed with a little cold water.
4. Heat the sauce, stirring all the time, until it foams and rises up the saucepan. Remove the pan from the heat and whisk the sauce for 3 to 4 minutes until cool.
5. Place spoonfuls of the sauce on the cold dessert. Serve immediately.

RED-BERRY COMPÔTE

Rote Grütze

INGREDIENTS (Serves 4)

1 cup freshly squeezed orange juice
³/₄ cup sugar
¹/₂ pound each strawberries, raspberries, red currants, and cherries, stems and pits removed
2 tablespoons cornstarch

METHOD

1. Put the orange juice and the sugar into a medium saucepan with two-thirds of the fruit and cook over low heat until the juices run.
2. Line a strainer with damp cheesecloth and pour in the stewed fruit. Allow the juice to drip through the cloth into a saucepan.
3. Mix the cornstarch with a little cold water, stir into the juice, and bring to a boil. Add the remaining fruit and cook briefly; refrigerate. Serve with soft whipped cream or custard sauce.

Hot Morning Rolls

Heißwecken

INGREDIENTS

4 cups all-purpose flour
2 cakes (0.6 ounce each) fresh
    compressed yeast or 2 enve-
    lopes active dry yeast
Grated zest of 1 lemon
³/₄ cup sugar
Pinch of salt
1 cup unsalted butter, melted
3 eggs
1 cup raisins
1 egg yolk

TO SERVE
¹/₂ cup unsalted butter
Pinch of ground cinnamon or
    ground cloves
2 cups milk, heated

METHOD

1. Sift the flour into a large bowl and make a well in the center. Cream the yeast in a little lukewarm water and pour into the well. Add the lemon zest, sugar, salt, 1 cup butter, and eggs and knead to form a smooth dough. Leave the dough to rise until it has doubled in size.

2. Preheat the oven to 400°F. Rinse the raisins and knead them into the dough. Form the dough into a sausage and cut off even-sized pieces of dough. Shape the pieces into balls. Place on a greased baking sheet and leave in a warm place until risen by about two-thirds.

3. Mix together the egg yolk and 1 teaspoon water and brush this on the tops of the rolls. Bake for 15 minutes until golden brown.

4. To serve, place the rolls in a deep plate. Cut off the tops, put a generous pat of butter on the cut surface, sprinkle with cinnamon or cloves, and replace the lid. Pour hot milk over the rolls.

GERMAN BAKERS: WORLD CHAMPIONS FOR QUALITY AND CHOICE

HANNELORE KOHL:
My husband and I are enthusiastic hikers. Hiking and sandwiches go together so well, don't they?

ALFONS SCHUHBECK:
Yes, because after an exhausting hike the body primarily needs the carbohydrates from starch, and it can obtain these most easily from bread and rolls. If you were to eat a huge pork roast during your hike, you wouldn't feel like walking anymore; instead, you'd want a bench to sit down on to have forty winks! Big meals tend to make people lethargic, while bread, on the other hand, makes them bright and lively. Whenever possible, you should eat a couple of raw carrots or a piece of radish with bread.

HANNELORE KOHL:
I know that many officials at German embassies abroad ask visitors to bring them German bread. Could our bakers ask for a better compliment?

ALFONS SCHUHBECK:
Indeed, no other country has such a wide choice of breads—over 300 types—in addition to another 1,200 varieties of cake and pastries. Germany is the world champion, and consumers value the choice. Statistically, each citizen of the Republic consumes about 180 pounds of bread and rolls each year!

From little bread rolls to a splendid loaf, master bakers Klaus-Peter Dung (left) and Joachim Becker have complete mastery of their craft.

HANNELORE KOHL:
On a visit to a bakery I learned that the *Brotprüfer- und Beratungsdienst* (Bread Inspection and Advisory Service) is what German bakeries rely upon for voluntary self-regulation.

These experienced master bakers inspect, among other things, the crust, crumb texture, taste, smell, and acidity level of unmarked bread samples.

ALFONS SCHUHBECK:
The inspection standards are strict, but superior products are rewarded with silver and gold medals. These awards, which bakers proudly hang in their shops, provide customers with clear proof of the highest quality.

HANNELORE KOHL:
I'm away from home a lot, so bread is often left for a couple of days. A tip from my own personal experience is that dark bread containing rye with a hard crust stays fresh much longer than soft white bread. Frequently I reserve half a loaf, cut it into slices right away, and freeze it. They thaw out in the toaster in no time.

By Helmut Kohl

Few cities in our country mirror the ups and downs of German history as much as Berlin does. I have often looked out from the Reichstag building toward the Berlin Wall and the East of the city, where the French cathedral is a reminder of an age of tolerance and openness. It was here that religious refugees such as the Huguenots made a new home.

One of the most important German architects, Karl Friedrich Schinkel, adorned the city with unmistakable highlights: the New Watchtower, the Playhouse, and the Old Museum.

▶

Despite this splendor, the citizens of Berlin are very modest folk as are the people of Brandenburg. Since time immemorial, they have made the best of a rather barren soil through hard work and imagination.

Many recipes from the area around Berlin are a reminder that Frederick II, or "Old Fritz" as he is still fondly called today, once gently set in motion the triumphal march of the potato. Potato soup, potato pancakes, and potato salad with meat balls are still part of traditional Berlin cuisine today. There is also *Currywurst,* a curried sausage, which tastes particularly good and is best eaten at one of the numerous snack bars in the city. Frikadellen (meat balls or patties) are popular under other names throughout Germany today, but they were supposedly served in 1903 for the first time in a Berlin bar.

The writer Theodor Fontane, born in Neuruppin, and an enthusiast for good food, immortalized the chatter of voices and the colorful array of fruit and vegetables at the Brandenburg markets. The plump, perfumed, golden-yellow pears enjoyed by Herr von Ribbeck have made generations of German schoolchildren's mouths water in literature classes. Havelland has today lost none of its charm and importance as a luxuriant fruit and vegetable garden. "Berlin-style Liver" is nothing without its classic accompaniments of onion rings and apple slices.

Fruit and vegetable growers are aware of their dependence on nature. The farmers from the Spree area proved early on how man can help himself with a little inventiveness. As early as the seventeenth century farmers started pickling their plentiful cucumber harvests, thus preserving them for the winter. Spree gherkins are still a specialty today. Sold in local markets as a snack, they are eaten on the spot with the fingers.

Mecklenburg-Upper Pomerania is the most sparsely populated Federal state. Observers are fascinated by the sweep of the landscape. If you want to vacation on a farm here, you can still find old-fashioned farmhouses secluded in the middle of fields. It is a country with innumerable lakes, each a little gem in itself. The untouched countryside provides space for bird preserves.

Fish lovers can really enjoy themselves on the Baltic coast. Cod, herring, mackerel, plaice, sea eel, and turbot can be bought straight from the trawler and are served up fresh from the sea at coastal guesthouses. Smoked fish, especially smoked eel, is a specialty of Mecklenburg. More unusual is the garfish or needlefish, which stands out because of its green fins.

Even today, many fields and farmhouses in the Spree River area can only be reached by punt.

PORK GOULASH WITH BEER AND MUSTARD-PICKLED GHERKINS

Schweinegulasch mit Bier und Senfgurke

INGREDIENTS (Serves 4)

2 pounds boneless pork
   shoulder
2 tablespoons pork drippings
1 pound onions
Salt and pepper to taste
1 cup beer
$1/2$ cup water
2 tablespoons paprika
2 pounds tomatoes
$1/2$ pound gherkins pickled
   with mustard seeds
$1/2$ cup crème fraîche

METHOD

1. Cut the meat in chunks. Seal in very hot drippings, browning well. Peel the onions, cut into wedges, add to the meat, and brown well.
2. Season with salt and deglaze with beer and water. Add the paprika and leave to simmer for about 1 hour 10 minutes.
3. Blanch the tomatoes and remove skins. Quarter the tomatoes, remove seeds, and add to the meat. Simmer for a little longer.
4. Cut the gherkins in strips and add to meat. Thicken the goulash with crème fraîche and season to taste. Serve with noodles.

STUFFED LOIN OF PORK

Gefüllte Schweinebrust

INGREDIENTS (Serves 4)

*2 pounds loin of pork, boned
(ask your butcher to cut a
hollow in it)*
Salt and pepper to taste
1 stale roll
5 ounces ground beef
5 ounces ground pork
1 bunch of fresh parsley, chopped
1 egg
Chopped fresh marjoram
1 garlic clove, minced
1 onion, minced
1/4 cup clarified butter
1 piece of parsley root or parsnip
1 carrot
1 onion, coarsely diced
1 cup stock

METHOD

1. Preheat the oven to 350°F.
Rub salt and pepper into the
pork, inside and out.
2. Soften the roll in lukewarm
water. Mix the ground meats
with the parsley, egg, marjoram, garlic, minced onion,
and seasoning. Squeeze out
the roll and crumble into the
meat. Fill the pork loin with
the meat mixture and sew up
the cavity with kitchen thread.
3. On stovetop seal in hot
clarified butter, then place in
oven and roast for about
1 hour 10 minutes, basting
frequently with the meat
juices.
4. Peel the parsley and carrot,
cut into pieces, and add to the
meat with the diced onion,
after 40 minutes.
5. Remove the roast and keep
warm. Pour the stock into the
pan juices and stir vigorously
to deglaze the juices. Bring to
a boil, then strain, and season
to taste. Serve the pork in
slices, with grilled tomatoes
and mashed potato.

CHOPS IN CAPER SAUCE

Koteletts in Kapernsauce

INGREDIENTS (Serves 4)

*4 boned pork loin chops, each
weighing 5 ounces*
Salt and pepper to taste
2 tablespoons clarified butter
1 tablespoon minced onion
4 ounces white wine
1 tablespoon tomato paste
2 tablespoons capers
*1 tablespoon chopped pickled
gherkin*
*1 tablespoon chopped fresh
parsley*

TO GARNISH

Lemon wedges
4 small fresh parsley sprigs

METHOD

1. Season the chops with
salt and pepper. Fry in hot
clarified butter, remove, and
keep warm.
2. Fry the onion for 1 to
2 minutes in the pan juices.
Add the wine, tomato paste,
capers, gherkin, parsley, and
a pinch of salt. Simmer the
sauce over low heat for about
20 minutes. Season to taste.
3. Pour the sauce over the
chops and garnish with lemon
and parsley.

HANNELORE KOHL

"*In order to give the dish a Mediterranean flavor, just
use olive oil instead of clarified butter. The sauce should
then be seasoned with lemon juice.*"

CARAWAY PORK

Kümmelbraten (photo above)

INGREDIENTS (Serves 4)

*2 pounds pork shoulder butt
    roast*
*Whole or ground caraway
    seeds to taste*
Salt and pepper to taste
1 tablespoon drippings
2 onions
²/₃ cup meat stock
2 cups small mushrooms
1/2 bunch of fresh parsley
1 garlic clove
1 cup diced Canadian bacon
Heavy cream

METHOD

1. Preheat the oven to 350°F.
Rub the caraway and salt
into the meat. On the stovetop heat the drippings in a
casserole and seal the meat
on all sides in it.

2. Peel the onions, quarter,
and add to the pot. Pour a
little meat stock over the
roast, so it doesn't brown
too quickly. Put in the oven
to cook.
3. Clean the mushrooms; chop
the parsley; and peel and
crush the garlic. Add all these
to the pot with the bacon
after 30 minutes cooking
time. Pour the remaining
meat stock over the roast.
Cover the casserole and cook
the roast for a further
30 minutes.
4. Lift the meat out of the
casserole. Mix the cream with
the pan juices, bring to a boil
again, and season to taste.
Serve with bread dumplings
and coleslaw.

SMOKED PORK LOIN WITH PURÉED SPLIT PEAS

Kasseler mit Erbspüree

INGREDIENTS (Serves 4)

FOR THE PEA PURÉE
*2 cups dried green or yellow
    split peas*
1 quart water
*1 bunch of vegetables for soup,
    e.g., carrots, leeks, celery*
1 onion
1 bouquet garni
2 tablespoons unsalted butter
Salt and pepper to taste

FOR THE PORK LOIN
*2 pounds smoked pork loin
    (Canadian bacon)*
1 onion
1/2 cup red wine
Salt and pepper to taste

METHOD

1. Soak the peas overnight in
the water.
2. Bring the peas and soaking
water to a boil in a large soup
pot. Peel or trim the soup

vegetables and onion, chop,
and add to the peas with the
bouquet garni. Simmer over
low heat until the peas are
soft, about 45 minutes.
3. Preheat the oven to 325°F.
Put the pork loin on a rack in
a roasting pan and roast for
about 45 minutes.
4. As soon as the meat juices
start to brown, add a little hot
water and deglaze the meat
juices. Baste the meat with
the juices.
5. Peel the onion, quarter, and
add to the pan 25 minutes
before the end of the cooking
time.
6. Purée the peas. Enrich with
the butter and season to taste.
7. Remove the roast. Deglaze
the meat residues with a little
hot water and bring to a boil.
Add the red wine, season to
taste, and simmer to reduce
slightly.

PORK SHOULDER WITH BRAISED CUCUMBER

Schweinenacken mit Schmorgurke

INGREDIENTS (Serves 4)

1³/₄ *pounds boneless pork arm*
   roast
Salt and pepper to taste
4 *onions*
¹/₄ *cup clarified butter*
3 *cups meat stock*
1 *tablespoon cornstarch*
1³/₄ *pounds cucumbers*
¹/₂ *cup diced Canadian bacon*
1 *tablespoon flour*
1 *tablespoon sugar*
1 *tablespoon tomato paste*
1 *tablespoon vinegar*

METHOD

1. Preheat the oven to 350⁰F.
Season the meat with salt
and pepper. Peel and quarter
2 onions. Heat 2 tablespoons
of the clarified butter in a
roasting pan on the stovetop
and seal the meat on all sides.
2. Add the onions to the
roasting pan and fry briefly.
Bring 2 cups of meat stock to
a boil and pour onto the roast;
braise in the oven for about
1 hour.
3. Remove the roast and keep
warm. Mix the cornstarch
with 2 tablespoons water and
use to thicken the meat juices.
4. Peel the cucumbers, cut in
pieces, salt lightly, and leave
to drain for about 10 minutes.
Peel the remaining onions and
cut in wedges.
5. Melt the remaining 2 tablespoons clarified butter in a
medium pan. Sweat the bacon
and remaining 2 onions in it.
Add the pieces of cucumber
and dust with flour. Stir in the
sugar and leave to caramelize.
6. Mix the remaining meat
stock with the tomato paste,
add to the cucumbers, and
simmer for 15 minutes longer.
Season to taste with the
vinegar.
7. Slice the meat and serve
with the braised cucumber
and the gravy. Accompany
with boiled potatoes.

SMOKED LOIN OF PORK WITH PLUMS

Kasseler mit Pflaumen (photo below)

INGREDIENTS (Serves 4)

1 pound plums
4 slices smoked loin of pork (Canadian bacon), each weighing about 6 ounces
2 tablespoons clarified butter
1 cup medium red wine
Salt and pepper to taste

METHOD

1. Wash the plums, remove pits, and quarter the flesh. Season the pork with pepper.
2. Heat the clarified butter in a pan. Cook the pork loin in it for 1 to 2 minutes on each side. Remove from the pan, wrap in foil, and keep warm.
3. Deglaze the meat residue in the pan with the red wine and reduce by about a third. Add the plums to the sauce, bring to a boil briefly, and season to taste with salt and pepper. Serve with the smoked loin of pork.

PANFRIED PORK AND CUCUMBER

Schweinefleisch-Gurken-Pfanne

INGREDIENTS (Serves 4)

1½ pounds pork tenderloin
2 tablespoons clarified butter
1 cup vegetable stock
Salt and pepper to taste
1 pound cucumbers
1 small onion
¾ cup sour cream
Bunch of fresh dill, chopped

METHOD

1. Cut the meat in strips. Heat the clarified butter in a pan and seal the meat in the butter in batches.
2. Gradually deglaze with vegetable stock and continue simmering for about 40 minutes. Season with salt and pepper.
3. Peel the cucumbers, cut in half lengthwise, remove seeds with a spoon, and slice. Peel the onion and slice in rings.
4. Add the vegetables to the meat 10 minutes before the end of cooking time and cook until tender. Thicken with the cream and season to taste with dill, salt, and pepper. Serve with baked potatoes.

LOIN OF PORK WITH APPLES

Schweinebrust mit Äpfeln

INGREDIENTS (Serves 4)

2 pounds pork loin roast with
  rind
Salt and pepper to taste
4 apples, totalling about 1 pound
1 cup prunes
Sugar
1 tablespoon breadcrumbs
2 egg yolks
6 tablespoons clarified butter
1½ pounds red cabbage
1 onion
1 clove
1 tablespoon vinegar
Beef extract or concentrated
  stock
1 to 2 tablespoons red currant
  jelly

METHOD

1. Ask your butcher to cut a
pocket in the pork loin. Score
the rind, and season the meat
lightly with salt.
2. Peel the apples, quarter,
and remove cores. Cut 3
apples in eighths or slice;
grate 1 apple. Remove pits
from prunes.
3. Sprinkle a little sugar over
the sliced apples and prunes.
Mix in the breadcrumbs and
egg yolks. Use the mixture to
stuff the meat, and sew up the
cavity with kitchen string.
4. Preheat the oven to 350°F.
Seal the pork in 3 tablespoons
of the hot clarified butter.
Roast in the oven for about
30 minutes, with the rind
underneath.
5. Turn the roast and brush
the rind with cold salted
water. Roast for 30 minutes to
1 hour longer.
6. Clean the red cabbage and
chop finely. Peel the onion
and dice. Fry both briefly in
the remaining 3 tablespoons
clarified butter with the clove,
grated apple, 1 tablespoon
sugar, and the vinegar.
7. Add about a finger of water
and simmer the red cabbage
for 15 minutes. Season to taste
with beef extract and red currant jelly. Braise for 15 minutes longer. Serve with the
pork and boiled potatoes.

ROAST PORK WITH CARAWAY

Schweinebraten mit Kümmel

INGREDIENTS (Serves 4)

2½ pounds pork sirloin roast
  with rind
Salt and white pepper
Dried marjoram
3 tablespoons clarified butter
About 2 cups water
8 onions
1 garlic clove
1 teaspoon caraway seeds
½ bay leaf

METHOD

1. Score the pork rind in a
diamond pattern. Rub the
meat with salt, pepper, and
marjoram and leave to rest
for about 1 hour.
2. Preheat the oven to 400°F.
Heat the clarified butter in a
pan. On the stovetop seal the
meat all over in it. Then, with
the rind underneath, place in
a deep casserole. Add 1 cup
of boiling water.
3. Peel the onions and cut in
rings. Add a quarter of the
onions to the pot and cook
the meat in the oven for
about 40 minutes.
4. Turn the meat over. Add
the remaining onions, the
garlic, caraway seeds, bay
leaf, and pepper. Cook the
pork for 40 minutes longer.
5. Remove the pork from the
oven. Remove the bay leaf.
Add enough water to the
meat juices to make 2 cups.
Allow the gravy to reduce a
little and season with salt
and pepper.
6. Slice the meat and serve
with the gravy. Accompany
with sauerkraut with mushrooms and potato croquettes.

PORK MEDALLIONS WITH CARROTS

Schweinemedaillons mit Möhren

INGREDIENTS (Serves 4)

1¹/₄ pounds pork tenderloin
¹/₂ teaspoon dried thyme
2 to 3 carrots
1 onion
2 tablespoons clarified butter
¹/₂ cup white wine
¹/₂ cup meat stock
2 tablespoons crème fraîche
1 tablespoon lemon juice
Cayenne to taste
Salt and pepper to taste
Chopped fresh parsley

METHOD

1. Cut the tenderloin in finger-thick medallions, flatten a little, and rub with thyme. Peel the carrots and cut in matchsticks. Peel and mince the onions.

2. Preheat the oven to very low. Fry the medallions in hot clarified butter over high heat for 4 to 5 minutes on each side. Keep warm in the oven.

3. Fry the carrots and onion in the pan, pour on the white wine and meat stock, and allow to reduce slightly. Stir in the crème fraîche and lemon juice.

4. Season the carrots to taste with cayenne and salt. Mix in the parsley. Serve the carrots with the pork medallions.

SMOKED PORK HOCKS WITH SAUERKRAUT

Eisbein mit Sauerkohl

INGREDIENTS (Serves 4)

3 quarts water
4 smoked pork hocks, each
  weighing about 14 ounces
4 onions
5 bay leaves
12 white peppercorns
5 juniper berries (optional)
1¹/₂ teaspoons sugar
3¹/₂ cups sauerkraut
2 cloves

METHOD

1. Bring the water to a boil in a large pan. Rinse the pork hocks in cold water and add to the pan.
2. Peel the onions and cut in wedges. Add 2 onions with 3 bay leaves, the peppercorns, juniper berries, and ¹/₂ teaspoon sugar to pan. Cover and simmer over low heat for about 1¹/₂ hours.
3. Remove the pork hocks and keep warm. Strain the stock and reserve. Return the pork hocks to the pan and pour on 2 cups of the stock.
4. Add the sauerkraut, cloves, and remaining onions, bay leaves, and sugar to pan. Cover and cook for 40 minutes longer.

ROAST PORK IN A BLACK-BREAD CRUST

Schweinebraten im Schwarzbrotmantel

INGREDIENTS (Serves 4–6)

3 pounds shoulder of pork roast
Salt and pepper to taste
¹/₂ cup boiling water
¹/₂ cup meat stock
1 cup red wine
³/₄ cup grated black (rye) bread
¹/₂ cup cranberries
Pinch of ground cloves
¹/₂ pound shallots
Unsalted butter
¹/₂ teaspoon sugar
¹/₂ cup canned chanterelle
  mushrooms
4 tablespoons sour cream

METHOD

1. Preheat the oven to 350⁰F. Rub the meat with salt and pepper. Put into a baking dish and pour on the water. Roast for about 1¹/₄ hours. Baste the meat frequently with a little of the stock and wine.
2. Mix together the black bread, ¹/₃ cup cranberries, and cloves. Spread the mixture over the meat 15 minutes before the end of cooking time.
3. When cooked, remove the meat and keep warm. Deglaze the meat residue with the remaining red wine and stock, to make a gravy.
4. Peel the shallots and caramelize in the butter and sugar. Add to the gravy with the chanterelles. Thicken slightly with the sour cream and add the remaining cranberries.

MARKISH BEEF POT ROAST

Märkischer Rinderschmorbraten (photo below)

INGREDIENTS (Serves 4)

2 pounds beef bottom round
   roast
3 tablespoons clarified butter
Salt and pepper to taste
1 bunch of vegetables and herbs
   for soup, e.g., carrots, onions,
   leeks, parsley, thyme
1 small bay leaf
4 red or other peppercorns
2 cups boiling stock or water

METHOD

1. Seal the meat thoroughly
all over in the hot clarified
butter in a casserole. Season
with salt and pepper.
2. Peel or trim the vegetables
and herbs, chop coarsely, and
add to the meat with the bay
leaf and the peppercorns.
3. Add boiling stock or water.
Cover the meat and braise
over low heat for 1½ to
2 hours, until cooked. Serve
with potato dumplings and
red cabbage.

BRAISED BEEF IN BEER GRAVY

Ochsenfleisch in Biersauce

INGREDIENTS (Serves 4)

FOR THE STUFFING
2 tablespoons German mustard
1 tablespoon each chopped
   parsley, dill, and chives
1 tablespoon breadcrumbs
Salt and pepper to taste

2 pounds boneless ox or beef
   shoulder roast
Pepper to taste
3 thin slices bacon
3 tablespoons clarified butter
Salt to taste
2 cups dark beer
1 leek, weighing about
   ½ pound
3 carrots
1 fennel bulb, weighing about
   ¾ pound
2 to 3 onions
½ pound mushrooms
2 tablespoons crème fraîche

METHOD

1. To make the stuffing, mix all
the ingredients together in a
small bowl. Make three cuts
lengthwise down to the center
of the meat and season with
pepper. Push the stuffing into
the cavities. Cover each with a
slice of bacon and tie up with
kitchen string.
2. Heat the clarified butter and
fry the meat until well browned.
Season with salt. Deglaze with
1 cup of the beer, then cover
and braise for about 1½ hours
over medium heat. Gradually
add the remaining beer.
3. Peel or trim the vegetables.
Cut the leek in rings, dice the
carrots and fennel, and chop the
onions. Add them to the meat.
Braise for a further 30 minutes.
Add the mushrooms for the last
15 minutes.
4. Remove the meat and keep
warm. Strain the stock and put
some of the vegetables back in.
Stir in the crème fraîche and
season.

VEAL WITH GNOCCHI AND MOREL CREAM SAUCE

Kalbshüfte mit Morchelrahmsauce (photo right)

INGREDIENTS (Serves 4–6)

FOR THE VEAL

2 pounds veal rump roast
Salt and pepper to taste
2 tablespoons clarified butter
2 ounces dried morels
1 onion, chopped
1 cup sour cream
Chopped fresh chervil for garnish

FOR THE GNOCCHI

1 quart milk
Salt to taste
1¹/₃ cups semolina flour
2 egg yolks
¹/₂ cup grated cheese
Clarified butter for frying

METHOD

1. Preheat the oven to 350°F. Season the meat with salt and pepper. On the stovetop heat the clarified butter in a roasting pan and seal the veal in the butter. Roast the meat for about 1 hour. Baste frequently with the meat juices.

2. Soak the morels in a little warm water to soften. Shortly before the end of the cooking time add the onion to the roasting pan and brown lightly. Remove the veal and keep warm. Deglaze with the strained soaking liquid from the morels and reduce a little.
3. Stir in the sour cream, then strain. Coarsely chop the morels and add to sauce. Simmer the sauce briefly. Season to taste with salt and pepper.
4. To make the gnocchi, bring the milk to a boil in a saucepan with a little salt. Stir in the semolina, bring back to a boil quickly and then leave to cool.
5. Stir in the egg yolks and cheese. Spread out to about ³/₄ inch thick. Cut out oval gnocchi and fry in clarified butter on both sides until golden brown.
6. Slice the meat and cover with the sauce. Garnish with chervil. Serve the gnocchi separately.

HOLSTEIN VEAL

Schnitzel Holsteiner Art

INGREDIENTS (Serves 4)

4 veal cutlets, each weighing
  5 ounces
Salt and pepper to taste
¹/₄ cup clarified butter
2 tomatoes, sliced
4 slices of hard cheese, cut in
  strips
4 eggs
1 tablespoon unsalted butter
Minced fresh chives

METHOD

1. Rub the cutlets with salt and pepper. Fry for 3 minutes on each side in the hot clarified butter.
2. Cover the cutlets with the tomato slices and cheese strips. Fry 4 eggs in a buttered pan and place on the cutlets.
3. Garnish the cutlets with chives and serve with potato croquettes and a green salad.

VEAL WITH RAISINS AND CAPERS

Kalbfleisch mit Rosinen und Kapern

CALVES' LIVER, BERLIN-STYLE

Kalbsleber Berliner Art

INGREDIENTS (Serves 4)

*1 bunch of vegetables and
herbs for soup, e.g., carrots,
leek, parsley, thyme*
1/4 cup clarified butter
Salt and pepper to taste
5 cups water
*11/4 pounds boneless veal
round or rump roast*
1 cup raisins
3 tablespoons breadcrumbs
1 cup dry white wine
Juice of 1/2 lemon
2 teaspoons sugar
32 capers

METHOD

1. Peel or trim the vegetables and herbs and mince them. Heat 3 tablespoons of the clarified butter in a large pan and gently brown the vegetables in it.

2. Season with salt and pepper. Add 4 cups of the water and bring to a boil. Add the veal and simmer gently for about 1 1/2 hours.

3. Remove the meat, cut in strips, and keep warm; reserve the veal stock. Heat the remaining water in a pan, add the raisins, and leave to swell.

4. Heat the remaining tablespoon clarified butter and fry the breadcrumbs until golden brown. Stir in 2 cups of the veal stock.

5. Mix in drained raisins and meat. Leave to reduce a little. Pour in the white wine. Adjust the seasoning with lemon juice and sugar. Add the capers shortly before serving. Serve with boiled potatoes and a green salad.

INGREDIENTS (Serves 4)

*4 slices of calves' liver, each
weighing 5 ounces*
Seasoned flour for dredging
3 tablespoons clarified butter
Salt and pepper to taste
4 small onions
2 apples
3 tablespoons unsalted butter

METHOD

1. Rinse the liver, pat dry, and coat in flour. Heat the clarified butter in a frying pan and fry the liver for about 3 to 4 minutes on each side. Season with salt and pepper. Keep warm.

2. Peel the onions and cut in rings. Peel the apples, quarter, core, and cut into thin slices. Melt the butter in a frying pan and fry the onion rings and apple slices for about 5 minutes, until softened.

3. Arrange the liver with the onion rings and apple slices. Serve with mashed potato.

BERLIN VEAL ROAST

Berliner Kalbsbraten

INGREDIENTS (Serves 8–10)

5 1/2 to 7 pounds veal sirloin roast
4 cloves
Salt and pepper to taste
1/4 pound bacon (about 8 slices)
1 1/2 cups stock
1 bay leaf
1 pound small onions
1/2 pound small apples
1/2 cup white wine
1/2 cup sour cream

METHOD

1. Preheat the oven to 400°F. Spike the meat with the cloves and rub with salt and pepper. Lay half the bacon on the bottom of a deep baking dish.
2. Place the meat on top of the bacon and put the remaining bacon on top of meat. Add the bay leaf. Roast the meat for about 2 hours. Gradually add the stock, basting the meat.
3. Peel the onions and add about 20 minutes before the end of cooking time. Peel the apples, quarter, core, and cut in wedges; add 10 minutes before the end of cooking time.
4. Remove the roast. Deglaze the meat juices with wine, thicken with the cream and season to taste.
5. Arrange the roast on a platter and serve the sauce separately. Serve with boiled potatoes and glazed carrots.

BRANDENBURG LAMB

Brandenburger Lammfleisch (photo right)

INGREDIENTS (Serves 4)

1 3/4 pounds boneless lamb
2 onions
Clarified butter
1/2 cup red wine
2 cups stock
1 pound green beans
1 pound potatoes
Fresh savory sprigs
Salt and pepper to taste

METHOD

1. Wash the meat, pat dry and dice.
2. Peel the onions and cut into small pieces. Heat the clarified butter in a pan and fry the diced meat to seal until golden brown.
3. Deglaze the pan with the red wine, add the onions, and season with salt and pepper. Pour in the stock, cover, and braise on medium heat for about 1 hour.
4. Clean the beans and cut in half if large. Peel the potatoes and cut in dice. Add the beans and potatoes to the meat 20 minutes before the end of cooking time. Season to taste with savory.

HANNELORE KOHL

"To make glazed carrots, use young carrots with the green tops. Peel the carrots and leave a little of the top on. Soften in melted butter, sprinkle with a little confectioners' sugar, and leave to caramelize. Instead of confectioners' sugar, you can also use honey."

HANNELORE KOHL

"The intense flavor of savory remains at full strength, even after drying. The peppery, spicy taste is a little reminiscent of thyme and oregano. If the herb is picked in summer, the leaves are soft, whereas the leaves of winter savory are hard and tough."

Lamb Cutlets with Beans

Lammkoteletts mit Bohnengemüse (photo below)

INGREDIENTS (Serves 4)

*12 lamb rib chops, weighing
  about 3 ounces each*
5 tablespoons wine vinegar
Fresh tarragon sprigs
Salt and pepper to taste
1 pound green beans
2 tablespoons clarified butter
1/2 cup heavy cream
*1 teaspoon green peppercorns
  in brine*
1 small garlic clove
3 tablespoons butter
1 bunch fresh savory, chopped

METHOD

1. Marinate the cutlets in the vinegar, tarragon, salt, and pepper.
2. Trim the beans, wash, and cook for about 8 minutes in salted water. Drain and keep warm.
3. Fry the cutlets in the melted clarified butter for about 5 minutes on each side; keep warm. Deglaze the pan with the marinade and cream. Add the peppercorns, season, and bring to a boil.
4. Peel and crush the garlic and brown briefly in the melted butter. Toss the beans in the garlic butter and stir in the savory. Serve the cutlets with the cream sauce and beans.

Lamb Chops with Pears

Lammkoteletts mit Birnen

INGREDIENTS (Serves 4)

*8 lamb loin chops, cut about
  1 inch thick*
1 garlic clove
1 teaspoon salt
2 allspice berries
8 white peppercorns
1 tablespoon soy sauce
4 medium pears
1 cup dry white wine
1 tablespoon sugar
1/4 cup clarified butter
1/4 cup cranberry jelly, warmed

METHOD

1. Snip the fat on the chops at 1-inch intervals.
2. Peel the garlic, chop coarsely, and crush to a fine paste in a pestle with the salt, the allspice, and peppercorns. Stir in the soy sauce. Brush onto the chops. Wrap in foil and leave to marinate in the refrigerator for 2 hours.
3. Peel the pears, halve, and carefully remove cores. Bring the white wine to a boil, with the sugar. Poach the pear halves in the wine for about 5 to 10 minutes.
4. Drain the lamb chops. Heat the butter in a pan. Fry the chops until brown on both sides and then continue frying for a further 5 minutes each side.
5. Arrange the pear halves on plates with the chops. Fill the pears with the warmed cranberry jelly. Serve with green beans or fresh shelled peas tossed in butter and mashed potato with chives.

HANNELORE KOHL

"Instead of the wine vinegar, you could make the marinade with lemon or lime juice. Discard the tarragon sprigs before making the sauce."

Baked Ham

Gebackener Schinken

INGREDIENTS (Serves 4)

3 pounds partially cooked boneless ham, any rind and most of the fat removed
Whole cloves
Salt to taste
1 1/2 cups fresh breadcrumbs
1 teaspoon ground cloves
1 to 2 tablespoons sugar

METHOD

1. Preheat oven to 300°F. With a knife, score the ham fat in 1/2-inch diamonds. Insert a clove at each intersection. Season the meat with salt.
2. Fill a deep baking dish with about 1 inch of water and place the ham in it. Put the dish in the oven, increase the temperature to 400°F and bake the ham for about 2 hours. Add hot water to the dish from time to time. There should always be sufficient water in the bottom.
3. Mix the breadcrumbs with the ground cloves and sugar. Remove the ham from the oven and take out the cloves. Spread the bread mixture over the fat.
4. Replace the ham in the baking dish. Bake until the crust is crisp.
5. Serve the sliced ham with glazed carrots, roasted onions, and a potato gratin.

Piquant Kidneys

Pikante Nieren

INGREDIENTS (Serves 4)

1 pound veal kidneys
2 cups buttermilk
1/4 cup clarified butter
1 can (1 pound) of tomatoes
1 onion
1 jar of pickled gherkins with mustard seed, drained
Paprika to taste
Salt and pepper to taste
1/4 cup cream
1 bunch fresh parsley, chopped

METHOD

1. Slice the kidneys in half lengthwise. Remove the cores. Soak the kidneys for 1 hour in the buttermilk.
2. Remove the kidneys from the buttermilk, pat dry, and cut into strips. Fry in the hot clarified butter until brown. Remove and keep warm.
3. Pour the tomatoes into a strainer, collecting the juice. Peel the onions and dice finely; dice the gherkins.
4. Soften the onions and gherkins in the butter left in the pan from the kidneys. Pour on the tomato juice. Season with salt, pepper, and paprika and simmer for 10 minutes.
5. Coarsely chop the tomatoes and add to the pan with the cream. Stir in the strips of kidney, and sprinkle with chopped parsley. Serve with parsley potatoes.

POT ROAST

Schmorbraten

INGREDIENTS (Serves 4)

$1/2$ cup prunes
2 cups red wine
1 cup diced bacon
$13/4$ pounds boneless beef
    pot roast
Salt and pepper to taste
2 bunches vegetables and herbs
    for soup, e.g., carrots, leeks,
    parsley, etc.
$3/4$ cup onions
4 peppercorns
1 clove
6 juniper berries (optional)
1 cup meat stock
2 tablespoons Scotch whisky
$2/3$ cup ground hazelnuts
2–3 tablespoons apple purée

METHOD

1. A day in advance, remove
the pits from the prunes and
soak in 1 cup of the red wine.
2. Fry the bacon to render the
fat. Rub the salt and pepper
into the beef and fry in the
bacon fat until well browned
on all sides.
3. Peel and dice the onions.
Clean the soup vegetables and
herbs and mince them. Add
the prepared ingredients and
spices to the meat and pour
on the remaining wine and
the stock. Braise for about
$11/2$ to 2 hours over low heat.
4. Shortly before the end of
cooking time, heat the prunes
and wine in a flambé pan.
Pour on the whisky, flambé
and while still burning, pour
over the pot roast. Add the
hazelnuts at the same time.
5. Remove the pot roast, place
on a serving dish and keep
warm. Reduce the gravy a
little and strain it. Flavor to
taste with the apple purée.
Serve the roast with the
prunes and the gravy and
with bread dumplings.

BEEF AND KOHLRABI STEW

Kohlrabi-Eintopf

INGREDIENTS (Serves 4)

2 onions
$13/4$ pounds beef for stew (chuck)
1 bay leaf
$11/2$ quarts water
$21/2$ pounds kohlrabi (with green
    leaves)
1 pound potatoes
Salt to taste
Grated nutmeg
Squeeze of lemon juice
Chopped fresh parsley

METHOD

1. Peel the onions, quarter
and place in a large saucepan
with the beef, bay leaf, and
water; bring to a boil. Cover
and simmer for an hour over
medium heat.
2. Cut off the kohlrabi leaves
and reserve the young leaves.
Peel and slice the kohlrabi.
Peel and dice the potatoes.
3. Remove the meat from the
stock. Add the kohlrabi and
potatoes to the stock and cook
for 30 minutes. Coarsely chop
the kohlrabi leaves and add to
the stew about 10 minutes
before the end of cooking
time. Return the meat to the
stew and reheat. Season to
taste with salt, nutmeg, and
lemon juice and sprinkle
with parsley.

CABBAGE ROULADEN

Kohlrouladen

INGREDIENTS (Serves 4)

1 large head white cabbage
2 slices stale multigrain bread
10 slices bacon
About 2 cups water
2 teaspoons beef extract or
    concentrated stock
$11/2$ cups chopped peeled
    tomatoes
1 tablespoon flour
1 cup sour cream
2 tablespoons paprika
6 tablespoons chopped fresh
    parsley
Salt and pepper to taste

FOR THE STUFFING
$1/2$ pound ground beef
$1/4$ pound ground pork
2 slices of white bread, softened
2 teaspoons salt
2 teaspoons pepper
$1/4$ cup diced bacon

METHOD

1. Make a deep cut in the
white cabbage around the
stem. With the stem down-
wards, boil with the multigrain bread and 1 tablespoon
salt for 30 minutes.
2. To make the stuffing, mix
all the ingredients together.
Carefully remove the leaves
from the head of cabbage.
Make a bed out of 3 to 4
leaves, spread some meat
mixture on top, roll up the
leaves, and tie with kitchen
string. Make 4 rolls in all.
3. Fry the bacon slices. Place
the rouladen on top of the
bacon and fry over low heat.
Add 1 cup of the water and
the beef extract, cover, and
braise for 30 minutes.
4. Mix the flour with the
remaining water. Add to the
rouladen after 20 minutes
with the cream and tomatoes.
Season with salt, pepper,
and paprika. Sprinkle with
parsley. Serve with boiled
potatoes.

MEAT STEW WITH PUMPKIN

Fleischtopf mit Kürbis

INGREDIENTS (Serves 4)

$3/4$ pound smoked pork loin
    (Canadian bacon)
$3/4$ pound boneless beef brisket
4 tablespoons butter
1 cup hard cider
1 cup meat stock
Salt and pepper to taste
$11/2$ pounds pumpkin
$11/4$ cups chopped onion
$1/2$ pound apples
2 cups chopped celery
$1/2$ bunch of fresh sage, minced
Coarsely ground pepper

METHOD

1. Cut the pork and beef in
chunks. Brown in the melted
butter. Deglaze with the cider
and stock. Season with salt
and pepper, cover, and braise
for about an hour.
2. Peel the pumpkin, remove
the seeds and dice the flesh.
Peel the apples, quarter, core,
and cut in wedges.
3. Add the vegetables and
apples 20 minutes before the
end of cooking time and cook
with the meat. Season to
taste with minced sage, salt,
and pepper. Sprinkle with
coarsely ground pepper,
if desired.

BERLIN CORIANDER AND BACON ROLLS
Berliner Koriander-Speck-Wecken

INGREDIENTS

FOR THE DOUGH

2 cakes (0.6 ounce each) fresh
   compressed yeast or 2 envelopes active dry yeast
$1/2$ teaspoon sugar
$1/2$ cup lukewarm milk
4 cups whole wheat flour
1 cup all-purpose flour
$3/4$ cup butter
$1/2$ teaspoon salt
2 eggs

FOR SPREADING AND
SPRINKLING

2 egg yolks, beaten
$3/4$ cup minced Canadian bacon
1 teaspoon crushed coriander
   seeds
$1/2$ teaspoon coarse sea salt

METHOD

1. Crumble the yeast and mix with the sugar and milk. Work into the remaining dough ingredients to form a smooth dough. Shape into a ball, place in a bowl, dust with a little flour, cover, and leave to rise in a warm place until doubled in size (this takes about 30 to 60 minutes).

2. Knead the dough again thoroughly by hand. Divide all the dough into even pieces, shape into small balls, and place on a buttered baking sheet.

3. Brush the rolls with beaten egg yolk, press in the minced bacon, sprinkle with coriander, and a little sea salt. Cover and leave to rise in a warm place for 20 minutes.

4. Preheat the oven to 400°F. Bake the rolls on the middle shelf for about 30 minutes until golden brown.

CARP WITH RED CABBAGE

Karpfen mit Rotkohl (photo below)

INGREDIENTS (Serves 2)

*3/4 pound "fresh" pickled red
    cabbage (sauerkraut) from
    a jar*
1 tablespoon lemon juice
5 tablespoons vegetable oil
Salt and sugar to taste
*1 carp, weighing 2 to 3 pounds,
    cleaned*

METHOD

1. Drain the red cabbage
and season with the lemon
juice, 1 tablespoon oil, salt,
and sugar.
2. Stuff the carp with the
cabbage; close the belly
with toothpicks. Brush the
carp with the remaining oil,
place on a piece of foil, and
wrap the foil around the
carp like a parcel.
3. Preheat the oven to 400°F
and bake the carp for about
50 to 60 minutes. Serve with
boiled potatoes, melted
butter, and lemon slices.

SPREE FOREST POPPY SEED PUDDING

Spreewälder Mohnpielen

INGREDIENTS (Serves 4–6)

1 cup raisins
*2 tablespoons orange liqueur,
    e.g., Cointreau or Grand
    Marnier*
2 cups poppy seeds
1 cup sugar
1 quart milk
*1 pound stale white bread, cut in
    small pieces (16 to 17 cups)*
1/2 cup sliced almonds

METHOD

1. Soak the raisins in the
liqueur in a saucepan. Bring
the poppy seeds, raisins,
1/2 cup sugar, and 2 cups of
the milk to a boil. Remove the
pan from the heat and leave
the mixture to cool
and thicken.
2. Put the bread pieces in a
bowl and sprinkle with the
remaining 1/2 cup sugar. Warm
the remaining 2 cups milk
and pour over the bread. Mix
the almonds into the poppy
seed mixture.
3. Alternately layer the poppy
seed mixture and white bread
in a mold. Leave to chill
thoroughly overnight in the
refrigerator. Serve with fruit
or a wine sauce.

BREAD PUDDING WITH WINE SAUCE

Semmelpudding mit Weinschaumsauce

INGREDIENTS (Serves 4–6)

1/2 cup unsalted butter
2 tablespoons sugar
6 egg yolks
2 1/2 cups breadcrumbs
1 cup milk
1 cup raisins
1 1/2 cups ground almonds
7/8 cup rum
6 egg whites
Salt to taste
Breadcrumbs

FOR THE WINE SAUCE

4 eggs
2 tablespoons cornstarch
1 cup sugar
2 cups white wine
Grated zest and juice of 1 lemon

METHOD

1. Beat the butter, sugar, and egg yolks until pale and fluffy in a mixing bowl. Gradually add the breadcrumbs and milk. Fold in the raisins, almonds, rum, and a pinch of salt.

2. In a separate bowl beat the egg whites with a little salt until stiff. Fold lightly into the egg-yolk mixture. Grease a quart mold well and sprinkle with breadcrumbs. Fill about three-quarters full with the mixture and cover tightly.

3. Place the mold in a saucepan and fill the pan with water to come halfway up the mold. Put the lid on the saucepan. Bring the water to a boil and then reduce the heat immediately. Gently simmer the pudding for about an hour. Turn off the heat and leave to firm up for 15 minutes.

4. To make the sauce, place all the ingredients in a heavy saucepan and mix thoroughly with a whisk. Bring the sauce to a boil over low heat, whisking all the time. Then remove from the heat immediately, stand in a bowl of cold water, and continue whisking until the sauce has cooled a little.

Egg Custard with Pears

Milchsuppe mit Birnen

INGREDIENTS (Serves 4)

1 pound pears
3/4 cup sugar
Juice and grated zest of
  1/2 lemon
3 tablespoons cornstarch
1 quart milk
1 1/2 tablespoons vanilla-
  flavored sugar
1 clove
1 teaspoon ground cinnamon
Pinch of salt
2 egg yolks
3 tablespoons butter, cubed

METHOD

1. Peel the pears, quarter and remove cores. Place the pears in a saucepan and cover with water. Add 1/3 cup of the sugar and the lemon zest and juice. Cook the pears in the liquid until tender but still firm.

2. Mix the cornstarch with a little milk. Bring the remaining milk, vanilla sugar, remaining sugar, spices and a pinch of salt to a boil.

3. Stirring constantly, add the cornstarch to the boiling milk and mix in thoroughly. Stir in the egg yolks and remove from the heat.

4. Whisk the butter into the custard. Add the quartered pears to the custard, with 1/2 cup of the cooking liquid. Serve hot.

Oat Dumpling Soup

Haferklößchensuppe

INGREDIENTS (Serves 4)

FOR THE SOUP

1 1/2 tablespoons clarified butter
1 onion, diced
1 carrot, sliced
1 leek, cut into rings
1 cup milk
1 vegetable bouillon cube
1 1/2 cups watercress
Salt and pepper to taste
1/2 cup heavy cream, stiffly
  whipped

FOR THE OAT DUMPLINGS

4 tablespoons unsalted butter
1 vegetable bouillon cube
1 cup coarse-ground oat flour or
  ground rolled oats
1 bunch of fresh parsley, chopped
1 egg, beaten
Salt, pepper, and grated nutmeg
  to taste

METHOD

1. Heat the clarified butter and fry the vegetables for 2 minutes until brown. Add the milk, 1 cup water, and the bouillon cube and simmer for 15 minutes.

2. Add the cress to the soup (reserve a few sprigs), purée, and season to taste with salt and pepper. Fold in the cream.

3. To make the dumplings, bring 7/8 cup of water to a boil with the butter and bouillon cube. Stir in the oatmeal and boil for 1 minute. Stir in the chopped parsley and egg. Season to taste with salt, pepper, and nutmeg.

4. Make dumplings out of the mixture and cook until done in salted water. Add the dumplings to the soup and garnish with remaining cress.

WITHOUT EQUAL: FRESH, YOUNG VEGETABLES

HANNELORE KOHL:
The arguments for and against organic vegetables have confused many consumers. What does a professional cook think?

ALFONS SCHUHBECK:
I think shoppers should rely on their common sense. My advice is look carefully at the vegetables and trust your nose. In the case of tomatoes, for example, you can often really smell the difference in quality.

HANNELORE KOHL:
It's also worthwhile sticking with the same market or farm. As a regular customer, you get the best advice, and if you do have a complaint, it is taken more seriously.

ALFONS SCHUHBECK:
The seasons themselves are also a good guide to menu-planning and shopping. In December, a baked apple for dessert must taste better than imported strawberries that have traveled for hours by plane. This is why we eat red cabbage with our goose at Martinmas and not asparagus.

HANNELORE KOHL:
What's your tip for the healthiest possible way to prepare vegetables?

ALFONS SCHUHBECK:
It's a very simple trick: "Cut up small and cook quickly" is my motto. I cut carrots into small dice, divide broccoli into tiny florets and put everything in the pan with

Choose vegetables that are in season and which are thus very fresh. If you do, you can't go wrong!

a pat of butter and a cup of water.

Then I bring it to a boil and take the pan off the hot-plate right away. In a few minutes, the vegetables have continued cooking to the point where they are tender but still crisp.

HANNELORE KOHL:
So you don't advise cooking a whole head of cauliflower?

ALFONS SCHUHBECK:
Of course it always looks nice, but something has to give. Either the tiny florets on the surface are

cooked to perfection, but the stem is still hard, or the stem is soft, and then the rest is overcooked. This is why I prefer removing the little florets from the stem. The stem is still perfectly suitable for making cauliflower soup.

SAXON ALPS AND THURINGIAN FOREST

By Helmut Kohl

Now that Germany's divisions have been overcome, Saxony and Thuringia are once again what they were for centuries: countryside in the heart of Germany and, simultaneously, focal points of German intellectual and literary history.

Martin Luther translated the Bible in Thuringia and worked for religious reform from there. Goethe and Schiller had lifelong homes in Weimar and Jena. From the eighteenth century onward, Dresden could compare itself to Florence. At one time, the great Italian artist Canaletto was the Dresden Court painter. With international aid, the Frauenkirche in Dresden, which was destroyed by Allied bombings in 1945, is now being restored.

It is not only these focal points of German and European history which attract visitors.

▶

SAXON ALPS AND THURINGIAN FOREST

The impressive mountainous region between the Erz mountains and Lausitz is just as accessible to city dwellers for walking and relaxation as the expanses of the Thuringian Forest. Intellectual and culinary delights are combined here in the best possible way.

Saxony is famed far and wide for its cuisine and its baking as well. Even in times of want, traditional recipes have been preserved and handed down, as I know from my own rare visits to Saxony in the 1960s. At that time, my wife and I went on a private trip to Leipzig, where she showed me her old primary school and the grammar school which she attended until she fled. It was then I learned to treasure this region's dishes, which have something to suit every taste, from gourmets with refined tastebuds to fans of hearty fare.

One of the most well-known dishes is Leipzig Allerlei—mixed, young, tender vegetables, originally made with crayfish tails. Anyone who visits Saxony must try this and, of course, the cakes and pastries for which the "sweet Saxons" are renowned throughout the world—Dresden Stollen and baked cheesecake. Saxony cherry bread pudding, made from a mixture of white bread, eggs, milk, and butter, is not as sweet and is baked in the oven.

As the filter paper was invented in 1908 by a practical Dresden housewife, Melitta Benz, it is hardly chance that the Saxons' favorite drink is coffee. As early as the eighteenth century, a coffee-house atmosphere was carefully cultivated in the "Coffee Bush" in Leipzig. In his "Kaffee-kantate" (Coffee Cantata) Johann Sebastian Bach good-humoredly mocked fashionable Leipzig society's obsession with coffee, while Johann Wolfgang von Goethe raved about the traditional onion market in Weimar. Could there be any better proof that intellect and enjoyment are by no means mutually exclusive?

If you have a chance, enjoy Thuringian dumplings—tasty proof of widespread potato cultivation throughout the area. Also don't miss the legendary Thuringian sausages at one of the traditional forest festivals. Then you will understand why their aroma is also called "Thuringian incense."

Beautiful farmhouses are plentiful in Vogtland. The area around Plauen is known for its bobbin lace and other traditional handicrafts.

Moritzburg Farmer's Chop

Moritzburger Bauernkotelett (photo above)

INGREDIENTS (Serves 4)

*4 pork chops, each weighing
    about ¹/₂ pound*
Salt and pepper to taste
7 tablespoons clarified butter
¹/₂ cup diced bacon
1 cup meat stock
1¹/₂ pounds potatoes
1 egg
Flour
2 onions, minced
1 pound (4 to 5 cups) spinach
¹/₂ onion, diced
Butter

METHOD

1. Season the chops with salt
and pepper and brown in
4 tablespoons of the clarified
butter. Keep warm on a
roasting rack in the oven.
2. Fry the bacon in the pork
fat until it renders its fat.
Deglaze with the stock, strain
the sauce through a sieve, and
season to taste.
3. Peel and grate the potatoes.
Mix with the egg, pepper, salt,
flour, and finely chopped
onion. Heat the remaining
clarified butter and fry spoonfuls of the potato mixture to
make little cakes.
4. Wash the spinach and
soften it in a frying pan, with
a little butter and the diced
onion. Season to taste with
salt and pepper. Serve the
chops with the sauce and
vegetables.

Saxon Onion Soup

Sächsisches Zwiebelfleisch

INGREDIENTS (Serves 4)

1 pound meaty pork bones
2 pounds onions
2 tablespoons butter
*³/₄ pound chuck or skirt steak,
    cut in strips*
*3 to 4 stale bread rolls, sliced
    in strips*
Pinch of sugar
*Salt, pepper, and caraway seeds
    to taste*

METHOD

1. To make the stock, boil the
bones in plenty of water for
about an hour. Strain.
2. Mince the onions and fry
briefly in the butter with just
enough water to cover. Place
the strips of meat on top of
the onions and braise them
until tender, which will take
20 minutes to 1 hour, depending on the cut.
3. Break up the bread rolls.
As soon as the meat is cooked,
add the bread. Pour on the
stock and cook everything
together briefly. The soup
should only now be stirred,
seasoned with salt, sugar,
pepper, and caraway seeds
and served.

HANNELORE KOHL

"*With farmer's chops I always serve a freshly cooked
potato rösti and a mixed leaf salad, using different
greens, depending on the time of year.*"

LOIN OF PORK WITH LEEKS

Schweinerücken mit Lauchgemüse

INGREDIENTS (Serves 4)

*2 pounds pork loin roast
   with rind
Salt, pepper, and chopped fresh
   marjoram to taste
2 tablespoons clarified butter
2 carrots
1 piece of parsley root or parsnip
1 fennel bulb
1 small onion, weighing about
   3 ounces
2 cloves
2 bay leaves
1 cup beef stock*

FOR THE LEEKS

*4¹/₂ pounds leeks
2 tablespoons unsalted butter
1 cup veal stock
¹/₄ cup cream
Salt and pepper to taste*

FOR THE SAUCE

*2 shallots
3 tablespoons unsalted butter
¹/₂ cup dry white wine
¹/₂ cup chilled butter, cubed
Bunch of fresh chervil, chopped
Salt, pepper, and sugar to taste*

METHOD

1. Rub the pork loin all over with salt, pepper, and marjoram. Score the rind in a diamond pattern.

2. Heat the clarified butter in a large flameproof casserole and fry the meat until sealed and well browned on all sides.
3. Wash and prepare the carrots, parsley root, and fennel and chop into small pieces. Add the vegetables to the meat. Pour on the stock, cover, and braise for 1¹/₄ hours.
4. Peel the onion, halve, and spike each half with the cloves and bay leaves. About 15 minutes before the end of cooking, add the onion halves. Brush the pork with salted water and continue cooking, uncovered.
5. Clean the leeks, and slice into strips. Melt the butter in a large saucepan and fry the leeks briefly. Season with salt and pepper and add the stock and cream. Cover and simmer for 5 minutes.
6. To make the sauce, peel and mince the shallots and fry in melted butter. Deglaze with the wine and leave to reduce a little. Whisk in the butter. Season the sauce with salt, pepper, a pinch of sugar, and chervil.

SHOULDER OF PORK ON A BED OF VEGETABLES

Schweinenacken auf Gemüse (photo right)

INGREDIENTS (Serves 4)

*2 pounds boneless pork butt
   roast
2 to 3 carrots
1 fennel bulb
5 ounces parsley root or parsnip
1 large onion
1 large garlic clove
4 to 6 parsley sprigs, tied
5 cups dry white wine
2 small leeks, weighing about
   ¹/₂ pound*

METHOD

1. Remove any fat and tendons from the meat. Wash and coarsely chop the carrots, fennel, and parsley root. Mince the onion and garlic.
2. Bring the white wine to a boil with one cup of water. Add the meat and the prepared ingredients and simmer gently for about 50 minutes, skimming frequently.
3. Slit the leeks lengthwise, but do not cut completely in half. Wash thoroughly, cut into 2¹/₂ inch long pieces and tie up again with kitchen string. Add the leeks to the meat 20 minutes before the end of cooking.
4. When all the vegetables are cooked, remove, baste with a little stock, cover, and keep warm. To serve the meat, slice thickly and arrange it with the vegetables.

POTATO CAKE

Kartoffelkuchen

INGREDIENTS (Serves 4)

*¹/₂ pound potatoes
¹/₂ cup raisins
3 tablespoons rum
6 eggs, separated
³/₄ cup sugar
Salt to taste
Grated zest of 1 lemon
3 tablespoons cornstarch
1¹/₂ tablespoons unsalted butter
1 tablespoon breadcrumbs*

FOR THE GLAZE

*6 tablespoons unsalted butter,
   melted
2 tablespoons sugar
1 teaspoon cinnamon*

METHOD

1. Boil the potatoes for about 25 minutes. Refresh and peel them. Leave overnight.
2. Preheat the oven to 350°F.

Soak the raisins in the rum. Grate the potatoes. Mix the egg yolks with ³/₄ cup sugar, salt, and lemon zest until foamy. Mix with the potatoes and raisins.
3. Beat the egg whites until stiff and add to the potato mixture. Sift in the cornstarch and fold together carefully.
4. Grease a springform pan

with 1¹/₂ tablespoons butter and sprinkle with breadcrumbs. Fill with the potato batter. Bake the cake for about an hour.
5. Remove the cake from the pan and leave to cool. Brush with 6 tablespoons melted butter and sprinkle with 2 tablespoons sugar and cinnamon.

VEAL KIDNEYS WITH PORCINI

Kalbsnieren mit Steinpilzen (photo below)

INGREDIENTS (Serves 4)

1¼ pounds veal kidneys
1 red and 1 green bell pepper
1 tablespoon unsalted butter
1 onion, minced
5 ounces fresh cèpes or
    2 tablespoons dried porcini
    (cèpes), rehydrated
Salt, pepper, and paprika to taste
½ cup white wine
Clarified butter
½ cup fresh parsley, chopped

METHOD

1. Cut the kidneys in half
lengthwise, remove any fat,
tendons, and veins and wash
carefully.

2. Wash the peppers, cut them
in half, and remove the core
and seeds. Cut the halves into
thin strips. Melt the butter in
a saucepan and fry the
peppers and onion until soft,
for about 3 minutes.
3. Add the cèpes, season with
paprika, salt, and pepper,
pour on the white wine, and
simmer for 10 minutes.
4. Slice the kidneys and fry on
all sides in hot clarified butter
for 5 minutes. Season with
salt and pepper.
5. Arrange the calves' kidneys
with the vegetables and
sprinkle with parsley. Best
served with noodles.

VEAL WITH GOOSEBERRIES

Kalbfleisch mit Stachelbeeren

INGREDIENTS (Serves 4)

2 pounds veal shoulder roast
2 tablespoons unsalted butter
1 cup gooseberries, as firm
    as possible
6 tablespoons white wine
1 tablespoon sugar
Pinch of ground cinnamon
½ cup cream

METHOD

1. Simmer the veal shoulder
on low heat in plenty of water
for 45 minutes.
2. Drain the meat well. Melt
the butter and seal the meat
all over in the hot butter.
3. Reserving a few of the
gooseberries, add the rest to
the meat, with the white
wine, sugar, and cinnamon.
Simmer over low heat for
about 45 minutes. Add a little
veal stock, if necessary.
4. Remove and slice the meat.
Add the reserved gooseberries
to the gravy and cook for
2 minutes. Enrich the gravy
to taste with the cream.

SADDLE OF LAMB

Lammrücken (photo above)

INGREDIENTS (Serves 4)

2 garlic cloves

2 onions

2 tomatoes

2 pounds saddle of lamb (double loin roast)

Salt and pepper to taste

3 tablespoons clarified butter

1 fresh thyme sprig, chopped

1 fresh rosemary sprig, chopped

METHOD

1. Preheat the oven to 350°F. Peel and mince the garlic. Peel the onions and cut into quarters. Blanch the tomatoes, peel and quarter.

2. Rub the saddle of lamb with salt and pepper. On the stovetop heat the clarified butter in a roasting pan and seal the lamb all over in it.

3. Add the vegetables, garlic, and chopped herbs. Place in oven and roast for 15 to 20 minutes (the meat should still be pink). Accompany with zucchini and bell peppers.

MARINATED LAMB SHANKS

Lammhaxen

INGREDIENTS (Serves 4–6)

FOR THE MARINADE

1/4 cup lemon juice

Minced fresh mint

1/2 cup dry red wine

1/4 cup vegetable oil

1/2 cup minced onion

1 tablespoon each minced fresh dill, parsley, and chives

FOR THE LAMB SHANKS

4 lamb shanks

Salt and black pepper to taste

3 tablespoons clarified butter

1 cup red wine

1 cup meat stock

2 leeks, chopped

2 carrots

1/2 cup crème fraîche

METHOD

1. Mix the ingredients for the marinade. Add the lamb shanks and refrigerate for a few hours.

2. Preheat the oven to 325°F. Remove the lamb from the marinade and season with salt and pepper. Heat the clarified butter in a roasting pan and fry the meat on all sides, until sealed and well browned. Roast for 45 minutes. Add wine and stock to the roasting pan a little at a time during cooking.

3. Add the vegetables and roast for 30 more minutes.

4. Remove the meat and keep warm. Strain the meat juices, pushing the soft vegetables through the strainer to purée them. Enrich the sauce with the crème fraîche, season to taste with salt and pepper, and serve with the meat.

LOIN OF LAMB WITH LEMON

Lammfilet mit Zitrone

INGREDIENTS (Serves 4)

1¼ pounds boneless loin of lamb
Salt and pepper to taste
2 tablespoons clarified butter
½ cup meat stock
½ bell pepper
½ lemon
Lemon slices
Fresh mint leaves

METHOD

1. Slice the loin thinly and press flat. Season with salt and pepper.
2. Heat the clarified butter in a frying pan. Seal the meat on both sides, remove, and keep warm. Deglaze the meat residue with the stock.
3. Remove core and seeds from the pepper and cut into thin strips. Wash the lemon and slice thinly. Add both to the stock and simmer gently for 15 minutes.
4. Add the lamb slices and heat through for 5 minutes. Season to taste. Garnish with lemon slices and mint leaves. Serve with mashed potato and a Belgian endive salad.

STUFFED LEG OF LAMB

Gefüllte Lammkeule

INGREDIENTS (Serves 4)

1 leg of lamb, about 3½ pounds boned
Salt and white pepper to taste
½ pound blue cheese
1⅓ cups chopped onions
1 garlic clove
2 tablespoons clarified butter
1 cup stock
Chopped fresh rosemary to taste
1 cup sour cream

METHOD

1. Preheat the oven to 350°F. Season the leg of lamb with salt and pepper. Stuff with the blue cheese in the cavities made by the bones and sew up with kitchen string.
2. Peel and chop the garlic. On the stovetop heat the clarified butter in a roasting pan and seal the leg of lamb on all sides. Add the onions and garlic and allow to braise together briefly. Pour on the stock and season with rosemary.
3. Place in oven and roast the meat for about 70 minutes on the lowest shelf. Baste occasionally with the meat juices.
4. Remove the leg of lamb and keep warm. Bring the meat juices to a boil, strain, and stir in the sour cream. Season to taste. Slice the leg of lamb and serve with the gravy, wilted spinach, and potato balls.

ROAST LAMB

Lammbraten

INGREDIENTS (Serves 4)

2 pounds boneless lamb leg roast
Salt and pepper to taste
¼ cup clarified butter
1 carrot, peeled and minced
2 onions, peeled and minced
1 parsley root or parsnip, finely diced
1 to 2 garlic cloves, minced
Minced fresh rosemary to taste
Meat stock
2 tablespoons cream

METHOD

1. Preheat the oven to 325°F. Season the leg of lamb with salt and pepper and seal on the stovetop in hot clarified butter.
2. Add the finely chopped vegetables and rosemary and deglaze with stock. Place in oven and roast for about 1¼ hours.
3. Pour the juices through a sieve, enrich with cream, and season to taste.
4. Slice the meat. Serve with the gravy, duchesse potatoes, and a green salad.

> HANNELORE KOHL
>
> "I often purée the vegetables which were cooked with the meat, add them to the gravy, and then press through a strainer. This makes the gravy even tastier."

POTATO AND HAM BAKE

Schinkenkartoffeln

INGREDIENTS (Serves 4)

1¾ pounds potatoes, cooked
½ pound cooked ham
2 onions
2 tablespoons clarified butter
1 cup cream
4 eggs
Salt, pepper, and grated nutmeg to taste
1¼ cups grated cheese

METHOD

1. Preheat the oven to 400°F. Remove the skins from the potatoes and slice thinly. Cut the ham into thin strips.
2. Peel the onions, cut into rings, and fry until translucent in 1 tablespoon of clarified butter. Grease a gratin dish with the remaining clarified butter. Layer the onions, potatoes, and ham in the dish.
3. Mix together the cream and eggs and season with salt, pepper, and nutmeg. Mix in half the cheese. Pour the mixture over the potatoes and ham and bake for about 30 minutes. Ten minutes before the end of cooking time, sprinkle with the remaining cheese.

PORK CHOPS WITH MUSHROOMS

Koteletts im Pilzgemüse
(photo left)

INGREDIENTS (Serves 4)

4 pork loin chops, $^1/_2$ pound each
Salt and pepper to taste
$^1/_3$ cup vegetable oil
1 pound mushrooms
2 tablespoons lemon juice
$^1/_4$ cup white wine
$^2/_3$ cup sour cream
2 tablespoons chopped fresh
herbs, e.g., thyme and
marjoram, or $^1/_2$ teaspoon
each dried herbs

METHOD

1. Preheat the oven to 400°F.
Season the chops with salt
and pepper. Heat the oil in a
casserole with a heavy base.
Seal the chops briefly on the
stovetop and remove.
2. Slice the mushrooms and
soften them in the casserole
with the lemon juice. Stir in
the white wine, sour cream,
and herbs.
3. Add the chops to the mushrooms. Cover the casserole.
Cook in the oven for about
15 minutes. Serve straight
from the casserole with a
white cottage loaf or garlic
bread.

PORK WITH PEARS AND PAN DUMPLING

Schweinefleisch mit Pfannen-Kloß

INGREDIENTS (Serves 4)

$1^1/_4$ pounds boneless pork loin
roast
Salt and pepper to taste
1 cup milk
$1^1/_4$ cakes (0.6 ounce each) fresh
compressed yeast or $1^1/_4$ enve-
lopes active dry yeast
4 cups all-purpose flour
1 teaspoon salt
1 egg
Pinch of grated nutmeg
$^1/_2$ cup unsalted butter, cubed

10 nice pears
1 tablespoon sugar
2 cups water

METHOD

1. Rub the pork with the salt
and pepper. Cover and refrigerate for about 24 hours.
2. Gently heat the milk in a
saucepan. Crumble the yeast
into the milk, add $^1/_4$ cup of
flour, and mix together. Cover

with a cloth and leave to
proof for about 30 minutes.
3. Mix in the remaining flour,
salt, the egg, and nutmeg.
Add the butter. Work everything into a smooth dough
and leave to rise for an hour.
4. Preheat the oven to 350°F.
Peel the pears, halve, remove
cores, and sprinkle with
sugar. Knead the dough again
and shape it into a dumpling.
5. Place the meat in the mid-

dle of a large pan with a
tightly fitting lid. Place the
pears on one side of the meat
and the dumpling on the other.
Cover with water and put on
the lid. Cook in the oven for
about 2 hours. If the gravy
boils away, add a little water.
6. Slice the meat and divide
the dumpling into portions.
Arrange on a serving dish,
with the pears and the meat
juices.

THURINGIAN RED CABBAGE ROLL

Thüringer Rotkrautwickel

BLOOD SAUSAGE WITH SWEET AND SOUR LENTILS

Rotwurst mit süß-sauren Linsen

INGREDIENTS (Serves 4)

8 nice red cabbage leaves
1 tablespoon wine vinegar
Pinch of sugar
1/2 onion
1 clove
1 1/2 pounds ground round
1/2 pound fresh cèpes or chanterelles, sliced and sautéed
1/4 cup breadcrumbs
1 egg, beaten
Salt and pepper to taste
3 tablespoons unsalted butter
1 cup stock
2 tablespoons sour cream

METHOD

1. Put the cabbage leaves in a saucepan with the vinegar, sugar, onion, and clove with salt and enough water just to cover and cook until just soft.
2. Mix the ground beef with the mushrooms, breadcrumbs, egg, salt, and pepper. Put some of the stuffing on each of the cabbage leaves. Fold in the leaves on the left and right, roll up and tie with kitchen string.
3. Heat the butter, add the stock, and cook the rolls in it until done. Remove the rolls and keep warm. Enrich the gravy with sour cream and season to taste. Serve with mashed potato.

INGREDIENTS (Serves 4)

1 1/3 cups lentils
1 cup minced soup vegetables, e.g., leek, parsley root, fennel, and carrots
1 to 3 tablespoons wine vinegar
2 onions
2/3 cup diced bacon
1 pound fresh Rotwurst *(cooked blood sausage)*
Salt, pepper, and sugar to taste

METHOD

1. A day in advance, cover the lentils with lukewarm water and leave to soak overnight.
2. Cook the lentils and soaking liquid with the minced vegetables over low heat until soft. Season to taste with vinegar, salt, pepper, and sugar.
3. Chop the onion into small dice with the bacon. Brown in a frying pan. Put a spoonful of lentils on a plate and top with bacon and onion. Slice the blood sausage and put it on the plate. Serve with fresh crusty bread.

HANNELORE KOHL

"The cabbage rolls taste especially good if a little cooked rice is mixed in with the stuffing."

HANNELORE KOHL

"With the blood sausage dish cut a small apple into a fine dice or grate coarsely, and then fry it with the bacon and onion."

STEW WITH SMOKED LOIN OF PORK

Eintopf mit Kasseler (photo above, left)

INGREDIENTS (Serves 4)

1¹/₂ quarts stock
*1 pound smoked pork loin
   (Canadian bacon)*
1 small head savoy cabbage
³/₄ pound carrots
³/₄ pound potatoes
2 leeks
Pepper to taste

METHOD

1. Heat the stock. Dice the smoked loin of pork and add to the stock.
2. Wash the savoy cabbage and cut into coarse ribbons. Peel the carrots and potatoes, slice the carrots and dice the potatoes. Slice the leeks. Add the vegetables to the stock and cook for 30 to 40 minutes. Season to taste with pepper.

HANNELORE KOHL

"**E**nrich this stew with cream or crème fraîche. You can vary the vegetables as you like, depending on the time of year."

VEGETABLE STEW WITH BEEF

Gemüse-Eintopf mit Rindfleisch (photo above, right)

INGREDIENTS (Serves 4)

*1 pound boneless beef chuck
   or round*
1¹/₂ quarts boiling water
Bunch of fresh parsley
1 onion, halved
2 bay leaves
2 cloves
10 peppercorns
³/₄ pound carrots
2 parsley roots or parsnips
³/₄ pound green beans
³/₄ pound white cabbage
Salt and pepper to taste

METHOD

1. Put the meat in the boiling water in a large saucepan. Add the parsley, halved onion, bay leaves, cloves, and peppercorns. Simmer over low heat for about an hour.
2. Remove the meat and dice. Strain the stock through a sieve. Peel the carrots and parsley roots or parsnips and dice. Clean the beans and cut into pieces. Clean the cabbage and cut into ribbons. Add the vegetables to the stock and cook for about another 20 minutes.
3. Add the meat. Season with salt and pepper. Serve garnished with parsley and bay leaves with French bread.

BRAISED MEAT WITH VOGTLAND DUMPLINGS

Schmorfleisch mit Vogtländer Klößen

INGREDIENTS (Serves 4)

FOR THE MEAT

4 slices bacon

2 pounds boneless ox or beef
  pot roast

Salt and pepper to taste

2 tablespoons clarified butter

1 onion

Bunch of vegetables for soup

1 tablespoon flour

1 bouillon cube

3 tablespoons tomato paste

FOR THE DUMPLINGS

3 1/2 to 4 pounds potatoes

1 egg

1/2 cup hot milk

4 cups white bread, cut in
  cubes

2/3 cup diced Canadian bacon

Salt to taste

METHOD

1. Cut the bacon into strips and use to lard the meat. Rub with salt and pepper. Heat the clarified butter and seal the meat until brown all over.

2. Peel the onion, dice, add to the pan, and brown also. Coarsely chop the soup vegetables, add to the pan and dust with flour. Pour on boiling water to cover. Add the bouillon cube and tomato paste, cover, and cook until the beef is tender.

3. To make the dumplings, peel and grate the potatoes. Put them in a bowl, smooth the surface, and pour on 1 to 2 cups cold water. Cover and leave to stand for a day.

4. Spread a dish towel loosely over a bowl, put the potato mixture onto it and then thoroughly squeeze the water out of the potatoes.

5. Leave the drained liquid to stand a minute or two so the potato starch settles to the bottom of the pan. Drain off the water and add the squeezed potatoes to the starch.

6. Mix together the egg and milk and season to taste with salt. Add to the potatoes. Add to the potatoes. Fry the bacon to render the fat. Brown the bread cubes in the fat and add to the dumpling mixture. Shape even-sized dumplings from the mixture, with the diced bacon in the centers. Cook in water at a rolling boil until tender.

HANNELORE KOHL

"*If there are any dumplings left over, the next day I cut them into slices and fry them in melted butter until golden brown.*"

68

SPICY ROAST PORK WITH MUSHROOMS

Würziger Braten mit Pilzen

INGREDIENTS (Serves 4)

1 ounce dried cèpes (porcini)
1 bay leaf
4 peppercorns
2 cloves
1½ cups stock
1¾ pounds boneless pork
  shoulder roast
3 tablespoons unsalted butter
1 onion
1¼ pounds button mushrooms
Bunch of fresh parsley, chopped
2 tablespoons sour cream
Salt and pepper to taste

METHOD

1. A day in advance, bring the cèpes, bay leaf, peppercorns and cloves to a boil in the stock; then leave to cool. Place the meat in a dish, pour the marinade over, cover, and refrigerate overnight.
2. Preheat the oven to 350°F. Remove the meat from the marinade, leave to drain, and then pat dry with paper towels. On the stovetop seal on all sides in the melted butter.
3. Peel the onion, dice, add to the meat, and fry until translucent. Put the roast into the oven. Strain the marinade. Baste the roast with the marinade every 10 minutes.
4. Clean the mushrooms. Season sparingly with salt and pepper. After 30 minutes cooking, add the mushrooms to the meat.
5. After 1 hour remove the meat from the oven, season with salt and pepper, turn off the oven, and leave the meat to rest in it for about 15 minutes.
6. Season the meat juices to taste with parsley and cream. Serve the gravy with the roast. Serve with new potatoes and salad.

LEIPZIG MIXED VEGETABLES

Leipziger Allerlei (photo below)

INGREDIENTS (Serves 4)

6 tablespoons unsalted butter
1/2 teaspoon salt
1/2 teaspoon sugar
1/2 pound each young carrots, kohlrabi, peas, and green beans, peeled and chopped as necessary
5 ounces small onions, peeled
1 pound white asparagus, chopped
1/2 pound fresh chanterelle mushrooms
1/4 pound fresh morel mushrooms
Grated nutmeg
2 tablespoons chopped fresh parsley

METHOD

1. In a large saucepan bring 1 quart of water to a boil with the butter, salt, and sugar. Add the carrots. After 5 minutes, add the asparagus, onions, kohlrabi, and beans. After a further 5 minutes, add the peas and cook everything together for 5 minutes more.
2. Drain the vegetables, reserving the liquid. Add the chanterelles and morels to the boiling liquid and simmer for 5 to 8 minutes.
3. Remove and reserve the mushrooms. Pour 2 cups of the vegetable stock into a clean pan, bring to a boil again, and reduce for 5 to 10 minutes. Season with nutmeg.
4. Heat the vegetables and mushrooms in the stock and sprinkle with parsley.

CREAM OF CUCUMBER SOUP

Gurkencremesuppe

INGREDIENTS (Serves 4)

1 medium cucumber
1 1/2 pounds potatoes
3 cups water
1 1/2 teaspoons salt
1/4 teaspoon black pepper
1 cup cream
1 cup milk
1 tablespoon grated onion
1 tablespoon minced fresh dill
Salt and pepper to taste

METHOD

1. Peel the cucumber, slice in half lengthwise, remove seeds, and cut in 1/4-inch dice.
2. Peel the potatoes and cut in 1/2-inch dice. Bring the water to a boil with the salt and pepper and add the potatoes. Cook the potatoes until soft and easy to mash.
3. Purée the potatoes and cooking liquid by pressing through a strainer. Return the purée to the pan and stir in the cream, milk, onion and diced cucumber.
4. Cook the diced cucumber in the soup for 5 minutes. Add the dill and season with salt and pepper to taste.

HANNELORE KOHL

"*In the original recipes for* Leipziger Allerei, *crayfish were an indispensable ingredient, but nowadays the vegetables are eaten with meat and potatoes.*"

Paprika Carp
Paprika-Karpfen

Carp in Dark Beer
Karpfen in Dunkelbier

INGREDIENTS (Serves 4)

*1 carp (3¹/₂ to 4 pounds), cleaned
and filleted*
Lemon juice
2 tablespoons soy sauce
1 tablespoon paprika
2 tablespoons diced onion
Salt to taste
Flour for coating
2 tablespoons butter
²/₃ cup plain yogurt
Bunch of fresh parsley, chopped
Lemon slices

FOR THE SAUCE

1 cup diced bacon
2 cups chopped onions
1 garlic clove, crushed
1 tablespoon paprika
2 tablespoons flour
2 cups vegetable stock
3 tablespoons tomato ketchup
1 bay leaf
Lemon juice
Salt to taste

METHOD

1. Cut the carp into 4 portions.
Drizzle with lemon juice and
soy sauce; sprinkle with
paprika and onion. Leave to
marinate for about an hour.

2. To make the sauce, fry the
bacon to render the fat and
fry the onion until golden
brown. Add the crushed
garlic, sprinkle with paprika
and flour, and stir well.
3. Pour on the stock. Add the
ketchup and bay leaf, bring
to a boil, and simmer for
3 minutes over low heat.
Season to taste with lemon
juice and salt.
4. Drain the carp portions,
season with salt, coat in flour
and fry in the melted butter
on both sides until golden
brown. Place the carp portions
in a clean pan, cover with the
paprika sauce and leave for
the flavors to combine for
3 minutes over low heat.
5. Arrange the carp on plates
with the sauce. Place a spoonful of yogurt on each portion,
sprinkle with parsley and
garnish with lemon slices.
Serve with boiled potatoes
and a raw vegetable salad.

INGREDIENTS (Serves 4)

*1 carp (3¹/₂ to 4 pounds), cleaned
and filleted*
Juice of 1 lemon
¹/₂ cup red wine
*2¹/₂ cups Malzbier (malt beer) or
bock beer*
1 onion
1 bay leaf
1 clove
¹/₄ cup golden raisins
¹/₂ pound carrots
1 fennel bulb
4 tablespoons butter
*³/₄ cup crumbled Lebkuchen or
gingerbread*
Salt and pepper to taste
Sugar
¹/₃ cup almonds

METHOD

1. Remove the skin from the
carp and cut into 4 pieces.
Season with pepper, drizzle
some lemon juice and red
wine over, and refrigerate for
about 2 hours.
2. Place the carp in a
flameproof dish and season
with salt. Pour on the beer
and the marinade. Peel and
mince the onion and add to

the dish with the bay leaf and
clove. Bring to a boil and
poach the fish for about
10 minutes over low heat.
3. Soak the golden raisins in a
little hot water. Peel the carrots and fennel, cut into thin
matchsticks, and fry for about
5 minutes in the melted butter.
4. Remove the carp from the
stock and keep warm. Strain
the stock into a saucepan,
bring to a boil, and thicken
with crumbled *Lebkuchen* or
gingerbread.
5. Stir in the vegetable matchsticks and drained golden
raisins. Season with salt,
pepper, the remaining lemon
juice, and sugar to taste.
6. Coarsely chop the almonds.
Pour the sauce over the carp
and sprinkle with almonds.
Serve with parsley potatoes.

NOTE

German malt beer is dark,
slightly sweet, and full-
bodied.

Leg of Lamb Cooked in Hay

Lammkeule im Heu gegart

INGREDIENTS (Serves 4)

5 1/2 pounds leg of lamb
5 garlic cloves
Fat for frying
2/3 cup vegetable oil
1/2 cup brandy
Grated zest of 1 lemon
Chopped fresh marjoram,
  rosemary, and thyme
Hay for lining the dish
Salt and freshly ground black
  pepper

FOR THE SAUCE

A few lamb bones, chopped
1/2 cup red wine
1/2 cup stock
4 tablespoons chilled unsalted
  butter, cubed
Lemon juice
Chopped fresh marjoram,
  rosemary, and thyme

METHOD

1. Season the lamb with pepper as well as the garlic cloves crushed with salt. Heat the fat in a roasting pan, add the lamb, and fry to seal on all sides.

2. Mix together the oil, brandy, lemon zest, and chopped herbs. Brush the leg of lamb all over with the marinade.

3. Preheat the oven to 350°F. Roast the lamb for 25 minutes, basting frequently with the marinade. Line a second pan with hay. Put the leg of lamb in the hay-lined pan and cover with more hay. Cook for a further 25 to 30 minutes in the oven.

4. To make the sauce, roast the bones in the meat juices left in the first pan. Gradually deglaze with red wine and stock and reduce a little each time. Remove the bones. Enrich the sauce with the butter, piece by piece, season to taste with a little lemon juice and herbs.

5. Remove the lamb from the hay. Slice the meat and serve with the sauce. Serve with Thuringian dumplings and green beans with bacon.

Wend Potato Salad

Wendischer Kartoffelsalat

INGREDIENTS (Serves 4)

2 pounds potatoes
3 tablespoons vinegar
3 tablespoons goose fat
Salt and pepper to taste
2 tablespoons sugar
1 pound apples
1 large onion
2 sour pickled cucumbers
Bunch of fresh chives

METHOD

1. Cook the potatoes in plenty of boiling, salted water. Drain, peel while still hot, slice, and keep warm.

2. Heat the vinegar gently and melt the goose fat in it. Do not allow to boil! Season to taste with salt, pepper, and sugar—it should be highly seasoned.

3. Wash the apples, quarter, remove cores, and dice finely. Peel the onion and dice; dice the cucumbers. Mix the apples, onion, and cucumber with the potatoes. Pour the hot vinegar mixture over and mix in thoroughly.

4. Cut the chives into short lengths, sprinkle over the potato salad, and serve warm. Serve with crispy meatballs.

ELDERBERRY SOUP WITH ALMOND DUMPLINGS

Holunderbeersuppe mit Mandelklößchen

INGREDIENTS (Serves 4)

FOR THE SOUP

1 pound (4 to 5 cups) elderberries
1 small cinnamon stick
1 piece of lemon zest
$^3/_4$ cup sugar
$^1/_2$ pound pears
$^3/_4$ pound plums
1 tablespoon cornstarch
$^2/_3$ cup white wine

FOR THE ALMOND DUMPLINGS

4 eggs
$^3/_4$ cup sugar
2 cups ground almonds
Breadcrumbs
Vegetable oil for deep frying

METHOD

1. Wash the elderberries, strip from stems, and boil in water for about 15 minutes. Pour into a strainer and press to extract as much juice as possible.
2. Bring the juice to a boil with the cinnamon, lemon zest, and sugar. Peel the pears, quarter, remove cores, cut into wedges, and add to juice. Cook the pears for 5 minutes over low heat.
3. Wash the plums, remove pits, quarter, add to juice, and cook briefly. Mix the cornstarch with a little cold water and use to thicken the soup. Stir in the wine, bring the soup to a boil, and check the sweetness.
4. To make the almond dumplings, beat the eggs and sugar until foaming. Stir in the almonds and enough breadcrumbs to make a soft, workable dough. Shape the dough into little dumplings and fry in the hot oil. Remove with a slotted spoon and drain on paper towels.
5. Divide the soup among soup plates. Place the dumplings in the soup and serve.

DRESDEN BAKED CHEESECAKE
Dresdner Eierschecke

INGREDIENTS (Serves 12)

FOR THE PASTRY

2 cups all-purpose flour
7 tablespoons unsalted chilled
    butter, cubed
3/4 cup sugar
1 tablespoon baking powder
1 egg
1 teaspoon vanilla-flavored sugar

FOR THE FILLING

1 pound Quark or ricotta
1/2 cup sugar
Grated zest and juice of 1/2
    lemon
6 1/2 tablespoons flour
1 egg
Pinch of salt
1 teaspoon vanilla-flavored sugar
Milk

FOR THE TOPPING

2 cups milk
1 package (42.5 g) vanilla
    pudding mix
1 cup plus 2 tablespoons sugar
14 tablespoons unsalted butter,
    at room temperature
3 eggs, separated
1 teaspoon vanilla-flavored sugar

METHOD

1. To make the pastry, quickly mix together the flour, cubed butter, sugar, baking powder, egg, and vanilla sugar to form a dough. Wrap the dough in plastic and refrigerate for 20 minutes. Preheat the oven to 400°F.

2. Grease a 10-inch diameter springform pan. Roll out the dough on a floured work surface and line the bottom and sides of the pan with the pastry. Prick the bottom all over with a fork.

3. To make the filling, mix together all the ingredients, adding enough milk to form a creamy mixture.

4. To make the topping, mix together the milk, pudding mix, and 2 tablespoons sugar. Cook until thickened, as directed on the package. Stir until cool.

5. In a mixing bowl beat the butter, remaining sugar, and egg yolks until foaming. Stir in the pudding a spoonful at a time. In a separate bowl beat the egg whites with the vanilla sugar until stiff and fold into the topping mixture.

6. Pour the filling into the pastry shell, cover with the topping, and smooth the surface. Bake for 10 minutes.

7. Reduce the temperature to 350°F and bake the cake for about an hour and 20 minutes or until done. If the cake starts to brown too much, cover with parchment paper.

HANNELORE KOHL

"*The Saxons love desserts. Dresden baked cheesecake is the most famous of innumerable cakes and tortes.*"

DRESDEN CHRISTMAS STOLLEN

Dresdner Christstollen

INGREDIENTS
(Makes 2 Stollen)

2 vanilla beans

1 cup sugar

1/4 cup rum

2 1/3 cups raisins

2/3 cup skinned, chopped almonds

1/3 cup diced candied lemon peel

2/3 cup diced candied orange peel

10 cups all-purpose flour

*6 cakes (0.6 ounce each) fresh
    compressed yeast or 6 enve-
    lopes active dry yeast*

1 3/4 cups lukewarm milk

2 eggs, beaten

Grated zest of 1 lemon

1 teaspoon salt

*2 cups (1 pound) plus 4 table-
    spoons unsalted butter, at
    room temperature*

METHOD

1. Split open the vanilla beans, remove the seeds, and mix well with the sugar. Half of the vanilla sugar is used for the mixture, and the rest is used for sprinkling over the Stollen.

2. Pour the rum over the raisins, almonds, lemon and orange peel and leave to soak for several hours.

3. Sift 4 cups of flour into a bowl and make a well in the center. Crumble the yeast and mix with 2/3 cup of the milk and a pinch of sugar, and then pour into the well. Mix with a little flour. Leave to proof in a warm place for about 15 minutes.

4. Add half of the prepared vanilla sugar, the remaining milk, eggs, lemon zest, and salt to the yeast mixture and knead to form a smooth dough. Leave the dough in a warm place to rise for 20 to 30 minutes.

5. In the meantime, knead 3/4 cup plus 2 tablespoons of the butter with the remaining flour. Knead the mixture into the risen yeast dough. Leave the dough to rise for a further 15 minutes.

6. Quickly work small batches of the rum-soaked fruits and nuts into the dough. Put the dough in a warm place again to rise for 15 minutes.

7. Divide the dough in half. Roll out each half of the dough to form a rectangle about 5 by 12 inches. On the longer edges form two bulges, one small and one large. Fold the edge with the small bulge in toward the other edge, so that both bulges lie next to each other. Gently smooth the Stollen into shape.

8. Place the Stollen on a well greased baking sheet and cover with a cloth. Leave to rise in a warm place for about an hour.

9. Preheat the oven to 400°F. Bake the Stollen on the bottom shelf for about an hour. If the Stollen browns too much, cover with foil or parchment paper.

10. Melt the remaining 6 tablespoons butter to brush over the Stollen while still warm. Dust with the remaining vanilla sugar.

QUARK CAKES

Quarkkeulchen

INGREDIENTS (Serves 4)

1 pound potatoes
1/2 pound (about 1 cup) low-fat Quark or ricotta
1 egg, beaten
About 1/2 cup all-purpose flour
Pinch of salt
1/4 cup sugar
1/2 teaspoon cinnamon
1/4 teaspoon vanilla-flavored sugar
Grated zest of 1 lemon
2/3 cup currants
7 tablespoons unsalted butter
Confectioners' sugar for dusting

METHOD

1. A day in advance, boil the potatoes. Peel and grate them.

2. Mix the Quark, egg, 6 tablespoons of the flour, salt, sugar, cinnamon, vanilla sugar, and lemon zest with the potatoes.

3. Pour a little hot water over the currants and leave to soak. Then drain, pat dry, and work into the potato mixture. If the dough is still a little sticky, add the remaining flour.

4. Using a tablespoon, scoop out portions of the dough and shape into ovals. Melt the butter in a large frying pan. Fry the potato cakes on all sides, until golden brown. While still hot dust with confectioners' sugar. Serve with apples.

TIPSY PEARS

Beschwipste Birnen

INGREDIENTS (Serves 4)

1 1/2 pounds pears
6 tablespoons sugar
1 1/2 tablespoons vanilla-flavored sugar
2 tablespoons apple or quince jelly
1/2 pound zwieback
Grated zest and juice of 1 lemon
2/3 cup pear juice
1 cup milk
2 egg yolks
1/2 cup blackberry liqueur (crème de mûre)
6 tablespoons unsalted butter

METHOD

1. Preheat the oven to 400°F. Peel, halve, and core the pears and cut diagonally into thin slices. Layer in a round baking dish.

2. Sprinkle the sugar and vanilla sugar over the pears. Spread the jelly on top. Crush the zwieback and sprinkle over the pears.

3. Mix the lemon juice and zest with the pear juice and use to moisten the zwieback. Beat together the milk and egg yolks. Mix with the liqueur and pour over the zwieback.

4. Dot the top with butter and cover with foil. Bake for about 15 minutes. Remove the foil and bake for 10 more minutes to brown the top.

Verger's Pudding

Küsterpudding (photo below)

INGREDIENTS (Serves 4)

6 egg whites
1 tablespoon cold water
1/2 cup plus 2 tablespoons sugar
7 ounces semisweet chocolate
1/2 cup cream
1/2 cup milk
Orange sections to garnish
Shredded orange zest to garnish

METHOD

1. Preheat the oven to 350°F. In a large bowl whisk the egg whites with the water and sugar until stiff. Butter a dome-shaped heatproof mold. Fill the mold with the meringue mixture.
2. Cover the mold with foil and place in a roasting pan containing gently boiling water (a *bain marie*). Bake the pudding for 20 minutes, until set. Remove the foil and bake the pudding for 25 more minutes until brown.
3. Unmold the pudding onto a glass serving plate and refrigerate. In the meantime, break the chocolate into small pieces and melt with the cream and milk mixture over low heat. Mix well and serve warm with the pudding.

Suhl Cream Slice

Suhler Rahmkuchen

INGREDIENTS (Serves 10–12)

FOR THE DOUGH
4 cups all-purpose flour
1/4 cup sugar
Pinch of salt
7 tablespoons unsalted butter, cubed
1 1/2 cakes (0.6 ounce each) fresh compressed yeast or 1 1/2 envelopes active dry yeast
1 cup lukewarm milk

FOR THE TOPPING
1 quart milk
3/4 cup sugar
2 packages (42.5 g each) of vanilla pudding mix
5 cups golden raisins
3 eggs
4 1/2 cups heavy cream

METHOD

1. Mix together the flour, sugar, salt, and butter. Cream or combine the yeast with the milk, cover, and leave to proof for a few minutes.
2. Mix everything to form a smooth dough. Cover and leave to rise in a warm place until doubled in size (about 20 minutes).
3. Grease a baking sheet with butter. Knead the dough, roll out on the baking sheet to about 1/2 inch thick, and leave to rise again briefly. Preheat the oven to 400°F.
4. Make up the pudding with milk and 1/2 cup of the sugar according to the directions on the package. Spread over the dough. Sprinkle the golden raisins on top. Mix together the eggs and remaining sugar. Stir in 4 cups of the cream and spread over the raisins.
5. Bake on the bottom oven shelf for about 45 minutes. Whip the remaining cream until stiff and pipe rosettes on the cooled cake.

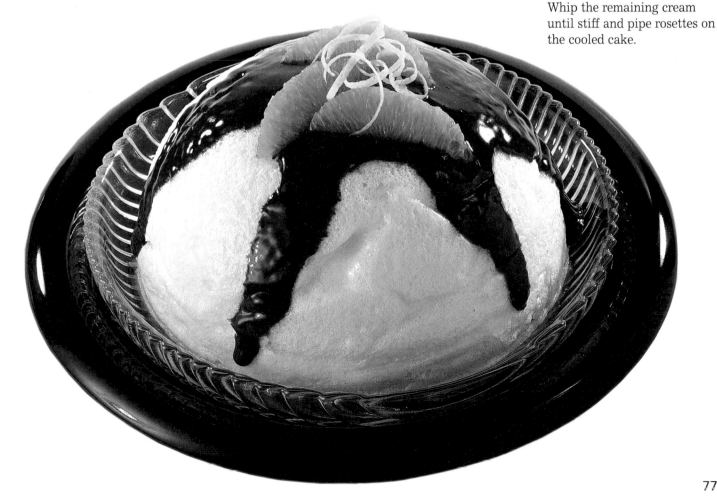

PEAR DUMPLINGS

Birnenklöße

INGREDIENTS (Serves 4)

3¼ cups all-purpose flour
1½ cakes (0.6 ounce each)
fresh compressed yeast or
1½ envelopes active dry yeast
3 tablespoons sugar
1½ tablespoons lukewarm milk
Grated zest and juice of 1 lemon
Pinch of salt
1 egg
3 tablespoons unsalted butter,
at room temperature
4 fully ripe, sweet pears
¼ cup brown sugar
1½ tablespoons pear schnapps
½ cup cinnamon sugar
½ cup beurre noisette (browned
butter)

METHOD

1. Sift the flour into a bowl and make a well. Cream or combine the crumbled or dry yeast with 1 teaspoon of the sugar in a little of the lukewarm milk. Pour the yeast into the well and mix with a little flour. Leave to proof for about 30 minutes.
2. Then work in the remaining milk and sugar, lemon zest, salt, egg, and butter to form a smooth dough. Knead the dough thoroughly. Leave to rise in a warm place until doubled in size.

3. Knead the dough again and then press out until about ½ inch thick and cut out squares of dough 3 by 3 inches.
4. Peel the pears, quarter, remove cores, and dice. Sprinkle with brown sugar and marinate in the lemon juice and pear schnapps.
5. Heap a spoonful of pears on each of the squares of dough. Press the edges of the dough together and shape into a ball. Leave to rise in a warm place for about 10 minutes.
6. Bring water to a boil in a large saucepan. Add the pear dumplings and poach for 12 minutes, covered. Turn the dumplings and cook for a further 6 minutes until done.
7. Remove the pears with a slotted spoon, dredge with cinnamon sugar and drizzle *beurre noisette* over. Serve immediately.

NOTES

To make cinnamon sugar, just mix ground cinnamon to taste with sugar. To make *beurre noisette*, heat the requisite amount of butter (preferably unsalted) gently in a pan until it turns a hazelnut brown color. Be careful not to let it burn.

ALMOND PUDDING

Mandel-Pudding

INGREDIENTS (Serves 4)

FOR THE PUDDING

4 eggs
¾ cup sugar
1½ tablespoons vanilla-flavored
sugar
3½ tablespoons cornstarch
1 cup milk
6 leaves of gelatin or
1½ packages powdered
unflavored gelatin
2 tablespoons almond liqueur
1 cup chopped almonds with
½ cup toasted
¼ cup grated chocolate

FOR THE SAUCE

3 egg yolks
6 tablespoons sugar
1 cup milk
1 tablespoon unsweetened cocoa
powder

METHOD

1. Separate the eggs. In a large bowl beat the sugar and vanilla sugar with the egg yolks until foamy. In a small bowl mix the cornstarch with the milk and add to the egg mixture.

2. In a separate bowl soften the gelatin in cold water.
3. Beat the egg mixture over hot water until thick and pale. Add the almond liqueur, gelatin, and untoasted almonds. Allow the custard to cool, stirring all the time. In a medium bowl beat the egg whites until stiff. Carefully fold the egg whites into the custard.
4. Rinse a desert mold with cold water and sprinkle with the toasted almonds. Pour the custard into the mold and leave in the refrigerator to set.
5. To make the sauce, beat the egg yolks and sugar in a small saucepan until foamy. Add the milk. Over low heat, beat the sauce with a balloon whisk until it turns creamy. Finally, stir in the cocoa powder.
6. Unmold the pudding on to a serving dish, sprinkle with grated chocolate, and pour around a pool of chocolate sauce.

AT THE MEAT COUNTER:
RELY UPON THE BUTCHER'S ADVICE

HANNELORE KOHL:
I can still remember during the war when a nice piece of meat seemed like an unobtainable delicacy. Many people today simply can't imagine it.

ALFONS SCHUHBECK:
Nowadays, meat is much more accessible and affordable. You can buy it from a butcher, at the supermarket, or from a farmer. Many different types of meat are available in a wide range of fatty or lean options.

HANNELORE KOHL:
Marbled meat is particularly tasty . . .

ALFONS SCHUHBECK:
That's right. It's the fat which contains the flavor. Gradually the word has spread, so that more and more consumers prefer marbled meat.

HANNELORE KOHL:
Which cut of meat is suitable for which purpose? Even experienced cooks often have difficulty in deciding.

ALFONS SCHUHBECK:
Your butcher or the expert at the meat counter in the super-market can help. It's a pity that many shoppers don't take advantage of their advice often enough. When several cuts could be used for the same dish, I would rely on the butcher's recommendation.

HANNELORE KOHL:
What tips are important when handling meat?

A carving steel is an essential piece of equipment in any kitchen. Meat knives should be sharpened regularly, so they cut perfectly.

ALFONS SCHUHBECK:
Meat should not be left in the packaging after you've bought it. Instead, you should place it in a china or glass bowl and cover it with a plate. If you have to buy the meat a few days before you are going to use it, for example, before a holiday, beef is a good choice. You should brush it with oil and leave it in the refrigerator so it continues to mature, and then it will be nice and tender.

HANNELORE KOHL:
Sealing meat properly so that the pores close immediately is also important.

ALFONS SCHUHBECK:
Using the right kind of fat is crucial so it is able to reach a high temperature and not burn. Clarified butter, for example, is very good for sealing meat. At the end of the cooking time meat should rest for an additional 15 min-utes or so before carving to prevent it from drying out. Otherwise, it loses too many delicious juices.

BY HELMUT KOHL

A Roman leader, a Celtic soldier, a Swedish knight, a Black Forest miner, a French actor, a Bohemian musician are just some of the colorful ways in which Carl Zuckmayer describes the origins of the inhabitants of the Rhineland in his novel *Des Teufels General:* "From the Rhine—that means from the West." For visitors interested in history the towns in the Rhine area are real treasure troves. Many of them were founded and built up by the Romans and can look back proudly on two thousand years of history. In Cologne the Roman-Germanic Museum next to the cathedral delves into the past, and in Bonn the history of the Federal Republic of Germany can be traced in the new "History House."

The oldest choir stall in the traditionally Catholic Rhineland can be seen in the cathedral at Xanten.

FROM THE LOWER RHINE TO THE EIFEL MOUNTAINS

It dates back to the thirteenth century. The chancel and altar in Xanten Cathedral have both recently been redesigned by a very good friend of mine, Professor Gernot Rumpf, from Neustadt. Up until 1531, German kings were crowned in the cathedral at Aachen, the city of Charlemagne.

In the Rhineland there are five seasons because in between winter and spring comes Carnival time. Here, to the surprise of many visitors, a *Halve Hahn* (half a chicken) turns out to be a rye-bread roll with cheese, and *Kölsche Kaviar* (Cologne caviar) is *blutwurst* (blood sausage) with mustard. The Rhinelander laughs merrily at people who are ignorant of local customs, breaking the ice in no time at all.

Good company and hospitality play a very important part in the Rhineland. Many little wine-growing towns strung out along the River Rhine, celebrate wine festivals and crown queens of the vintage; some songs from the Rhine are even known throughout the world. "Pützchen's Fair," the famous annual fair on the river bank opposite Bonn, has been celebrated since the fourteenth century, and the Anna Kermis, the fair in Düren, attracts visitors from all over Germany every year.

Crisp rösti and *Himmel un Äd* (Heaven and Earth), a specialty made from mashed potato, apples, and blood sausage are traditional dishes that go well with a freshly poured *Kölsch*. Like all top-fermented beers, Kölsch is quite light and thus fits in with the Rhinelander's light-hearted lifestyle. The history of the Cologne breweries, where the staff served in long aprons and which often had their own butcher next door, can be traced back in part to the fifteenth century.

Aachener Printen, famous throughout the world (and whose existence is documented as early as 1483), is sweetened with sugar-beet syrup, which is also used as a seasoning for Rhineland spiced beef. During May and June, asparagus from the foothills near Bonn and from the Lower Rhine is especially popular and often features at official dinners.

For outings and rambles there are the Eifel mountains on the left bank of the Rhine with their dormant volcanoes and volcanic lakes, as well as Bergish Land on the other side of the Rhine. It is worth popping into a café where *Bergische Kaffeetafel* (Bergish coffee and cakes) is still served, including waffles with hot cherries, rice pudding with cinnamon and sugar, black bread with liver sausage, fruit cake, jam, and *Klatsch-käse* or curd cheese. This colorful array is supposed to stem from the formerly poverty-stricken conditions in this area when hosts brought out whatever their pantries had to offer.

I also enjoy visiting the Maria Laach monastery on Lake Laach just to the south of Bad Neuenahr. This is the start of the famous Ahr valley, one of the major growing areas for delicious German wine. During the Nazi period, Konrad Adenauer, first Chancellor of Germany after World War II, found sanctuary and safety here with the Benedictine monks of Maria Laach.

In the area around Krefeld there are beautiful windmills just like those found in Holland.

Pea Soup

Ähzesupp (photo above)

INGREDIENTS (Serves 4)

2 shallots
1¹/₂ cups shelled peas
2 tablespoons unsalted butter
Salt, pepper, and sugar to taste
2 cups stock
¹/₄ cup cream
2 tablespoons diced bacon

METHOD

1. Peel and mince the shallots. Wash the peas.
2. Melt a little of the butter in a saucepan and fry the shallots and peas. Season with sugar, salt, and pepper and pour in the stock. Cook over low heat for 5 to 8 minutes.
3. Purée the soup. Add the cream and the remaining butter and mix together thoroughly. Blend briefly until foamy. Quickly reheat.
4. Fry the bacon until crisp in its own fat. Drain and sprinkle on the soup.

Cabbage and Sausage Soup

Pitter un Jupp

INGREDIENTS (Serves 4)

Unsalted butter
1 small head savoy cabbage, cut in ribbons
4 carrots, peeled and diced
1 pound potatoes, peeled and diced
Some vegetables and herbs for soup, e.g., leek, fennel, thyme, parsley, chopped
3 cups stock
Salt, pepper, and grated nutmeg to taste
4 Mettwurst lean minced pork or beef sausages
Small bunch of fresh parsley, minced

METHOD

1. Melt a little butter in a large saucepan and soften the cabbage. Add the remaining vegetables in layers and pour in the stock. Simmer the soup for 35 to 40 minutes on low heat. Gently mash the vegetables and season to taste with salt, pepper, and nutmeg.
2. Cook the sausages in boiling water for about 10 minutes. Slice the sausages, add to the soup, and leave for the flavors to blend for about 5 minutes. Serve sprinkled with finely chopped parsley.

BITBURG BEER SOUP

Bitburger Biersuppe

INGREDIENTS (Serves 4)

Unsalted butter
2 slices rye bread, cubed
2³/4 cups lager-type beer
2 tablespoons raisins
¹/4 cinnamon stick
2 egg yolks
1 cup heavy cream
Sugar, salt, pepper, and grated
  nutmeg to taste
Chopped fresh parsley to garnish

METHOD

1. Melt a little butter in frying pan and fry the bread cubes until golden brown. Put the beer, raisins, cinnamon, and a little sugar in a saucepan and bring quickly to a boil. Season to taste with salt, pepper, and nutmeg.
2. In a small bowl whip together the egg yolks and cream and add to thicken the soup. Do not allow to boil.
3. Divide the soup among warmed soup plates. Scatter the croûtons on top and garnish with parsley.

COLORFUL POTATO SOUP

Bunte Kartoffelsuppe

INGREDIENTS (Serves 4)

1 pound potatoes
2 onions
2 tablespoons pork drippings
1 quart stock
¹/2 fennel bulb
1 leek
3 carrots
2 tomatoes
1 piece parsley root or parsnip
1 cup diced bacon
2 tablespoons chopped fresh
  parsley to garnish

METHOD

1. Peel and dice the potatoes. Peel and mince the onions.
2. Melt the pork drippings and fry the onions until translucent. Add the stock.
3. Prepare the vegetables, chop into small pieces and add to the stock, with the potatoes. Cook the vegetables for about 30 to 40 minutes in the stock.
4. Fry the bacon until crisp in its own fat. Drain. Sprinkle the soup with bacon and parsley and serve.

HANNELORE KOHL

"**C**innamon is the bark of a tropical bay tree. To make cinnamon sticks, several sheets from the inner bark of young plants are layered together, rolled up, and then dried. Cinnamon from Sri Lanka is considered the best."

HANNELORE KOHL

"**Y**ou can also prepare the potato soup a day in advance. The soup can then infuse overnight and develop a particularly flavorsome aroma. Add the parsley just before serving."

SAUERKRAUT SALAD

Sauerkrautsalat (photo above)

INGREDIENTS (Serves 4–6)

1 pound mild fresh sauerkraut
   (from a jar)
2 red apples
3 pickled gherkins
1 small onion
3 tablespoons sour cream
Pinch of sugar

METHOD

1. Rinse the sauerkraut and loosen with a fork.
2. Quarter the apples (with peel), remove cores, and cut into small dice. Dice the gherkins. Peel the onion and slice into thin rings. Mix the prepared ingredients with the cream and sugar.
3. Serve the salad with cold roast meat or as an hors d'oeuvre. You can also hollow out tomatoes, fill them with the salad, and serve with dark rye bread.

MUSTARD CHOPS

Senf-Rippchen

INGREDIENTS (Serves 4)

3 slices white bread
1 cup milk
1 onion
1 pound ground meat
2 tablespoons mustard
3 eggs
2 tablespoons vegetable oil
Salt and white pepper to taste
4 tablespoons unsalted butter
4 thin pork chops
³/₄ cup grated cheese

METHOD

1. Preheat the oven to 400⁰F. Cut the white bread into large pieces and soak in the milk. Peel and mince the onion.
2. Squeeze the milk out of the bread, mix with the ground meat, the onion, and mustard. Beat the eggs and knead into the meat mixture with the oil and season with salt and pepper to taste.
3. Melt the butter in a frying pan and fry the chops for 2 minutes on each side to seal. Remove and place on a baking sheet.
4. Spread the meat mixture on top of the chops. Sprinkle with the cheese, and bake the chops for about 5 minutes. Serve with potato dumplings and peas or cauliflower.

STUFFED MEATBALLS

Frikadellen vom falschen Hasen (photo right)

INGREDIENTS (Serves 4)

3 to 4 stale bread rolls
Lukewarm milk
1 onion
2 tablespoons vegetable oil
3/4 pound ground beef
1/2 pound ground pork
1 egg
2 to 3 tablespoons wholegrain
*   mustard*
Fresh basil leaves, minced
Salt and pepper to taste
8 hard-boiled quail eggs
Breadcrumbs
1 1/2 tablespoons clarified butter
2/3 cup heavy cream
Lemon juice

METHOD

1. Preheat the oven to 350°F. Soak the bread rolls in a little milk and squeeze out. Peel and mince the onion and fry in the oil until translucent.
2. Thoroughly mix the ground meats, bread, onion, egg, and mustard. Season to taste with basil, salt, and pepper.
3. Divide the meat mixture into eight even portions and press lightly to flatten. Shell the quail eggs, place on top of the patties, and mold the meat mixture around the eggs, to enclose them.
4. Coat the stuffed meatballs in the breadcrumbs. Heat the clarified butter in a flame-proof pan. Fry the meatballs briefly, then bake for 25 minutes until done. Baste occasionally with the juices.
5. Remove the meatballs and keep warm. Deglaze the meat juices with the cream and allow to reduce a little. Season the sauce to taste with lemon juice and serve with the meatballs.

POTATO AND LEEK SOUP WITH SMOKED SAUSAGE

Kartoffel-Lauch-Suppe mit Grützwurst (photo above)

INGREDIENTS (Serves 4)

2 onions
5 ounces young leeks
3 tablespoons clarified butter
1 pound baking potatoes
2 cups concentrated beef stock
2 tablespoons unsalted butter
2 tablespoons cream
Grated nutmeg, salt, and white
*   pepper to taste*
Chopped fresh marjoram

FOR GARNISH

3 ounces Grützwurst *(coarse*
*   smoked sausage)*
Flour
4 heaped tablespoons whipped
*   cream*
Fresh parsley sprigs

METHOD

1. Peel the onions, clean the leeks, and cut both into thin rings. Melt half of the clarified butter and fry the leek and onions until soft.
2. Peel the potatoes and add to the leeks and onions. Pour in the beef stock and simmer until cooked.
3. Purée the soup. Then press through a chinois (fine conical sieve), or use a food mill (mouli) if you don't have a chinois.
4. Reheat the soup. Enrich with butter and cream, and season with nutmeg, salt, pepper, and a little marjoram.
5. Slice the sausage, toss in flour and fry on both sides in the remaining clarified butter.
6. Serve the soup in warmed soup plates and garnish with smoked sausage, whipped cream, and parsley.

HANNELORE KOHL

"*If you cannot obtain quail eggs, wrap quartered, hard-boiled hen's eggs in the meat mixture. You can give the meat extra flavor by adding tomato paste.*"

POTATO BAKE

Rheinischer Döbbekooche

SAUSAGES WITH APPLES

Bratwurst mit Äpfeln

INGREDIENTS (Serves 4–6)

2 bread rolls

1 cup milk

1 large onion

7 pounds potatoes

1 apple

2 to 3 eggs

1/2 teaspoon salt

Pepper to taste

1 cup diced bacon

METHOD

1. Preheat the oven to 400°F. Soak the rolls in the milk. Squeeze out and reserve the milk. Peel and dice the onion.

2. Peel the potatoes and apple, grate, place in a dish towel, and squeeze out as much liquid as possible. Collect the liquid and leave to stand for 5 minutes, so the potato starch settles.

3. Mix together the potatoes, apple, onion, bread, eggs, salt, pepper, and bacon. Drain off the potato liquid and mix the potato starch into the potato mixture. Add a little of the reserved milk if necessary.

4. Thoroughly butter a baking dish, fill with the mixture, and bake for 60 to 70 minutes.

INGREDIENTS (Serves 4)

1 1/2 pounds apples

2 tablespoons sugar

1/2 teaspoon ground cinnamon

1 cup raisins or currants

4 tablespoons unsalted butter

4 Bratwurst

1 teaspoon grated zest of a lemon

1/4 cup white wine or apple juice

METHOD

1. Peel the apples, quarter, core, and cut into eighths. Sprinkle with 1 tablespoon of sugar and the cinnamon.

2. Add the raisins or currants, mix together, and leave to stand for an hour.

3. Melt the butter in a casserole and fry the sausages. Add the apples, raisins, remaining sugar, and lemon zest. Braise for 20 minutes over low heat with the lid on. The apples should be tender but not mushy.

4. Flavor the juices with the wine or apple juice. Serve with potato, semolina, or bread dumplings.

HUNSRÜCK CHICKEN STEW

Eintopf vom Hunsrücker Hahn

INGREDIENTS (Serves 4)

1 chicken, about 4¹/₂ pounds
2 tablespoons vegetable oil
Salt and pepper to taste
1 medium onion
2 medium carrots
1 fennel bulb
3 cups sliced button mushrooms
1 garlic clove
2 cups Pinot Noir
2 cups chicken stock
1 fresh thyme sprig

1 fresh rosemary sprig
1 fresh basil sprig
1 bay leaf
¹/₂ cup chilled unsalted butter, cubed

METHOD

1. Rinse the chicken, pat dry, and divide into eight portions. To do this remove both legs and cut the breast and the wings in half.

2. Heat the oil in a casserole and brown the chicken on the skin side. Season with salt and pepper.

3. Peel the onion, carrots, and fennel, cut into ¹/₂-inch dice, and add to chicken. Clean the mushrooms, peel the garlic, and slice both. Add to the chicken and fry everything together briefly.

4. Remove the breast portions and place to one side. Deglaze the juices with the red wine and allow to reduce. Add the chicken stock. Cover the pot and leave to simmer for about 30 minutes over low heat.

5. Return the breast portions and herbs and cook for a further 10 minutes. Finally, stir in the butter and season to taste. Serve the stew straight from the casserole, with potatoes and strips of bacon.

FARMER'S BREAKFAST

Bauernfrühstück

INGREDIENTS (Serves 4)

2 pounds small, waxy potatoes
2 onions
1 cup diced bacon
3 eggs
3 tablespoons milk
Salt and pepper to taste
Bunch of fresh chives
1 tomato

METHOD

1. Boil the potatoes in their skins. Peel and leave to cool. Then dice.
2. Peel and dice the onions. Fry with the bacon until translucent. Add the diced potato and fry everything together until brown.
3. Beat together the eggs and milk, season with salt and pepper, pour over the potato mixture, and cook over low heat until set, loosening the edge of the omelette occasionally with a spatula so that the egg cooks evenly.
4. Cut the chives into short lengths and the tomato into slices. Use to garnish the omelette. Serve with a mixed salad including cucumber slices and grated carrot.

PANFRIED MEAT LOAF

Panhas (photo right)

INGREDIENTS (Serves 4)

3 onions
²/₃ cup diced bacon
1¹/₂ quarts meat stock
³/₄ pound Leberwurst *(liver sausage)*
³/₄ pound Blutwurst *(blood sausage)*
Salt and pepper to taste
¹/₂ teaspoon ground cloves
1 tablespoon rubbed dried marjoram
5 cups buckwheat flour
¹/₄ cup clarified butter

METHOD

1. Peel the onions and cut into small dice. Render the fat of the diced bacon in a frying pan. Fry the onions in the bacon fat. Pour off excess fat.
2. Add the stock. Remove the liver sausage and blood sausage from their skins and add to the stock; quickly bring to a boil. Season to taste with salt, pepper, ground cloves, and marjoram.
3. Add the buckwheat flour, stirring all the time. Bring to a boil and cook for about 10 minutes. Then leave to cook for 30 minutes on low heat.
4. Turn the meat mixture out into a bowl, level out, and leave to cool. Unmold onto a plate and slice. Fry on both sides in the hot clarified butter. Serve with parsley potatoes and rye bread rolls.

RÖSTI WITH BACON

Reibekuchen mit Speck

INGREDIENTS (Serves 4)

3¹/₂ pounds potatoes
2 onions
1¹/₃ cups diced bacon
2 eggs, beaten
Salt and pepper to taste
Clarified butter

METHOD

1. Peel the potatoes, wash, grate, and leave to drain in a sieve.
2. Peel the onions and chop finely. Chop the bacon into small dice. Mix together the potatoes, onion, and bacon. Mix in eggs and season with salt and pepper.
3. Heat the clarified butter in a frying pan. Using two tablespoons, place small heaps of the potato mixture in the pan and press flat. Fry the rösti on both sides until golden brown. Serve with apple compôte.

HANNELORE KOHL

"Rösti *are found throughout Germany, but nowhere are they as common as in the Rhine region. Freshly cooked* Rievekooche, *as they are called in the Rhine dialect, can be bought on any street corner."*

EIFEL POT ROAST

Eifeler Schmorbraten

INGREDIENTS (Serves 10)

4$1/2$ pounds boneless pork
  shoulder roast
Salt to taste
8 onions
2 bay leaves
8 allspice berries
$2/3$ cup wine vinegar
1 quart ale or bitter beer
$2/3$ cup honey
1 to 2 tablespoons flour

METHOD

1. Preheat the oven to 350°F.
Rinse the meat, pat dry and
rub with salt. Peel the onions,
slice into rings, and place in
a lidded roasting dish, with
the meat, bay leaves, and
allspice berries.
2. Mix together the wine
vinegar and beer, dissolve the
honey in the mixture, and
pour enough of the liquid
into the dish to cover the
meat halfway. Tightly cover
the dish and braise the meat
for 2 hours, or until meat
is done.

3. Remove the meat from the
dish and keep warm. Pour the
remaining vinegar and beer
mixture into the dish and
deglaze the meat juices.
4. Strain the gravy and
reduce. Mix the flour with a
little cold water and use to
thicken the gravy. Serve with
savoy cabbage and boiled
potatoes.

HANNELORE KOHL

"**H**alfway through the cooking time, add shallots and
tomatoes to the dish. Remove the vegetables from the
gravy before straining it and return them once the
gravy has been thickened."

POTATO PANCAKES

Schnippelkuchen

INGREDIENTS (Serves 4)

1 cup milk

3 tablespoons flour

5 eggs

1 1/2 pounds potatoes

Salt, pepper, and grated nutmeg to taste

4 shallots

2 tablespoons unsalted butter

3/4 pound boiled ham, sliced

1/2 pound corn salad (mâche)

2 tablespoons vinegar

1 tablespoon balsamic vinegar

6 tablespoons vegetable oil

METHOD

1. Mix the milk and flour together and beat in the eggs. Peel the potatoes and immediately grate or slice with a mandolin into the batter. Season to taste with salt, pepper, and nutmeg. Peel and mince the shallots and add to the batter.

2. Melt the butter in a pan and fry the ham briefly. Remove. Pour in half the potato mixture, put the ham on top, and then pour on the remaining potato. Fry the pancake on both sides, until crisp and golden brown. Keep warm.

3. Prepare the corn salad, wash thoroughly, and leave to drain. Mix together the vinegar, balsamic vinegar, oil, and a little water. Season to taste with salt and pepper. Dress the corn salad with the vinaigrette. Arrange on plates with the potato pancakes cut in wedges.

HEAVEN AND EARTH

Himmel un Äd

INGREDIENTS (Serves 4)

2 pounds potatoes

2 pounds apples

1 teaspoon sugar

2 onions

1 2/3 cups diced bacon

Salt, pepper, and grated nutmeg to taste

1 pound Blutwurst (blood sausage)

2 tablespoons unsalted butter

METHOD

1. Peel the potatoes, cut into chunks, and cook in salted water until tender. Peel the apples, quarter, core, and cook in a little water and the sugar until tender.

2. Place the potatoes in a large bowl. Push the apples through a sieve and add to the potatoes. Beat until smooth, using an electric mixer with a dough hook. Return to a saucepan and heat briefly.

3. Peel the onions and cut into small dice. Render the bacon fat in a frying pan, fry the onions in the bacon fat until golden brown, and stir into the potato and apple mixture. Season to taste with salt, pepper and nutmeg.

4. Cut the blood sausage into 1/2-inch thick slices. Melt the butter and fry the sliced sausage in it on both sides. Serve the potato and apple mixture with the blood sausage.

Rhineland Spiced Beef

Rheinischer Sauerbraten

INGREDIENTS (Serves 4)

2 pounds beef shoulder pot roast
2 carrots
1 large onion
1/2 cup wine vinegar
1 quart water
3 cloves
8 peppercorns
1 bay leaf
4 juniper berries (optional)
Pinch of sugar
Salt and pepper to taste
2 tablespoons clarified butter
1/2 cup crumbled Lebkuchen *or gingerbread*
1 tablespoon apple jelly
11/3 cups raisins
3 tablespoons sour cream

METHOD

1. Place the meat in a large dish. Peel the carrots and onion and chop them into small pieces. Bring the vinegar, water, carrots, onion, spices, bay leaf, and sugar to a boil and leave to cool. Pour over the meat and leave the meat to marinate for 2 to 3 days in the liquid, turning now and again.
2. Remove the meat from the marinade, pat dry, and rub with salt and pepper. Heat the clarified butter in a flame-proof casserole and sear the meat all over in it.
3. Add the crumbled *Lebkuchen* and apple jelly. Strain the marinade and add to the casserole. Braise for 1½ hours over medium heat, basting the meat frequently.
4. Wash the raisins and add to the casserole 15 minutes before the end of cooking.
5. Remove the meat and keep warm. Season the gravy to taste and enrich it with sour cream. Slice the meat and arrange on a serving dish. Serve with potato dumplings.

Rösti with Smoked Trout

Reibekuchen mit Räucherforelle

INGREDIENTS (Serves 4)

31/2 pounds potatoes
2 onions
2 eggs, beaten
Salt and pepper to taste
Clarified butter
1 cup heavy cream
1 tablespoon lemon juice
2 tablespoons freshly grated horseradish
1 sharp apple, finely grated
4 smoked trout fillets, halved

METHOD

1. Peel the potatoes, wash, grate, and leave to drain in a strainer. Peel and mince the onions. Mix together the potatoes and onions, stir in the eggs, and season with salt and pepper.
2. Heat a little clarified butter in a frying pan. Using 2 tablespoons, place little heaps of potato in the pan and press flat. Fry the rösti on both sides until golden brown. Keep 8 rösti warm, allow the rest to cool, and freeze them for thawing and cooking later.
3. Whip the cream until stiff and mix with the lemon juice, horseradish, apple, and salt to taste. Place two rösti on each plate and place half a trout fillet on each rösti.
4. Divide the cream among the trout fillets. If liked, garnish with apple slices or salad leaves and cherry tomatoes.

Martinmas Goose with Apples and Chestnuts

Martinsgans mit Äpfeln und Maronen

INGREDIENTS (Serves 4)

1 goose, about 11 pounds
Salt and pepper to taste
1 teaspoon chopped fresh marjoram
1 teaspoon chopped fresh mugwort (see note)
3 apples
2 onions
1/2 pound (1 1/2 cups) peeled chestnuts
2 cups stock

METHOD

1. Rinse the goose thoroughly inside and out and place in ice water for 4 to 5 hours.
2. Preheat the oven to 325°F. Pat the goose dry very carefully and rub inside and out with salt, pepper, marjoram, and mugwort.
3. Peel the apples, quarter, remove cores, and chop up small. Peel the onions and cut into eighths. Mix the onions and apples. Use half to stuff the goose. Sew up the cavity with kitchen string.
4. Place the goose, breast up, in a large roasting pan. Pour in 1 cup of water, place the roasting pan on the middle shelf, and roast the goose for 2 hours.

5. Increase the temperature to 400°F. Add the remaining stuffing mixture and the chestnuts and roast with the goose for a further 30 minutes. Baste the goose occasionally with the juices.
6. Remove the goose, apples, onions, and chestnuts from the pan and keep warm. Take off the wings and neck, chop finely, and seal in the roasting juices. Deglaze with the stock and simmer for 30 minutes.

7. Strain the gravy and season to taste. Slice the goose and serve with the apples, onions, chestnuts, and gravy.

NOTE

Mugwort (also known as St John's Wort, *Artemisia vulgaris*) is traditional in stuffings for goose but you could use any fresh herb you like. Mugwort has a slightly bitter taste and digestive properties.

HANNELORE KOHL

"*Placing the goose in ice water for a long time before roasting is an age-old trick. It makes the skin turn especially crisp when roasted. Of course, you can do the same with duck and chicken.*"

LIMBURGER ROLLS
Halve Hahn

INGREDIENTS (Serves 4)

4 rye bread rolls
Unsalted butter
2 Limburger cheeses
6 tablespoons wholegrain
    mustard
Black pepper to taste
Raw onion slices or radishes
    for garnish (optional)

METHOD

1. Slice the bread rolls in half
and spread each half with a
little butter.
2. Cut the Limburger cheese
into roughly 1/4-inch thick
slices and use to cover the
halved rolls.
3. Spread the mustard on top
of the cheese. Season with
pepper. Garnish with onions
or radishes, if desired.

APPLE JELLY
Apfelkraut

INGREDIENTS
(Makes about 5 quarts)

22 pounds sweet, ripe apples
1 vanilla bean, split
About 1/3 package powdered
    pectin (optional)

METHOD

1. Wash the apples well, quarter, core, and chop coarsely.
2. Place the chopped apple
in the upper section of a
steamer. Place a little water
in the lower section. Juice the
apples for a long time.
3. Bring the juice to a boil
with the split vanilla bean
and reduce to the desired
consistency (or add pectin to
speed jelling, if preferred).
Fill sterilized jars with apple
jelly while still hot.

HANNELORE KOHL

"*Apple jelly can be used in many ways other than as a
spread. Fruit juices taste wonderful if flavored with
apple jelly or try drizzling apple jelly over homemade
granola with yogurt.*"

DUCK-STUFFED BEER ROLLS WITH PLUM SAUCE

Rheinische Altbiertaschen mit Entenbrustfüllung und Pflaumensauce

INGREDIENTS (Serves 4)

FOR THE DOUGH
1¹/₂ cups whole wheat flour
3 cups rye flour
2 packages active dry yeast
2 teaspoons sugar
Pinch of salt
1¹/₄ cups ale or bitter beer

FOR THE STUFFING
4 boneless duck breast halves
1¹/₂ tablespoons clarified butter
Salt and pepper to taste

FOR THE SAUCE
¹/₂ cup meat stock
3 tablespoons puréed plums
3 tablespoons ale or bitter beer
1 tablespoon red wine vinegar
Salt, pepper, and cayenne to taste
5 prunes

METHOD

1. To make the dough, knead together all the ingredients, which should be at room temperature, to form a smooth dough. Cover the dough and leave to rise in a warm place for about 15 minutes. Preheat the oven to 350°F.

2. Seal the duck breast halves on all sides in the hot clarified butter. Season with salt and pepper.

3. Knead the dough, roll out as thinly as possible, and divide into 4 rectangles. Wrap each breast half in a dough rectangle and brush with a little water. Bake until golden brown.

4. In the meantime, deglaze the meat residues with the meat stock. Add the plum purée, beer, and vinegar. Season to taste with salt, pepper, and cayenne. Cut the prunes into strips, add to the sauce, and let them heat through.

5. Turn the oven off and leave the duck rolls to rest for 5 minutes. Slice thickly and serve with the plum sauce.

CARAMEL PUDDING

Karamelpudding

INGREDIENTS (Serves 4–6)

10 tablespoons confectioners'
* sugar*
Vegetable oil
1 cup milk
6 tablespoons unsalted butter
1/2 vanilla bean, split
1 cup all-purpose flour
8 egg whites
8 egg yolks

METHOD

1. Place 6 tablespoons of the confectioners' sugar in a nonstick saucepan and leave until golden brown and caramelized. Pour the caramel on to an oiled marble board and leave to cool. Crush finely.
2. Bring the milk, butter and split vanilla bean to the boil. Stir in the flour and cook for several minutes, stirring constantly. Remove the vanilla bean from the mixture.
3. In a large bowl whisk together the egg whites and sugar until foamy. Stir into the milk mixture with the egg yolks and caramel. Pour into a buttered and sugared dessert mold two-thirds full with the mixture and cover the mold tightly with foil. Cook the pudding for about 35 to 40 minutes in a covered pan half-filled with simmering water.
4. Remove the mold from the pan of water. Leave the pudding to rest for a little while and then unmold. Serve with vanilla custard sauce, fruit sauce, or caramel sauce.

MILK-CURD MOLD WITH BERRIES

Dickmilchgelee mit Beerenfrüchten

INGREDIENTS (Serves 4)

5 leaves of gelatin, or 1 package
* powdered unflavored gelatin*
1 pound Dickmilch (thick sour
* milk), yogurt, sour cream,*
* buttermilk, or fromage blanc*
1/4 cup sugar
1/2 pound mixed berries,
* e.g., raspberries, blackberries,*
* red currants, black currants,*
* strawberries*
Fresh mint leaves and mixed
* berries to garnish*

METHOD

1. Soften the gelatin for 10 minutes in a little cold water. Mix together the thick sour milk or its alternative and sugar. Put 2 tablespoons of the milk in a saucepan with the gelatin (drain leaf gelatin). Dissolve the gelatin over low heat. Stir the gelatin mixture into the remaining milk.
2. Wash the berries, sprinkle lightly with sugar, and use to fill 4 small molds. Cover with the still-liquid milk mixture and refrigerate until set.
3. Dip the molds briefly in hot water and unmold the desserts onto plates. Garnish with mint leaves and berries.

HANNELORE KOHL

"*If you don't have suitable molds, simply pour the mixture into coffee or teacups and leave to set.*"

RHINELAND CURRANT CAKE

Rheinischer Korinthenblatz

INGREDIENTS (Serves 10–12)

2¹/₂ cups currants
8 cups all-purpose flour
3 cakes (0.6 ounce each) fresh
    compressed yeast or 3 enve-
    lopes active dry yeast
³/₄ cup sugar
1 cup lukewarm milk
14 tablespoons unsalted butter
2 eggs
1 teaspoon salt
1 teaspoon ground cinnamon
1 egg yolk
1 tablespoon milk

METHOD

1. Soak the currants in lukewarm water for about 30 minutes. Leave to drain thoroughly.

2. Place the flour in a bowl and make a well in it. Crumble the compressed yeast and mix with a little sugar and the milk. Pour into the well, mix with a little flour, cover and leave to proof in a warm place for about 15 minutes.

3. Melt the butter and add to the yeast mixture with the remaining sugar, eggs, salt, cinnamon, and drained currants. Knead to form a smooth yeast dough. Knead for about 10 minutes.

4. Line a baking sheet with parchment paper and place the sides of a 10-inch diameter springform pan on top. Place the dough in the ring.

5. Mix together the egg yolk and milk and use to glaze the dough. Cut a cross in the surface of the dough. Cover and leave to rise for 1 to 2 hours in a warm place.

6. Preheat the oven to 400°F and bake for about an hour. The currant cake should be very crisp on the outside and meltingly soft inside.

BLUSHING VIRGIN

Errötende Jungfrau

INGREDIENTS (Serves 4)

1 cup buttermilk

³/4 cup sugar

2 cups heavy cream

2 tablespoons lemon juice

2 tablespoons fruit schnapps

*5 leaves of gelatin or 1 package
    powdered unflavored gelatin*

4 cups raspberries

Confectioners' sugar for dusting

Fresh mint leaves to garnish

METHOD

1. Whisk the buttermilk with half of the sugar and half the cream until light and fluffy. Stir in the lemon juice and schnapps.

2. Soften the gelatin for 5 minutes in cold water. Drain gelatin leaves, dissolve over a low heat, and stir into the buttermilk mixture. Leave in the refrigerator for about 30 minutes until thick.

(You should be able to make a trail with a fork that holds its shape.)

3. Wash the raspberries, mix with the remaining sugar, and leave to juice. Place the berries in a strainer, collecting the juice.

4. Whip the remaining cream until stiff and fold evenly into the setting buttermilk mixture. Divide the mixture in half and mix one half with

the raspberry juice. Divide this half among dessert plates.

5. Place some raspberries on top, spoon on the white cream, and sprinkle with the remaining raspberries. Refrigerate the dessert again until completely set.

6. Just before serving dust the plate with the confectioners' sugar and garnish with mint leaves.

IN A STIR ABOUT STEWS

HANNELORE KOHL:
I've noticed that soups and stews, which have their origins in modest cooking and often came into being as a way of using up leftovers, are becoming more and more fashionable. Have you experienced this in your restaurant as well?

ALFONS SCHUHBECK:
Among other things, we offer fish stew, stew made with beef skirt or flank, and cassoulet. They are always very popular. The trend is toward "good home-cooking." Traditional dishes made with home-grown produce in a time-honored fashion are in demand again. Because of this development, stews are being treated with greater importance. A big bowl of savory stew enjoyed round the table with friends is something truly special.

HANNELORE KOHL:
How important is it to make the base of the soup yourself with bones and meat? It's very time-consuming. Won't a ready-made stock or bouillon cube do?

ALFONS SCHUHBECK:
If you've planned having a stew or soup on your menu well in advance, I would always advise making your own stock. The flavor simply can't be beaten. If you need a stew to provide a quick meal, then use a bouillon cube. Often, though, the basis of a good soup or stew is the by-product of another dish, such as when you prepare roast beef.

Who's poking their nose in here? Doesn't matter, they both like the vegetable soup.

HANNELORE KOHL:
I often freeze portions of vegetable soup or stew. This way I always have a meal at hand if I don't have enough time to cook.

ALFONS SCHUHBECK:
This is another advantage of stews, that they freeze and reheat particularly well. Many people swear that pea soup, for example, or Swabian lentil stew with noodles, taste better when reheated. If you intend to reheat a vegetable stew, you should take care when cooking the stew that the vegetables retain plenty of "bite." Otherwise, they will quickly become soggy and unappetizing when reheated.

BETWEEN THE RHINE AND THE TEUTOBURG FOREST

BY HELMUT KOHL

On our way from the Ruhr area to Münster, we discover two completely different regions that have formed a happy union, and both have changed the course of history in Germany and farther afield.

In Münster, a city rich in tradition, the Thirty Years' War was brought to an end in 1648 with the Peace of Westphalia, a truly European peace. At this time, The Netherlands finally achieved popular recognition as an independent state.

Since August 1995, the 1st German-Dutch Corps has been garrisoned in Münster.

▶

Despite modern agricultural technology, the countryside around Münster still shows signs of traditional farming techniques and cultivation. When the ploughed fields and meadows of Eastern Westphalia are swathed in mist on an autumn day, it is a reminder that *"Spöken-kiekerei,"* or second sight, was once very prevalent here. Comical figures such as Baron von Bomberg, "the jolly Baron," rode through the countryside and Annette von Droste-Hülshoff was inspired by the eerie scenery to write her novel *Die Judenbuche* (The Jew's Beech).

There is proof that one traditional Westphalian recipe, *Pfefferpotthast,* a stew simmered with lots of onions and peppercorns and seasoned with capers, dates back over 600 years. This dish is still regarded as the region's culinary calling card. *Möppkenbrot,* sliced blood pudding, served hot from the frying pan with sautéed potatoes, should not be forgotten either, nor a special dessert—vanilla ice cream with pumper-nickel.

In the parish of Steinhagen on the southern slopes of the Teutoburg Forest, corn and juniper-berry brandies were produced as early as the sixteenth century. The quality at that time was so good that the brandies were regarded as a medicine. The people of Steinhagen can attribute their brandy's survival to its good reputation. In 1688 the Great Elector strictly limited the manufacture of corn-based brandy due to a lack of corn for bread-making, so the people of Steinhagen obtained special permission to continue making their prized brandy. A few of the distilleries still produce genuine "Steinhagen brandy."

For a total contrast, visit the Ruhr area. I never forget the fact that it was the men of the Ruhr who ensured that we had coal again after 1945. But even the Ruhr area has changed along with many of its traditional recipes. In order to earn a living as miners digging for the "black gold," Polish immigrants and Germans from Silesia or Pomerania once streamed into the area between Dortmund, Hamm, and Bottrop. Thus, recipes with varied origins have established themselves in the Ruhr's cuisine and have been adapted to local conditions. Numerous stews were devised to be taken to the pit in an individual metal lunch pail, to be eaten during the lunch break. On weekdays, creamy dishes such as *Schlabberkaps* (made of white cabbage and potato) as well as turnip, cabbage, and bean stews were popular. On the one hand, they were filling to sustain the men through the hard work ahead, and on the other they were easily spooned up thanks to their consistency. A good, strong beef consommé was only eaten on Sundays.

For most workers in the Ruhr area, such hearty meals became unnecessary a long time ago. Much of the heavy work has long since been automated, and the billy-can has been replaced by well-organized canteens. Many of these traditional dishes have thus taken on a new twist with much healthier and lower-calorie versions appearing on menus.

Münster is a paradise for cyclists: castles such as Wasserburg Hülshoff, above, near Havixbeck, offer respite.

PADERBORN CARROT SALAD

Paderborner Möhrensalat (photo above)

INGREDIENTS (Serves 4)

1 pound carrots
2 apples
Bunch of radishes
$1/4$ cup golden raisins
Bunch of fresh parsley
Juice of 2 lemons
$1/4$ cup vegetable oil
2 teaspoons sugar
$2/3$ cup plain yogurt
$1/2$ teaspoon white pepper
Salt to taste

METHOD

1. Peel the carrots, slice them thinly, and cook them for 1 to 2 minutes in a little salted water. Drain.
2. Peel and quarter the apples, wash and trim the radishes. Slice the apple quarters and radishes. Pick over the golden raisins to remove any stones or seeds and mince the parsley.
3. Mix together the lemon juice, oil, sugar, yogurt, and pepper, and mix it with the prepared salad ingredients. Season to taste with salt and more pepper.

CINNAMON FRENCH TOAST

Arme Ritter

INGREDIENTS (Serves 4)

8 slices slightly stale white bread
  or 4 halved bread rolls
1 cup milk
3 eggs
Pinch of salt
1 tablespoon sugar
Breadcrumbs
Unsalted butter
Cinnamon sugar (see note)

METHOD

1. Place the sliced bread or halved rolls in a shallow bowl. Beat together the milk, eggs, salt, and sugar. Pour the egg and milk mixture over the bread and leave it to soak in.
2. Carefully remove the slices of bread and coat them in breadcrumbs. Heat some butter in a frying pan and fry the bread in it on both sides, until golden brown and crisp.
3. Sprinkle the fried bread with cinnamon sugar and serve it hot. If liked, serve with fruit compôte.

NOTE

To make cinnamon sugar, mix ground cinnamon to taste into the required quantity of caster or granulated sugar.

PORK LOIN CHOPS

Lummerkoteletts (photo right)

INGREDIENTS (Serves 4)

Bunch of carrots
1 pound Brussels sprouts
1 shallot
1 tablespoon unsalted butter
1/2 cup heavy cream
Bunch of fresh parsley
Salt, pepper, and grated nutmeg
to taste
1 1/2 tablespoons clarified butter
4 pork loin chops, each weighing
about 7 ounces

METHOD

1. Peel the carrots. Cut large carrots into four pieces, cut smaller carrots in half and cook for about 10 to 15 minutes in salted water.
2. Wash and clean the Brussels sprouts and cook for 15 minutes in salted water. Peel the shallot.
3. Melt the butter in a frying pan and fry the shallot in it until soft. Pour the cream into the pan and bring to a boil.
4. Mince the parsley and add to the frying pan. Season the sauce to taste with salt, pepper, and nutmeg. Add the Brussels sprouts and carrots to the pan and reheat in the sauce.
5. Heat the clarified butter in another frying pan and fry the chops in it on both sides for about 6 minutes until golden brown. Season with salt and pepper. Arrange on a serving plate with the vegetables.

THICK FAVA BEAN SOUP

Suppe von dicken Bohnenkernen (photo above)

INGREDIENTS (Serves 10)

9 pounds fresh fava beans,
shelled
2 1/2 cups crème fraîche
1 quart strong beef stock
Salt and white pepper to taste
10 ounces dry-cured ham,
e.g., prosciutto
2 cups snipped fresh chives

METHOD

1. Blanch the fava beans and remove the thick outer skin. Place the beans in a blender or food processor with the crème fraîche and beef stock and purée until very smooth. Pour the purée into a saucepan, season to taste with salt and pepper, and then bring it to a fast boil.
2. Cut the ham including the fat into thin strips; snip the chives into short lengths.
3. Divide the soup among soup cups or soup plates. Sprinkle with strips of ham and chives. Serve with bread rolls studded with bacon.

HANNELORE KOHL

"Loin chops are sold on the bone often with the kidney included. They are particularly good for quick frying, broiling, or braising."

POTATO AND SAUSAGE LOAF

Sauerländische Potthucke

INGREDIENTS (Serves 4)

*3/4 pound boiled potatoes, cooked
    a day in advance*
1 1/4 pounds potatoes
3/4 pound Mettwurst
1 cup cream
4 eggs
*Salt, pepper, and grated nutmeg
    to taste*
2 tablespoons butter

METHOD

1. Preheat the oven to 350°F.
Mash the boiled potatoes
or press through a potato
ricer. Grate the raw potatoes
and squeeze out the liquid
in a dish towel. Dice the
Mettwurst.
2. Knead together the potatoes, cream, eggs, sausage,
and seasonings to form a
dough. Shape the dough into
a loaf and place in a well
buttered loaf pan. Bake in
the oven for 1 1/4 hours.
3. Remove the loaf from the
oven and leave to cool. Slice
the loaf and fry the slices
briefly on both sides in
melted butter. Serve with
Westphalian or other ham
and a mixed salad.

GLAZED PORK CHOPS ON A BED OF SAVOY CABBAGE

Glasierte Rippchen auf Wirsing

INGREDIENTS (Serves 4)

*2 pounds pork loin blade chops
    or country-style ribs*
Salt, pepper, and cayenne to taste
2 tablespoons clarified butter
1 1/2 pounds head of savoy cabbage
2 onions
1/4 pound boiled ham
1 1/2 tablespoons butter
2 1/2 tablespoons honey
1 tablespoon German mustard
1/2 cup beer
1/2 cup meat stock

METHOD

1. Season the chops with salt,
pepper, and cayenne. Heat
the clarified butter in a frying
pan and seal the chops
quickly in it on both sides.
Keep them warm.
2. Preheat the oven to 350°F.
Cut the cabbage in half, wash
it thoroughly and cut into
thin ribbons. Peel the onions
and cut into quarters; cut the
ham into thin strips.
3. Melt the butter in a roasting pan. Fry the onions in the
butter until translucent, add
the ham and cabbage, place
the chops on top of the onion,
ham and cabbage. Place in
the oven and cook for about
45 minutes.
4. Meanwhile, bring the honey
and mustard to a boil in a
saucepan and brush it on to
the chops, halfway through
cooking.
5. Remove the chops and
vegetables from the roasting
pan. Deglaze the meat juices
with the beer and stock and
leave to reduce a little. Season
the gravy to taste with salt
and pepper.

BUCKWHEAT BLINI

Buchweizenblini (photo below)

INGREDIENTS (Serves 4)

5 cups buckwheat flour
2 eggs, separated
1 cake (0.6 ounce) fresh com-
pressed yeast or 1 envelope
active dry yeast
2 cups lukewarm milk
2 tablespoons unsalted butter,
melted
3 heaped tablespoons stiffly
whipped cream
Clarified butter
Seasonal salad leaves
4 to 8 smoked trout fillets

METHOD

1. Put the flour and egg yolks in a bowl. Crumble the yeast and dissolve it in the milk. Pour the milk into the bowl and mix to form a batter. Leave to rest for 3 to 4 hours.
2. Beat the egg whites until stiff and fold into the batter with the butter and cream.
3. Heat the clarified butter in a frying pan. One by one, drop small spoonfuls of the batter into the frying pan. Fry the blini on both sides until golden brown.
4. Garnish plates with a few salad leaves. Arrange the trout fillets and blini on the plates.

SPANISH FRIKKO

Spanisch Frikko

INGREDIENTS (Serves 4)

1 pound boneless beef
4 tablespoons vegetable oil
Salt, pepper, and paprika to taste
1/2 cup stock
1 pound potatoes
1 pound onions
2 to 3 bay leaves
2 to 3 cloves
2/3 cup sour cream
1/2 cup crème fraîche

METHOD

1. Preheat the oven to 350°F. Cut the beef into small dice. Heat 2 tablespoons of the oil in a frying pan and fry the meat to seal it. Season to taste with salt, pepper, and paprika and cook for 10 minutes. Add the stock to the pan and cook for a further 10 minutes.
2. Peel the potatoes, cut into small dice, and cook for about 15 minutes in salted water. Peel the onions, slice them, and fry in the remaining oil until golden brown.
3. Butter an ovenproof dish and layer the meat, potatoes, and onions alternately, adding the bay leaves and cloves. Season the layers of potato with a little salt.
4. Pour the gravy from the frying pan on to the meat and potato layers. Bake in the oven for 10 minutes.
5. Mix together the cream and crème fraîche and pour it over the top. Bake for a further 30 minutes. Serve immediately.

Westphalian Ham on a Potato Rösti

Westfälischer Schinken auf Kartoffelpuffer

INGREDIENTS (Serves 4)

1¹/₄ pounds potatoes
1 onion
Bunch of fresh parsley
¹/₂ pound Westphalian ham
1 egg
Salt, pepper, and grated nutmeg
  to taste
¹/₂ cup vegetable oil
1 cup sour cream

METHOD

1. Peel the potatoes, grate them finely, place in a strainer and collect the liquid in a bowl. Leave the liquid to stand for a while, so that the starch can settle. Then carefully drain off the liquid.
2. Peel and grate the onion. Wash the parsley and chop two-thirds of it. Divide the remaining sprigs of parsley into 4 small bunches and tie each one up. Cut the ham into thin strips.

3. Add the potatoes, onion, and egg to the starch in the bowl. Mix everything together. Season to taste with salt, pepper and nutmeg.
4. Heat the oil in a frying pan and fry batches of the potato mixture to make 4 golden-brown potato rösti equal in size. Turn the rösti several times during frying.
5. Mix the sour cream with the chopped parsley and season to taste with salt and pepper.

6. Arrange the potato rösti on warmed plates. Divide the parsley and sour cream mixture among the rösti and place the strips of ham on top. Garnish with the bunches of parsley.

HANNELORE KOHL

"*In the summer you can also prepare the sour cream with fresh basil, and season it with garlic too, if you like. The rösti should then be fried in olive oil.*"

Hunter's Cabbage

Jägerkohl (photo above)

INGREDIENTS (Serves 4)

1³/₄ pounds head of white
  cabbage
1 onion
1 cup diced bacon
³/₄ pound mixed ground meats
Salt and pepper to taste
1 cup stock
1 pound potatoes

METHOD

1. Clean the white cabbage,
wash it, and shred it finely.
Peel and dice the onion.
2. Fry the bacon to render the
fat in a large frying pan, and
then fry the onions in the
bacon fat until translucent.
Add the ground meats and fry
them with the onions and
bacon. Season with salt and
pepper.
3. Add the white cabbage to
the pan, pour in the stock,
and cook over low heat for
20 minutes.
4. Meanwhile, peel and slice
the potatoes and add to the
cabbage. Cook the cabbage
and potatoes for a further
20 minutes.

Fried Blood Sausage

Möppkenbrot

INGREDIENTS (Serves 4)

2 cups fresh pig's blood
2 cups meat stock
About 2¹/₂ cups rye meal (coarse
  whole-grain rye flour)
²/₃ cup diced bacon
¹/₂ cup raisins
Pinch of sugar
Grated nutmeg to taste
Chopped fresh thyme to taste
Ground allspice and cumin
  to taste
Salt and black pepper to taste

TO SERVE
1 large onion, sliced
1 large apple, diced
2 tablespoons clarified butter

METHOD

1. Mix the pig's blood and
stock. Add the rye meal or
flour, to form a stiff dough.

2. Work the uncooked bacon
into the dough, with the
raisins. Season to taste with
the sugar, herbs, spices, salt,
and pepper. The mixture
should be spicy. Leave to
rest for 30 minutes.
3. Divide the mixture into
even portions, shape into
balls, and poach in salted
water for about 30 to 40
minutes. The sausages are
cooked when they float to the
surface of the water. Remove,
drain and leave to cool.
4. Slice the sausages. Melt the
clarified butter in a frying-
pan and fry the blood sausage,
onion, and apple together
briefly. Serve the blood sausage with sugar beet syrup (or
maple syrup), pumpernickel,
and coffee or tea.

Pork Stew

Schlodderkappes

INGREDIENTS (Serves 6)

2 pounds potatoes
2 pounds boneless pork
  shoulder butt
2 pounds head of white cabbage
2 cups light stock
Salt and white pepper to taste
Caraway seeds
Minced celery leaves

METHOD

1. Peel the potatoes and cut into even cubes. Do the same with the pork. Wash the cabbage, separate the leaves, and cut out the thick core. Blanch the cabbage leaves.
2. In a large flameproof casserole, alternately layer the potato, cabbage leaves, and pork. Season each layer with salt and pepper. Add the stock to the pot, cover with a lid, and braise on medium heat for 1 hour.
3. Shortly before the end of cooking, add the caraway and celery leaves to the casserole.

Beef Stew

Pfefferpotthast

INGREDIENTS (Serves 4)

1 pound onions
1³/4 pounds beef for stew
1/4 cup clarified butter
2 cups beef stock
1 bay leaf
3 cloves
Salt and pepper to taste
2 cups hot water
3 tablespoons rye breadcrumbs
1 tablespoon capers
2 tablespoons lemon juice
1 pickled gherkin, sliced
  lengthwise
1 lemon, cut in 8 wedges

METHOD

1. Peel the onions and dice them. Do the same with the meat. Heat the clarified butter in a casserole and seal the meat in the butter. Remove the meat and keep it warm.
2. Fry the onion in the meat juices until soft. Add the stock to the onions. Add the bay leaf and cloves and season with salt and pepper. Return the meat to the pot and braise for about 1 hour on medium heat.
3. Gradually add the water to the pot. Stir in the breadcrumbs, capers, and lemon juice and simmer for a further 15 minutes.
4. Garnish the stew with the gherkin and lemon slices.

NOTE

If you can't get rye bread for crumbs, substitute the darkest, coarsest-textured whole wheat bread you can find.

VEAL STEAKS WITH MOREL SAUCE

Kalbssteaks mit Morchelsauce

INGREDIENTS (Serves 4)

Scant 1/2 ounce dried morel mushrooms

3 tablespoons unsalted butter

2 tablespoons brandy

1 cup heavy cream

Salt, black pepper, white pepper, and lemon juice to taste

1 1/2 tablespoons clarified butter

4 boneless veal steaks, each weighing about 7 ounces

1 tablespoon cream sherry

METHOD

1. Soak the morels in 1 cup of lukewarm water for 1 1/2 hours.

2. Pour the morels into a coffee filter paper or a strainer lined with paper towels. Collect the liquid. Rinse the mushrooms thoroughly under cold running water because they are often very gritty. Pat the mushrooms dry and chop, if wished.

3. Melt the butter and soften the mushrooms in it for about 5 minutes. Season with salt, black pepper, and a few squeezes of lemon juice.

4. Pour in the brandy, add a little cream, and allow the sauce to reduce. Gradually add the remaining cream and the liquid from the mushrooms, until it has all been used up and the sauce is pale brown and creamy.

Season to taste with salt, white pepper, and lemon juice. Cover and place to one side.

5. Heat the clarified butter and fry the veal steaks in it for about 5 minutes on each side. Season with salt and pepper.

6. Reheat the mushroom sauce, flavor with sherry, and serve it with the veal steaks.

HANNELORE KOHL

"Morels are wild mushrooms with smooth, columnar, mostly white stems and bell- or beehive-shaped, honey-combed caps. The mushrooms are available fresh, canned, and, more usually, dried."

SAUERLAND BAY LEAF POT ROAST

Sauerländischer Lorbeerbraten

INGREDIENTS (Serves 4)

1 teaspoon coriander seeds
2 cloves
6 allspice berries
3 juniper berries (optional)
1 teaspoon white peppercorns
Pinch of ground ginger
Ground nutmeg to taste
Ground cinnamon to taste
Paprika to taste
5 ounces slab bacon
1½ tablespoons cognac
2 pounds beef sirloin tip roast
¼ cup clarified butter
Flour for dusting
3 carrots
2 onions
1 cup red wine
1 to 2 cups meat stock
1 slice black bread
6 bay leaves
½ to 1 cup crème fraîche
Salt and pepper to taste

METHOD

1. Grind the coriander, cloves, allspice berries, juniper berries, and peppercorns to a fine powder in a pestle and mortar or spice mill. Mix the powder with the ginger, nutmeg, cinnamon, and paprika.
2. Cut the bacon into strips, sprinkle the bacon with the prepared spices, drizzle the cognac over, cover it, and refrigerate. Allow the bacon to marinate for 30 minutes.
3. Preheat the oven to 350°F. Lard the beef with the strips of bacon and rub salt and pepper into the beef. On the stovetop heat the clarified butter in a casserole, seal the beef on all sides, then drain off the fat from the pot.

4. Dust the meat with a little flour. Peel the carrots and onions, dice them, and add them to the tin. Add the red wine and meat stock, so that the liquid comes halfway up the joint of meat. Heat the meat and liquid.
5. Crumble the slice of bread and add it to the pan. Place the bay leaves on top of the meat and braise for 2 to 3 hours on the stovetop or in the oven.
6. Baste the meat frequently with the stock and top up the pan from time to time, with red wine and stock. After an hour, turn the meat and cover the top again with the bay leaves.
7. Remove the meat and keep it warm. Pass the meat juices through a sieve and add a little stock to it. Stir in the crème fraîche and reduce the sauce until it is creamy. Season the sauce with salt and pepper. Serve the braised meat and the sauce separately. Serve with dumplings, red cabbage, or a salad.

GAME-STYLE ROAST BEEF

Rinderbraten auf Wildbretart (photo right)

INGREDIENTS (Serves 4)

½ carrot
½ piece parsley root (see note) or parsnip
½ fennel bulb
2 onions
10 juniper berries
1 bay leaf
2 cups dry red wine
¼ cup water
Juice of ½ lemon
1¾ pounds boneless beef rump roast
Salt and pepper to taste
½ teaspoon paprika
¼ pound bacon, cut in strips
¼ cup clarified butter
1 cup sour cream
1 teaspoon flour
Sugar

METHOD

1. Peel and chop the carrot, parsley or parsnip, fennel, and onions. Crush the juniper berries.
2. Place the prepared vegetables and juniper berries in a large saucepan with the bay leaf, red wine, a few drops of lemon juice, and some water. Bring them to a boil and then remove the pan from the heat.
3. Put the meat into the marinade and leave it to marinate in a cool place for 2 days. Turn the meat occasionally.
4. Preheat the oven to 400°F. Remove the meat from the marinade and pat dry. Rub the meat with salt, pepper, and paprika. Lard the meat with strips of bacon. On the stovetop heat the clarified butter in a casserole and fry the meat in it to seal it on all sides.

5. Strain the marinade. Using half the marinade, deglaze the casserole, then place it in the oven and braise for about an hour. Gradually add the remaining marinade.
6. Remove the meat and keep it warm. Mix together the cream and flour and use to thicken the meat juices. Season to taste with salt, sugar, and lemon juice. Slice the meat and serve with the sauce, red cabbage, and dumplings.

NOTE

Parsley root, also called Hamburg parsley, is the variety *Petroselinum crispum* 'Tuberosum'.

MUSTARD POT ROAST WITH VEGETABLES

Senfbraten mit Gemüse

INGREDIENTS (Serves 4)

3 pounds pork shoulder roast
¹/₄ cup medium-hot mustard
Salt and pepper to taste
¹/₂ teaspoon paprika
2 onions
1 shallot
1 carrot
1¹/₄ cups dry white wine
Fresh marjoram sprig
¹/₄ cup sour cream

METHOD

1. Preheat the oven to 475°F. Brush the mustard on to the pork and season it with the salt, pepper, and paprika.
2. Peel and mince the onions and shallot. Peel the carrot and slice into thick strips.
3. Place the meat in a casserole and arrange the onion, shallot, and carrot around it. Season with a little salt and pepper. Pour the white wine into the pot and add the sprig of marjoram. Cover.
4. Braise the meat in the oven for about an hour or until it is done, turning it and basting it frequently with the meat juices.
5. At the end of the cooking time, switch off the oven and leave the meat to rest in the oven for a further 15 minutes. Slice the meat and keep it warm.
6. Strain the meat juices into a saucepan. Bring the juices to a boil, stir the sour cream in and reduce over low heat for 5 minutes. Season the sauce to taste. Pour the sauce over the sliced meat.

BRAISED VEAL IN MUSTARD SAUCE

Kalbsbraten in Senfsauce (photo above)

INGREDIENTS (Serves 4)

3 pounds veal shoulder roast
3 tablespoons hot clarified butter
1 Spanish onion
1 cup hot meat stock
1¹/₂ cups dry white wine
2 tablespoons medium-hot mustard
2 egg yolks
1 cup cream
Salt and white pepper to taste
Pinch of sugar
2 tablespoons ice-cold unsalted butter, cubed

METHOD

1. Preheat the oven to 425°F. Season the veal with pepper, place it in a roasting pan, and pour the hot butter over the veal. Peel and chop the onion and add it to the pan.
2. Pour the meat stock over the veal, place the pan in the oven, and braise the veal for about 1¹/₂ hours. After 40 minutes, add the white wine to the pan.
3. Remove the meat from the roasting pan and keep it warm. Deglaze the meat residue with a little hot water and press the resulting liquid through a strainer. Heat the liquid, stir the mustard into it, and thicken with a mixture of the egg yolks and cream. Do not allow the sauce to boil.
4. Season the sauce to taste with salt, pepper, and sugar. Carefully stir the cold butter into the sauce, a cube at a time. Slice the meat and serve it with the mustard sauce. Serve with spinach and Parisienne or boiled potatoes.

> HANNELORE KOHL
>
> "*If you like, try different mustards like Dijon instead of medium-hot mustard. The meat tastes particularly good if you stir a variety of minced fresh herbs into the mustard.*"

Westphalian Beef in Burgundy

Westfälischer Schinken in Burgunder (photo above)

INGREDIENTS (Serves 8–10)

3 cups red Burgundy wine
3 bay leaves
6 peppercorns
5¹/₂ pounds boneless beef round
  rump roast
6 to 8 large slices of bacon

METHOD

1. Place the red wine in a bowl with the bay leaves and peppercorns. Marinate the meat for 12 hours.
2. Preheat the oven to 300°F. Remove the meat from the marinade, leave to drain, pat it dry, and wrap the meat in the bacon slices. Roast for about 2 hours. Baste the meat frequently with the marinade.
3. Take the meat out of the oven and leave it to rest for 15 minutes. Slice the meat and serve it with mustard and pumpernickel bread.

Fava Beans with Bacon

Dicke Bohnen mit Speck

INGREDIENTS (Serves 4)

1 teaspoon clarified butter
1 onion, peeled and chopped
2¹/₂ cups (750 ml) water
1 pound Canadian bacon
1³/₄ pounds fresh fava beans,
  shelled
Bunch of fresh savory, chopped
1 tablespoon unsalted butter
2 tablespoons flour
2 to 3 tablespoons coarsely
  chopped fresh parsley

METHOD

1. Heat the clarified butter in a saucepan. Fry the onion in the butter. Add 3 cups of water and the bacon and cook for 45 minutes.
2. Remove the bacon from the pan and keep it warm. Add the fava beans and savory to the meat stock, cover, and cook for 15 minutes.
3. Mash together the butter and flour, and use this *beurre manié* to thicken the stock. Slice the bacon and arrange it on a bed of fava beans. Sprinkle the bacon with parsley. Serve with boiled potatoes.

WESTPHALIAN MOCK CHICKEN

Westfälisches Blindhuhn

INGREDIENTS (Serves 4)

1 heaped cup dried lima beans

1 pound salt pork

³/4 pound green beans

³/4 pound carrots

³/4 pound potatoes

¹/2 pound cooking apples

¹/2 pound pears

4 tablespoons unsalted butter

2 onions

Salt and pepper to taste

*1 tablespoon chopped fresh
  parsley to garnish*

METHOD

1. On the previous evening, soak the lima beans in 2 quarts of water.

2. Next day, bring the lima beans to a boil in the soaking liquid with the salt pork and cook for about 60 to 70 minutes.

3. Wash and trim the green beans and remove any string. Peel and slice the carrots and potatoes. Add the carrots and potatoes to the stew with the green beans and cook for a further 30 minutes.

4. Peel the apples and pears and halve, core, and slice them. Add the fruit to the stew and cook for a further 30 minutes.

5. Melt the butter in a frying pan. Peel and mince the onion, and fry it in the melted butter until golden brown. Add the onions to the stew. Season the stew with salt and pepper and sprinkle it with parsley.

HANNELORE KOHL

"U*sing firm, sharp apples is very important. However, if you can only get sweet apples, add a little vinegar to the stew.*"

PUMPERNICKEL PUDDING

Pumpernickelpudding

INGREDIENTS (Serves 4–6)

14 ounces pumpernickel bread
1 cup hot milk
2/3 cup raisins
5 eggs, separated
1/2 cup sugar
2 ounces semisweet chocolate, grated
1/2 teaspoon ground cinnamon
2 tablespoons rum
Grated zest and juice of 1 lemon
1 1/4 cups ground hazelnuts
4 tablespoons unsalted butter
2 tablespoons breadcrumbs

METHOD

1. Crumble the pumpernickel into small pieces or chop it finely with a knife. Pour the milk over the bread, stir well and leave to soak for an hour. Meanwhile, soak the raisins in a little hot water.

2. Whisk the egg yolks and sugar until foaming. Add the chocolate, cinnamon, rum, lemon zest, lemon juice, and hazelnuts to the egg mixture and fold in.

3. Mix together the pumpernickel and egg yolk mixtures.

Beat the egg whites until stiff and fold into the mixture.

4. Butter a steaming mold and sprinkle it with breadcrumbs. Fill the mold three-quarters full with the pumpernickel mixture, cover it, and set in a pan half-filled with boiling water. Cover and steam for 1 hour.

5. Remove the pudding from the water and leave it to rest for a little while. Then unmold the pudding on to a warmed plate. Serve with vanilla custard sauce.

WESTPHALIAN AMBROSIA
Westfälische Götterspeise

INGREDIENTS (Serves 4)

2 apples
1 tablespoon unsalted butter
2 cups heavy cream
3 tablespoons confectioners'
  sugar
4 ounces pumpernickel bread
1 cup chopped hazelnuts
1 cup crumbled macaroons
2¹/₂ cups cherries, pitted

METHOD

1. Peel, quarter, core, and slice the apples. Melt the butter in a frying pan and fry the apples briefly over low heat. Cool.
2. Whip the cream with the confectioners' sugar until stiff. Grate the pumpernickel bread and mix together the hazelnuts and macaroons.
3. Fold half of the pumpernickel and half of the hazelnut and macaroon mixture into the cream. Make alternate layers of the cream, pumpernickel, and remaining hazelnut and macaroon mixture in 4 parfait or other tall glasses.
4. Garnish with apple slices and cherries. Cover and leave in the refrigerator for an hour, so the flavors can develop and combine.

MÜNSTERLAND QUARK DESSERT
Münsterländer Quarkspeise

INGREDIENTS (Serves 6)

1 pound (2 cups) full-fat Quark
  or ricotta
3 tablespoons brown sugar
2 cups milk
4 ounces pumpernickel bread
¹/₄ cup kirsch
4 ounces semisweet chocolate
1 jar of cherries in syrup,
  drained

METHOD

1. Mix the Quark with 2 tablespoons of the sugar and the milk until smooth.

2. Crumble the pumpernickel, sprinkle the remaining sugar on top, and moisten with the kirsch. Coarsely grate the chocolate and mix into the pumpernickel mixture.
3. Alternately layer pumpernickel, Quark mixture, and cherries in a bowl. Continue until all the ingredients are used up. Refrigerate the dessert for 1 to 2 hours.

HANNELORE KOHL

"I*nstead of using cherries, you can also prepare this dessert with stewed cranberries.*"

BAKED APPLE PUDDING

Apfelauflauf (photo above)

INGREDIENTS (Serves 4)

1/2 cup milk
4 1/2 tablespoons unsalted butter
1/2 cup flour
3 eggs, separated
1/3 cup sugar
*1/4 teaspoon vanilla pudding
    powder*
Grated zest of 1/2 lemon
2 pounds apples, e.g., pippins
Pinch of salt

METHOD

1. Bring the milk to a boil, with the butter and a pinch of salt. Add the flour and stir until the dough comes away from the bottom and sides of the saucepan. Leave to cool.

2. Preheat the oven to 350°F. Whisk the egg yolks with the sugar until pale and foamy. Stir in the pudding powder, lemon zest, and cooled dough, a spoonful at a time.

3. Peel the apples, quarter, core, and slice thinly. In a separate bowl beat the egg whites together with a pinch of salt until stiff. Carefully fold the egg whites into the dough mixture.

4. Place the apples in a buttered baking dish, spread the dough mixture on top and level off. Bake in the oven for about 45 minutes or until golden brown.

HENRIETTA'S RICE PUDDING

Henriettes Reispudding

INGREDIENTS (Serves 10)

1 1/4 cups short-grain rice
1 quart milk
Piece of cinnamon stick
*Zest of 1/2 lemon, pared in one
    strip*
1/2 cup unsalted butter
1/2 cup plus 2 tablespoons sugar
10 eggs, separated
7 ounces macaroons
Breadcrumbs

METHOD

1. Bring the rice to the boil with the milk, cinnamon, and lemon zest. Simmer for about 20 minutes. Leave it to cool.

2. Remove the cinnamon stick and lemon zest from the rice.

Beat the butter until fluffy, gradually add the sugar and egg yolks. Stir in the rice one tablespoon at a time. In a separate bowl beat the egg whites until stiff and fold in.

3. Butter a steaming mold and sprinkle it with breadcrumbs. Layer the rice mixture and macaroons in the mold and then cover it tightly. Cook the pudding for about 2 1/2 hours in a covered pan half-filled with boiling water.

4. Let the pudding cool briefly and then unmold onto a serving dish. Serve the pudding with mixed berry compôte or vanilla custard sauce.

LIPPER PUDDING
Lipper Pudding

INGREDIENTS (Serves 4)

FOR THE WHITE CUSTARD

2 cups milk
1/4 cup sugar
1 1/2 tablespoons vanilla-flavored
    sugar
1 cup ground almonds
5 tablespoons cornstarch
4 egg whites

FOR THE YELLOW CUSTARD

4 egg yolks
1 1/2 cups dry white wine
6 tablespoons sugar
Grated zest of 1/2 lemon
2 1/2 tablespoons cornstarch

TO SERVE

10 macaroons
1 cup heavy cream, whipped
1 tablespoon lemon zest cut
    in julienne

METHOD

1. To make the white custard, heat together the milk, 1/4 cup sugar, and vanilla sugar. Add the almonds to the milk. Mix the cornstarch with a little cold water and stir it into the milk. Bring the custard to a boil quickly and allow it to cool again.
2. In a medium bowl beat the egg whites until stiff and fold gently into the custard. Place the custard in a glass bowl and leave to set.
3. To make the yellow custard, beat together the egg yolks, white wine, and 6 tablespoons sugar. Add the grated lemon zest to the egg mixture. Stirring constantly with a balloon whisk, carefully heat the egg mixture. Mix the cornstarch with a little cold water and stir it into the egg mixture. Continue to cook the custard until it thickens.
4. Allow the yellow custard to cool a little and then spread it on top of the white custard. Refrigerate for several hours.
5. Garnish the cold custard with macaroons, whipped cream, and a *julienne* of lemon zest.

WESTPHALIAN FARMER'S LOAF
Westfälischer Bauernstuten (photo above)

INGREDIENTS (Makes 1 loaf)

8 cups all-purpose flour
2 1/2 cakes (0.6 ounce each) fresh
    compressed yeast or 2 1/2 enve-
    lopes active dry yeast
5 tablespoons sugar
2 cups milk
1 teaspoon salt
1/4 cup pork drippings

METHOD

1. Place the flour in a bowl and make a well in the center. Crumble the yeast, mix it with the sugar and milk (reserving a few tablespoons of the milk), and pour it into the well. Mix the yeast mixture with a little flour and leave the mixture to proof in a warm place for 15 minutes.
2. Knead together the yeast mixture and the remaining ingredients. Butter a loaf pan, shape the dough into a loaf, place it in the pan, and leave it to rise in a warm place until doubled in size.
3. Preheat the oven to 400°F. Brush the dough with the reserved milk. Bake for an hour.

HANNELORE KOHL

"**W**estphalian farmers usually crumbled this simple breakfast loaf into large coffee bowls, sprinkled it with sugar, and poured hot milk over it. Sometimes they spread butter on it and ate it with a slice of pumpernickel on top."

A to Z of Herbs and Spices

Even the best ingredients can taste bland without the proper seasoning. A wide choice of herbs and spices offers a wide range for personal preference. The following tips on seasonings are only suggestions. Let your imagination run wild!

ANISEED: for cakes, pastries, sweet sauces, fruit compôtes, and stewed plums.

BASIL: for roast goose and pork.

BAY LEAVES: with lentil dishes, in pickling and for marinades, with game dishes.

CARAWAY: with all types of cabbage, roast pork, potatoes, and for use in homemade bread.

CAYENNE: for all spicy soups and sauces, with meat and vegetable stews. Cayenne is very hot and therefore needs to be used sparingly.

CHERVIL: with all sauces and soups.

CINNAMON: with red cabbage, in stewed fruits, and for baking.

CLOVES: with red cabbage, in meat stocks and chicken soups, with pears and stewed plums.

CURRY: for rice dishes, veal and chicken, with fish and egg dishes.

LOVAGE: in herb sauces, with soups and stews.

NUTMEG: in meatloaf, spinach, cauliflower, and Brussels sprouts, in egg dishes.

OREGANO: with pizza, pork and lamb, in tomato dishes, with cucumber, and in stews.

ROSEMARY: with rabbit, poultry, and lamb.

SAVORY: for all recipes using beans, and in pea, lentil, or potato soups. Savory makes cucumber salad easier to digest.

PAPRIKA: in goulash and schnitzel, in tomato sauces and dips, and on cheese open sandwiches.

TARRAGON: in sauces and soups, with veal and asparagus.

THYME: in game dishes, liver dumplings, fish and mushroom dishes, pies, and with sautéed potatoes.

Mixed herbs and spices are very useful for giving chicken dishes, ground meat, steaks, and meat for barbecues and stews just the right flavor in an instant. Often, these herb and spice mixes already contain salt. If you are on a low-sodium diet, you can get special seasoning mixes which guarantee lots of flavor without the salt by using a skillful mix of herbs.

BY HELMUT KOHL

Self-confident, a little stubborn, forthright, sometimes a little crude, but full of likable warmth and hospitality—these are the typical characteristics of those who live in the Palatinate!

The people of the Palatinate enjoy the mildest climate in Germany, where tobacco, sweet chestnuts, figs, and almonds flourish and where, above all, excellent wine is made. They regard wine highly, enjoying and sharing it with their fellow men, because an open house, pleasant company, and good home-cooking are second nature.

▶

BETWEEN THE RHINE, MOSELLE, AND SAAR RIVERS

Wine is completely different from any other beverage. Wine represents a unique and important part of Western cultural history from the Greeks down through the Romans to the present. Viticulture in the Palatinate is thus proof that the area is an ancient cultural center in the heart of Europe.

Not just about enjoyment, wine is also associated with hard work in the vineyards, which have often belonged to the same family for generations; with worry about the grapes; with the seasons and sometimes setbacks caused by wind and weather. The men and women of the Palatinate have close ties to the soil, making them both easy-going and hard-working at the same time.

My parents first met in 1910 at the grape harvest in Burrweiler in the heart of the Palatinate between Landau and Neustadt. My preference for the Palatine wine and way of life was thus instilled in me from the cradle.

The Palatinate also stands for a past rich in tradition from the Palatine Counts to Elizabeth Charlotte of Bavaria, called the Princess Palatine, the sister-in-law of the Sun King, Louis XIV. Elizabeth lived at the court of Versailles, but is said to have been homesick for the Palatinate well into ripe old age. The Hambach festival, still a symbol of the birth of German democracy, took place here on May 27, 1832. Very few people know that the first time our black, red, and gold flag was used as a symbol of democracy was in Hambach. For centuries almost every generation from the Palatinate experienced war. Being an area that borders France, the people are most conscious of the valuable gift represented by Franco-German friendship. Because they have such close ties to their home, they are dedicated Europeans.

The solid, middle-class way of life of the Palatinate and its traditions is reflected in the cuisine, which is often flavored with wine. Liver dumplings on a bed of sauerkraut and, of course, the famous stuffed *Saumagen* are typical regional dishes. Those with a sweet tooth rave about *Kerscheplotzer,* a baked pudding made with bread and cherries or *Dampfnudel* (sweet yeast dumplings), which in the Palatinate are prepared using salted water, oil, and a wine sauce. The aromas of such dishes and the delicate flavors defy description. Let your tastebuds do the work instead! To get a true taste of the Palatinate, take a ramble through some of the vineyards and relax in a country inn.

A significant historical place to visit: Hambach castle on the Deutsche Weinstrasse (German Wine Route). The black, red, and gold flag flew here for the first time in 1832, as the symbol for the German patriots who were fighting for freedom and unity.

STUFFED PAUNCH

Pfälzer Saumagen

INGREDIENTS
(Makes 7–8 pounds)

FOR THE STUFFING

3¹/₂ pounds boneless pork
    shoulder and loin
3¹/₂ pounds potatoes
3¹/₂ pounds lean ground pork or
    sausage meat

FOR THE SEASONING MIX

2 to 3 tablespoons salt
¹/₂ teaspoon pepper
¹/₂ teaspoon ground nutmeg
1 teaspoon dried marjoram
¹/₂ teaspoon ground coriander
¹/₂ teaspoon ground cloves
¹/₂ teaspoon chopped fresh thyme
¹/₂ teaspoon ground cardamom
¹/₂ teaspoon dried basil
¹/₃ cup diced onion
Ground bay leaf

TO PREPARE

1 pig's paunch (order it in
    advance from your butcher)
Salt to taste
2 tablespoons clarified butter

METHOD

1. Coarsely chop the meat. Peel the potatoes, cut in ¹/₂-inch dice and blanch them. Mix together the meat, potatoes, and ground pork or sausage meat. Mix together the herbs and spices and use them to season the meat mixture.

2. Wash the pig's paunch thoroughly under cold, running water, then pat it dry. Tie up two openings tightly with kitchen string. Fill the paunch with the stuffing mixture, via the third opening. Tie up the third opening. (Don't stuff the paunch too full or it might burst.)

3. Bring plenty of salted water to a boil and reduce the heat. Place the stuffed paunch in the water and cook for 3 hours over low heat without boiling.

4. Remove the paunch from the cooking liquid, drain it, and place on a serving dish. Do not slice until serving the paunch at table.

5. If you like, heat some clarified butter in a roasting pan and seal slices of the paunch in the butter on both sides. Then preheat the oven to 400⁰F and bake the slices of paunch until crisp. Serve with fresh crusty bread, creamed potatoes or Palatine potatoes, white cabbage, and Palatine wine.

HANNELORE KOHL

"**I**f some of the stuffed paunch is left over, it can be sliced the next day and fried in melted butter until golden brown."

PANCAKE LAYER CAKE

Gefüllter Eierkuchen

INGREDIENTS (Serves 4)

1 pound boneless veal shoulder roast

2¹/₂ cups all-purpose flour

2 cups milk

3 eggs, separated

¹/₂ pound carrots

¹/₂ pound asparagus

¹/₂ pound peas, shelled

¹/₂ cup unsalted butter

Juice of ¹/₂ lemon

Salt and white pepper to taste

Bunch of fresh parsley, chopped

³/₄ cup grated young Gouda cheese

METHOD

1. Cook the veal in plenty of salted water for about 45 minutes. Remove the meat from the stock, reserving the stock, leave to cool, and dice.

2. Beat together about 2 cups of the flour, the milk, egg yolks, and salt with a balloon whisk to form a smooth batter. Leave it to rest for about 40 minutes.

3. Meanwhile peel the carrots and asparagus and chop finely; wash the peas. Cook the vegetables separately in salted water; remove while still crisp, reserving the water. Rinse the vegetables in cold water to refresh them.

4. Add sufficient veal stock to the vegetable stock to make 1 quart. Melt 4 tablespoons of butter in a saucepan, add the remaining flour, and cook to form a roux. Gradually add the stock to the roux, stirring all the time, and simmer for about 10 minutes.

5. Season the sauce to taste with salt, lemon juice, and pepper. Divide the sauce into four portions and reheat each of the vegetables and meat separately in the sauce. Sprinkle the meat and vegetables with chopped parsley.

6. Beat the egg whites until stiff and fold into the batter. Melt the remaining butter in a frying pan. Fry five large pancakes, one at a time.

7. On a serving dish, layer the pancakes alternately with meat and vegetables, to form a cake. Sprinkle generously with freshly grated Gouda. The cake should be cut just before serving. Serve with a green salad.

HANNELORE KOHL

"*These pancakes can be layered with any seasonal vegetables. Instead of veal, use ground beef seasoned with fresh herbs.*"

WINEMAKER'S SALAD
Winzersalat

INGREDIENTS (Serves 4)

*1 large head romaine or
  Cos lettuce*
¹/₂ cup sour cream
1 tablespoon grapeseed oil
2 tablespoons white wine vinegar
2 garlic cloves
Paprika, salt, and pepper to taste
*1 tablespoon chopped fresh
  chives*
4 slices of white bread
3 tablespoons unsalted butter
*2 heaped tablespoons shredded
  Allgäu cheese or any hard,
  well-aged cheese*

METHOD

1. Separate the lettuce leaves, wash them, and tear them into bite-sized pieces.
2. Place the sour cream, oil, and vinegar in a bowl. Peel the garlic, crush 1 clove, and add to the bowl. Season the dressing to taste with paprika, salt, and pepper. Stir the chives into the dressing.
3. Cut the white bread into cubes. Melt the butter in a frying pan and fry the cubed bread over medium heat until crisp. Crush the second clove of garlic and stir into the croûtons.
4. Toss the lettuce in the dressing, sprinkle the croûtons on top, and scatter the grated cheese over. Toss the salad again immediately before serving.

BEEF BRAISED IN RED WINE
Rinderbraten in Rotwein

INGREDIENTS (Serves 6)

1/2 pound slab bacon
3 1/2 pounds beef pot roast
2/3 cup vegetable oil
3 cups red wine
Bunch of fresh thyme
3 tablespoons clarified butter
4 onions
2 garlic cloves
*1 small package frozen soup
   vegetables*
1 calf's foot, halved
1 bay leaf
1/2 pound button mushrooms
1/2 pound carrots
1 pound shallots
2 tablespoons unsalted butter
Salt and pepper to taste

METHOD

1. Cut the bacon into thin strips and place in the freezer for a little while to firm them up. Lard the beef with the strips of bacon in the direction of the grain.

2. Mix together the oil, red wine, a sprig of thyme, and pepper. Place the meat in the marinade, cover, and leave to marinate overnight.

3. Remove the meat from the marinade and pat dry. Heat the clarified butter in a casserole and fry the meat in it on all sides to seal. Season the meat with the salt.

4. Peel and halve the onions and garlic and add them to the casserole, with the soup vegetables, calf's foot, remaining bunch of thyme, and bay leaf. Heat the marinade and add it to the pot.

5. Preheat the oven to 350°F. Put the lid on the casserole and place the meat on the bottom oven shelf. Cook for 3 hours. Skim off the fat frequently.

6. Wash the mushrooms, peel the carrots and shallots, cut the carrots into 1/2-inch dice. Melt the butter in a saucepan and fry the shallots and the carrots. Deglaze with a little water, put the lid on the saucepan and cook until crisp-tender. Add the mushrooms to the saucepan, toss with the other vegetables, and season them to taste with salt and pepper.

7. Remove the meat and calf's foot from the stock. Skim off the fat and strain the stock. Return the stock to the casserole and reduce for 10 minutes. Season. Add the beef, carrots, mushrooms, and shallots to the casserole and heat through in the gravy. Serve with potato gratin.

WINEMAKER'S BEEF STEW
Winzertopf mit Rindfleisch (photo above)

INGREDIENTS (Serves 4)

1 pound boneless beef rump
1/4 cup clarified butter
1 onion, minced
2/3 cup medium red wine
1 pound white cabbage
1/2 pound carrots
1/2 pound fennel bulb
1 leek
1 quart meat stock
1 bay leaf
1/2 pound potatoes
Salt and pepper to taste
*Bunch of chopped fresh parsley,
   for garnish*

METHOD

1. Preheat the oven to 350°F. Cut the beef in chunks. On the stovetop heat the clarified butter in a casserole and fry the beef in it for 5 minutes to seal it.

2. Add the minced onion to the pan and fry until caramelized. Deglaze the juices with the red wine. Trim or peel the vegetables, chop, and add to the meat. Pour the stock into the pot and add the bay leaf, pepper, and salt. Cover.

3. Braise the meat in the oven for an hour. Peel the potatoes, dice them and add to the meat, 10 to 15 minutes before the end of cooking. Sprinkle the stew with the chopped parsley just before serving.

PORK GOULASH WITH POTATOES

Schweinegulasch mit Kartoffeln (photo above)

INGREDIENTS (Serves 4)

1¹/₂ pounds boneless pork shoulder
3 tablespoons clarified butter
³/₄ pound onions
1 tablespoon paprika
1¹/₂ pounds small potatoes
1 tablespoon vinegar
1 tablespoon caraway seeds
3 cups meat stock
1 cup sour cream
Salt and pepper to taste

METHOD

1. Cut the meat into cubes. Heat the clarified butter in a casserole and fry the meat in it until sealed and browned. Remove the meat from the pot.
2. Peel the onions, cut into eighths, and fry them in the meat fat until translucent. Sprinkle the onions with paprika. Peel the potatoes and add them to the pot with the vinegar, caraway, stock, and meat. Put the lid on the casserole and simmer for 30 minutes.
3. Remove the pot from the heat. Stir the sour cream into the goulash and season it with salt, pepper, and more paprika.

PORK AND POTATO BAKE

Backesgrumbeere

INGREDIENTS (Serves 4)

2 pounds potatoes
1 tablespoon pork drippings
1 pound fresh side pork (belly)
Bunch of fresh chives
1 cup sour cream
Salt, pepper, and ground cinnamon to taste

METHOD

1. Preheat the oven to 475⁰F. Peel the potatoes and slice thinly. Grease an ovenproof dish with the pork drippings, layer half of the sliced potatoes on the bottom of the dish and season with salt and pepper.
2. Slice the pork and spread on top of the sliced potato. Mince the chives and sprinkle half over the meat. Cover with the remaining sliced potato, season with salt and pepper. Place the dish on the middle oven shelf and bake for 15 minutes.
3. Mix together the sour cream and cinnamon, pour it over the potatoes and return the dish to the oven. Bake for 30 minutes longer, until a brown crust has formed on top of the potatoes. Sprinkle the remaining chopped chives on top.

Quick Beef Sauté with Onions

Geschnetzeltes Zwiebelfleisch (photo below)

Leek Tart

Lauchkuchen (photo right)

INGREDIENTS (Serves 12)

FOR THE PASTRY
2 cups all-purpose flour
1/2 cup unsalted butter, cubed
Pinch of salt
Pinch of sugar
1 tablespoon water

FOR THE FILLING
3 tablespoons unsalted butter
3/4 pound slab bacon
3 1/2 pounds leeks, sliced
2 tablespoons flour
1 cup cream
4 eggs, beaten
Salt, pepper, and ground nutmeg to taste

METHOD

1. To make the pastry, work together all the ingredients, cover, and refrigerate for about 30 minutes.

2. Preheat the oven to 400°F. Melt the butter in a frying pan. Cut the bacon in small cubes and fry it in the butter, to render the fat. Add the thinly sliced leeks to the bacon and fry for 10 minutes. Sprinkle with the flour and mix it in well.

3. Roll out the pastry and line an 11-inch buttered spring-form pan. Fill the pastry shell with the leek mixture and bake for 10 minutes.

4. Mix together the eggs and cream and season to taste with the salt, pepper, and nutmeg. Pour over the leeks and bake for 30 to 40 minutes longer. Serve hot.

INGREDIENTS (Serves 4)

1 1/2 pounds beef tenderloin
4 tablespoons butter
1 pound onions
1 garlic clove
1 leek
1 cup meat stock
1/2 teaspoon ground caraway
1 teaspoon dried marjoram
Salt and ground black pepper to taste

METHOD

1. Cut the beef into strips. Melt the butter in a large frying pan and sauté the meat in it for 6 minutes. Remove the meat from the pan and keep it warm.

2. Peel and slice the onions. Peel and mince the garlic. Trim the leek, wash thoroughly, and slice.

3. Fry the onion and the garlic in the juices from the meat until caramelized. Add the meat stock to the pan and allow to reduce. Season with salt and pepper.

4. Add the sliced leek to the pan, season with caraway and marjoram, and simmer for 10 minutes.

5. Season the meat with salt and pepper, return it to the frying pan and heat it through with the vegetables. Serve the beef sauté with potato dumplings.

Beef and Onion Stew

Ochsenfleisch-Zwiebel-Topf

INGREDIENTS (Serves 4)

1/4 cup clarified butter
1 cup diced bacon
1 pound ox or beef for stew (chuck)
Salt and pepper to taste
1/2 teaspoon paprika
2 pounds onions
1 teaspoon ground caraway
2 cups meat stock
2 cups white wine
1 pound potatoes
2 triangles of cheese spread

METHOD

1. Heat the clarified butter in a frying pan and fry the bacon in it until the fat starts to run. Add the beef to the pan and brown it. Season the meat and bacon with pepper, salt, and paprika.

2. Peel and slice the onions. Add to the pan, with the caraway and mix everything thoroughly. Add the stock and wine to the pan. Bring to a boil, then simmer for about 50 minutes.

3. Peel and dice the potatoes. Add them to the frying pan. Cook the stew for a further 30 to 40 minutes. Finally, melt the cheese spread in the gravy and season the stew to taste.

BEEF AND PORK CASSEROLE WITH WINE

Weinfleisch mit Rind und Schwein

INGREDIENTS (Serves 4)

1/2 pound boneless pork shoulder
1/2 pound boneless pork loin
1/2 pound chuck steak
2 1/2 cups dry white wine
1 1/2 pounds potatoes
3/4 pound onions
Salt and ground black pepper
*   to taste*
Bunch of fresh parsley
Sprig of fresh thyme
Sprig of fresh marjoram
1 bay leaf
1 garlic clove

METHOD

1. Cut the meat into 1-inch cubes and marinate overnight in 2 cups of the white wine.
2. Preheat the oven to 425°F. Dampen a *Schlemmertopf* (clay cooking pot). Remove the meat from the marinade, allow it to drain and pat it dry. Reserve the marinade. Peel the potatoes and onions and slice thinly.
3. Line the clay pot with half of the sliced potato and season with salt and pepper.

Place the meat on top of the sliced potato, season the meat with salt and pepper, and cover with the onion rings.
4. Tie the parsley, thyme and marjoram together with kitchen string, to form a bouquet garni. Place on top of the onions, with the bay leaf. Peel the garlic, crush, and spread over the onions. Cover the herbs with the remaining potatoes.
5. Pour the marinade on top of the potatoes and cover the pot. Cook on the bottom shelf for 1 1/2 hours.
6. Add the remaining wine to the pot and reduce the oven temperature to 325°F. Put the lid on the cooking pot, return the pot to the oven, and cook on the middle shelf for 1 hour longer or until cooked. Remove the bouquet garni and check the seasoning before serving.

DÜRKHEIM BRAISED BEEF IN RED WINE

Dürkheimer Rotweinbraten

INGREDIENTS (Serves 4)

2 pounds boneless beef
*   pot roast*
3 cups red wine
2 carrots
Salt and pepper to taste
1/4 cup vegetable oil
2 onions
2 tablespoons tomato paste
1 cup meat stock
2 tablespoons flour
3 tablespoons cream

METHOD

1. Place the beef in a bowl with the red wine and leave to marinate in the refrigerator for 2 days.
2. Peel the carrots. Remove the beef from the marinade and leave it to drain, reserving the marinade. Using the handle of a wooden spoon, drill two holes in the beef and stick the carrots in the holes. Rub the beef with salt and pepper. Heat the oil in a flameproof casserole and seal the beef all over in the oil.
3. Peel the onions, dice, and fry with the meat. Add the tomato paste, meat stock, and marinade to the pot. Braise the meat for 1 1/2 hours.
4. Mix the flour with a little water and the cream, until smooth. Stir into the gravy. Serve the meat with seasonal vegetables and noodles.

BAKER'S POTATOES

Bäckerkartoffeln (photo above)

INGREDIENTS (Serves 4)

4 onions
2 pounds potatoes
1/2 pound beef for stew
1/2 pound lean pork for stew
1/2 pound lamb for stew
Salt and pepper to taste
Bunch of fresh chives
2 tablespoons clarified butter
3 tablespoons butter
1 cup dry white wine

METHOD

1. Preheat the oven to 425°F. Peel the onions and potatoes and slice thinly. Mince the chives.
2. Grease an ovenproof dish with the clarified butter. Line the dish with onion rings, then cover the onions with a layer of potato. Cover the potato with cubes of meat and sprinkle chives on top. Repeat the process, seasoning each layer with salt and pepper. Continue until all the ingredients are used up. The last layer should be potato.
3. Dot the butter over the potato and pour the white wine into the dish. Bake in the oven for 1 1/2 to 2 hours.
4. Serve straight from the oven with a crisp lettuce salad dressed with a herb vinaigrette.

LAMB GOULASH

Lammgulasch

INGREDIENTS (Serves 4)

1 1/2 pounds boneless lamb
  shoulder
3 tablespoons clarified butter
1/2 pound onions
1 pound green beans
1/2 pound pimientoes (from a can
  or jar)
Salt and black pepper to taste
4 teaspoons paprika
1 cup hot meat stock
2/3 cup plain yogurt
Small bunch of fresh parsley,
  chopped

METHOD

1. Cut the lamb in chunks. Heat the clarified butter in a flameproof casserole. Fry the lamb cubes for 15 minutes to seal.
2. Peel and slice the onions. Trim the beans and wash them. Drain the pimiento. Add everything to the meat. Season with salt, pepper, and paprika.
3. Pour the meat stock into the pan, put the lid on, and braise for 30 minutes.
4. Before serving, top the goulash with yogurt and chopped parsley.

HUNSRÜCK SPIT ROAST

Hunsrücker Spießbraten (photo right)

INGREDIENTS (Serves 4)

2 pounds boneless pork loin roast
6 large onions
Salt and pepper to taste
Chopped fresh marjoram
Vegetable oil
Beer for basting

METHOD

1. When buying the roast, ask your butcher to cut a 2-inch cavity in it. Preheat the oven to 400°F.

2. Peel and slice the onions. Season the onions with pepper, salt, and plenty of chopped marjoram. Stir a few tablespoons of oil into the onions and leave to infuse for a few minutes.

3. Stuff the loin of pork with the onion mixture. Tie up the meat with kitchen string, place on a spit, and roast the meat for about 1½ hours.

4. Baste the meat with beer frequently during cooking. Serve with baked potatoes and grilled tomatoes.

BEEF WITH RAISIN SAUCE

Rindfleisch mit Rosinensauce (photo above)

INGREDIENTS (Serves 4)

1 pound boneless beef sirloin tip roast
1 onion
Bunch of mixed vegetables, e.g., carrots, leek, celery, etc.
Salt to taste
1 cup golden raisins
½ cup grated or crumbled Pfefferkuchen (gingerbread)
1 cup chopped almonds
1 tablespoon sugar
1 tablespoon wine vinegar
Concentrated stock

METHOD

1. Bring 2 quarts of water to a boil. Place the meat in the water, bring to a boil again, and skim off the froth. Add the onion, vegetables, and salt to the pan, cover, and cook for about an hour. The meat should be tender but not falling apart.

2. Soak the golden raisins in a little water.

3. Remove the meat from the stock. Strain the stock and return it to the pan. Add the gingerbread, golden raisins, and almonds to the stock and reduce it until thick and creamy. Season with sugar, vinegar, and concentrated stock to give a spicy flavor.

4. Slice the meat, and serve with the sauce poured over the meat. Serve with potato dumplings.

BEEF GOULASH WITH CHESTNUTS

Rindergulasch mit Eßkastanien

INGREDIENTS (Serves 4)

2 pounds piece of beef round steak
2 tablespoons clarified butter
12 pearl onions, peeled
1 cup beer
1 tablespoon tomate paste
1 teaspoon dried thyme
Salt and pepper to taste
1 pound chestnuts
4 cups peeled, diced pumpkin
1 cup heavy cream
Chopped fresh parsley

METHOD

1. Heat the clarified butter in a flameproof casserole and fry the meat in it to seal. Add the button onions to the meat and fry briefly. Deglaze the pot with ½ cup of beer.

2. Add the tomato paste, thyme, salt, and pepper to the pan. Place the lid on the pan and braise the meat for about an hour.

3. Score the chestnuts, place in a saucepan with some water, bring to a boil, and cook for 15 minutes. Remove chestnuts from the water and take off the shell and brown inner skin immediately. Add the chestnuts and the pumpkin to the meat after an hour. Add the remaining beer to the pan and cook for 30 minutes longer.

4. Remove the meat, chestnuts and pumpkin from the pan, and reduce the gravy by half. Stir the cream into the gravy, bring it to a boil and pour the gravy over the meat. Season the meat and gravy to taste. Sprinkle the meat with chopped parsley before serving.

STUFFED CROWN ROAST OF LAMB

Gefüllte Lammkrone

INGREDIENTS (Serves 6)

2 racks of lamb, total weight
*   about 4¹/2 pounds*
Salt, garlic powder, and pepper
*   to taste*
1 cup hot meat stock
¹/2 cup white wine

FOR THE VEGETABLES
1 pound green beans
1 small head of cauliflower
6 tomatoes
Salt, garlic powder, and grated
*   nutmeg to taste*
4 tablespoons unsalted butter
1 heaped teaspoon flour
Crème fraîche

METHOD

1. Preheat the oven to 350⁰F.
Remove the layer of fat from
both racks of lamb. Rub the
meat with salt, garlic powder,
and pepper. Shape each rack
into a semicircle, and tie them
together with kitchen string
to form a crown (your butcher
can also do this for you).
2. Make incisions about
³/4 inch deep between the
bones. Place the lamb crown
in a roasting pan. Pour the
meat stock and white wine
into the pan. Cover with foil
and cook on the lower middle
shelf of the oven for 2 hours.
3. After an hour, remove the
foil. About 45 minutes from
the end of cooking time,
remove the strings from the

green beans and break them
into pieces. Divide the cauliflower into florets. Take the
stems off the tomatoes.
4. Bring a little water to a boil
with the salt and garlic powder. Add the beans to the pan
and cook for 10 minutes. In
another saucepan, bring some
water to a boil, with the salt
and nutmeg. Add the cauliflower to the pan and cook for
15 minutes.
5. Drain the beans and cauliflower. Dot 3 tablespoons of
butter over the vegetables and
keep them warm. Season the
tomatoes with salt and garlic
powder. Dot the remaining
butter over the tomatoes.
Place the vegetables on an
oiled rack in a roasting pan.

6. Remove the crown roast
from the oven and place it on
a serving platter. Cover with
foil and keep it warm. Make
up the meat juices to 1¹/2 cups
with hot water and bring to
a boil. As soon as the crown
roast is removed from the
oven, put the tomatoes, cauliflower and beans into the hot
oven to reheat for 5 minutes.
Mix together the flour and
some crème fraîche. Use the
flour mixture to thicken the
gravy and season to taste.
7. Remove the vegetables
from the oven and arrange
on the platter around the
crown roast. Serve the
gravy separately.

Saarbrücken Meat Pie

Saarbrücker Fleischpastete (photo right)

INGREDIENTS (Serves 8)

2 pounds boneless pork shoulder
  (blade)
1 large onion, finely diced
3 bay leaves
6 cloves
8 juniper berries
1 teaspoon ground coriander
3 cups red wine
1/2 cup mild wine vinegar
1/2 cup ground pork
1 cup sour cream
1 egg yolk
Salt and pepper to taste

FOR THE DOUGH

2 1/3 cups all-purpose flour
1 cake (0.6 ounce) fresh compressed yeast or 1 envelope
  active dry yeast
1 teaspoon sugar
1/2 cup lukewarm milk
6 tablespoons unsalted butter,
  melted
1 egg
Salt to taste

METHOD

1. Cut the pork into 3/4-inch cubes. Mix the meat with the onion, bay leaves, cloves, juniper berries, ground coriander, red wine, and vinegar and leave to marinate for about 24 hours.
2. On the next day make the yeast dough. Place the flour in a bowl and make a well in the center. Mix the yeast with the sugar and 1/4 cup of the milk and pour into the well. Mix the yeast with a little flour and leave to proof in a warm place for about 15 to 20 minutes.
3. Preheat the oven to 350°F. Mix the remaining milk with the butter, egg, and a pinch of salt. Add to the yeast mixture and knead to form a smooth yeast dough. Roll out two-thirds of the dough in a large rectangle. Use to line the bottom and sides of a buttered springform pan.
4. Remove the meat from the marinade, pat dry and mix with the ground pork. Season the meat with salt and pepper. Spread the meat mixture in the pie shell, and pour the sour cream on top.
5. Roll out the remaining dough to make a circle a little larger than the diameter of the pan. Use the dough to cover the meat. Lightly press together the edges.
6. Cut a little circle out of the center of the top crust lid. Decorate the crust with the dough trimmings and brush with beaten egg yolk. Bake the pie for about 1 1/2 hours. After an hour, cover the pie with parchment paper, to prevent it from getting too brown.

Potato Pancakes

Kartoffelpuffer

INGREDIENTS (Serves 4)

3 1/2 pounds potatoes
2 onions
2 eggs
Salt and pepper to taste
Clarified butter

METHOD

1. Wash the potatoes, peel, grate finely, and squeeze out in a cloth. Peel and mince the onions and add to the grated potato. Stir in the eggs and season with salt and pepper.
2. Heat some clarified butter in a frying pan. Using two tablespoons, drop little batches of the potato mixture into the frying pan. Press flat and fry on both sides, until golden brown.
3. Drain the potato pancakes on paper towels and keep warm until all the pancakes have been cooked. Serve with stewed apple.

Potato and Bacon Bake

Pfälzer Schales

INGREDIENTS (Serves 4)

4 1/2 pounds potatoes
Bunch of scallions
1/2 pound slab bacon
4 eggs
Salt and pepper to taste

METHOD

1. Preheat the oven to 350°F. Wash, peel, and grate the potatoes. Trim the scallions, wash them, and slice thinly. Dice the bacon.
2. Mix together the prepared ingredients and use to fill a buttered ovenproof dish. Beat the eggs together, season with salt and pepper, and pour over the bacon and potato mixture. Bake the potatoes and bacon for about 1 1/2 hours.

WINE SOUP

Weinsuppe

INGREDIENTS (Serves 4)

3 cups white wine, e.g., Riesling
$^1/_2$ cup water
1 piece of lemon zest
Piece of cinnamon stick
$^1/_2$ cup sugar
4 egg yolks
$^1/_2$ cup cream
Salt, white pepper, and grated
   nutmeg to taste
3 tablespoons chilled unsalted
   butter, cubed
Chopped fresh chervil to garnish
4 slices of white bread, toasted

METHOD

1. Place the white wine, water, lemon zest, cinnamon stick, and sugar in a saucepan and bring them to a boil. Then strain and pour back into the saucepan.
2. Beat together the egg yolks and cream, and slowly trickle it into the wine soup, stirring all the time. The soup should not boil. Season to taste with salt, pepper and nutmeg.
3. Finally, whisk the butter into the hot soup, a cube at a time. Pour the soup into warmed soup bowls and sprinkle with chopped chervil. Serve with toasted white bread.

CABBAGE ROULADEN

Krautwickel

INGREDIENTS (Serves 4)

1 head white cabbage
$^1/_2$ pound ground beef
$^1/_2$ pound ground pork
1 onion, minced
2 eggs
Salt, pepper, and grated
   nutmeg to taste
4 slices bacon
2 tablespoons clarified butter
$^2/_3$ cup meat stock
$^1/_2$ cup sour cream

METHOD

1. Blanch the whole head of white cabbage in boiling water, drain it, and then separate the leaves. Place 3 to 4 leaves on top of each other on paper towels to make several piles.
2. Mix together the ground meats, onion, and eggs and season with salt, pepper, and nutmeg. Divide the mixture among the piles of cabbage leaves. Fold in the sides of the cabbage leaves. Working from a long side, roll up the cabbage leaves. Place a slice of bacon on top of each roulade and tie the roulade up with kitchen string.
3. Heat the clarified butter in a frying pan and fry the cabbage roulade. Add the stock to the pan and simmer for about an hour.
4. Remove the cabbage rouladen from the stock and keep them warm. Thicken the gravy with the sour cream. The sauce should not be allowed to boil. Season to taste with salt, pepper, and nutmeg. Serve the gravy with the cabbage rouladen and mashed potato.

ONION QUICHE

Zwiebel-Quiche

INGREDIENTS (Serves 4)

$1^3/_4$ cups all-purpose flour
4 eggs
7 tablespoons unsalted butter
5 ounces slab bacon, diced
$^1/_2$ pound onions, finely diced
Salt and pepper to taste
$1^1/_4$ cups grated cheese

METHOD

1. Preheat the oven to 400°F. Quickly mix together the flour, 1 egg, salt, and butter. Butter an 11-inch diameter spring-form pan. Roll out the dough and line the pan with it.
2. Fry the bacon in a frying pan to render the fat. Gently fry the onions in the bacon fat until caramelized and golden; then leave to cool.
3. Beat the remaining eggs and stir in the bacon and onions. Season the egg mixture with salt and pepper.
4. Spread the egg mixture in the pastry shell and sprinkle the grated cheese on top. Bake the quiche in the oven for about 25 to 30 minutes.

SURPRISE APPLE KUCHEN

Falscher gedeckter Apfelkuchen

INGREDIENTS (Serves 8)

FOR THE PASTRY

2½ cups all-purpose flour
10 tablespoons butter, cubed
About ¼ cup water
1 egg yolk
Pinch of salt

FOR THE FILLING

2 cups chopped savoy cabbage
½ pound Blutwurst (blood
    sausage)
½ pound Leberwurst (liver
    sausage)
2 apples
Breadcrumbs
Confectioners' sugar
Apricot jam, melted

FOR THE SAUCE

2 shallots
2 cups chicken stock
½ cup white wine
1 bay leaf
½ cup heavy cream

4 tablespoons unsalted butter,
    chilled and cubed
Freshly grated horseradish
Salt and pepper to taste

METHOD

1. Mix together the flour, butter, water, egg yolk, and salt to make a dough. Cover and leave to rest for about an hour.
2. Preheat the oven to 350°F. Butter a 9-inch diameter springform pan. Roll out the dough thinly and use to line the bottom and sides of the pan. Leave about 1 inch of pastry hanging over the rim of the pan. Fill the pastry shell with ceramic baking beans and bake for 12 to 14 minutes.
3. Blanch the cabbage. Slice the blood sausage and liver sausage into ½-inch thick rounds. Peel, core, and slice the apples thinly.
4. Sprinkle the bottom of the pastry shell with breadcrumbs. Layer the cabbage, liver sausage, apple slices, and blood sausage in the pastry shell. Sprinkle more breadcrumbs over the top. Finish with a rosette of apple slices. Return the pastry shell to the oven and bake for 18 minutes longer.
5. Meanwhile, peel and mince the shallots. Put in a saucepan, with the chicken stock, white wine, and bay leaf. Bring to a boil and boil until reduced by half.
6. Pass the sauce through a sieve. Stir in the cream and bring the sauce to a boil again. Reduce the sauce a bit more. Beat in the cubed butter. Season the sauce to taste with grated horseradish, salt, and pepper.
7. Shortly before the end of the baking time, dust the top of the cake with a little confectioners' sugar and allow it to caramelize slightly. Glaze the sliced apples with the apricot jam.
8. Remove the cake from the pan and cut away the pastry edge. Whisk the sauce until thick and frothy.
9. Using an electric knife, slice the cake into portions. Place a slice of cake in the middle of each plate and surround with a pool of sauce. If desired, garnish with cranberries.

CARTHUSIAN DUMPLINGS

Kartäuserklöße

INGREDIENTS (Serves 4)

8 to 9 cups bread cut in even
    cubes
½ cup milk
1½ tablespoons vanilla-flavored
    sugar
Ground cinnamon
Breadcrumbs
Unsalted butter
Sugar
Salt

METHOD

1. Preheat the oven to 400°F. Season the milk with the vanilla sugar, ground cinnamon, and salt.
2. Soak the bread cubes in the spiced milk; drain gently and coat in the breadcrumbs.
3. Melt some butter in a frying pan and fry the bread cubes in it briefly. Then transfer to the oven and bake for about 5 minutes or until crisp. Mix together some cinnamon and sugar and toss the dumplings in the sugar mixture.
4. Serve the Carthusian dumplings with Sabayon sauce and ice cream.

SABAYON SAUCE

Weinschaumsauce

INGREDIENTS (Serves 4–6)

1¾ cups white wine
8 egg yolks
1⅔ cups sugar
Grated juice and zest of 1 lemon

METHOD

1. Put all the ingredients in a metal bowl. Set over a saucepan of hot water and whisk until foaming.

SABAYON ICE CREAM

Weinschaumeis

INGREDIENTS (Serves 4–6)

5⅓ cups wine
10 egg yolks
3 cups sugar
2 cups (1 pound) chilled unsalted
    butter, cubed

METHOD

1. Bring the wine to a boil in a saucepan. Beat together the egg yolks and sugar until foaming and stir into the wine.
2. Place the egg mixture in a food processor. Gradually add the butter.
3. Pour the mixture into a bowl and leave to cool. Put the bowl in the freezer and leave to set. Once the mixture is sludgy, but not fully set, take it out of the freezer and whisk it to break up the crystals. Return the mixture to the freezer. Repeat a couple of times to ensure it freezes evenly.

CARAMEL CREAM
Karamelcreme

INGREDIENTS (Serves 4)

1/4 cup sugar

5 egg yolks

1 cup cream

1/2 cup milk

METHOD

1. Cook the sugar in a saucepan until caramelized. Take care as the caramel will be very hot.

2. In a medium bowl whisk together the egg yolks, cream, and milk and carefully pour the mixture into the caramel. Stir well.

3. Transfer the caramel mixture to the top of a double boiler and cook gently over hot water, stirring all the time until the custard thickens. Pour the custard into dessert dishes and leave to cool.

RASPBERRY CRÊPES
Himbeer-Crêpes (photo above)

INGREDIENTS (Serves 4)

FOR THE CRÊPES

1 3/4 cups all-purpose flour

Pinch of salt

6 tablespoons sugar

6 eggs

2 cups milk

6 tablespoons unsalted butter, melted

3 tablespoons raspberry liqueur

FOR THE FILLING

2 cups medium white wine, e.g., Sylvaner

1/4 cup sugar

1/2 teaspoon ground cinnamon

2 pints (1 pound) raspberries

FOR THE SAUCE

5 tablespoons sugar

4 eggs

1 cup milk

1 cup macaroons, crumbled

6 tablespoons unsalted butter, melted

METHOD

1. Thoroughly mix together the flour, salt, sugar, eggs, and milk. Gradually add the melted butter and stir. Leave to rest for an hour.

2. Stir the raspberry liqueur into the batter. Lightly butter and heat a non-stick frying pan. Pour a little batter into the pan and spread thinly over the bottom of the pan. Fry the crêpes on both sides until golden brown. Remove from the pan and keep warm while you make the remaining crêpes.

3. Bring the wine to a boil with the sugar and cinnamon, remove it from the heat, place the raspberries in the pan, and leave to infuse for 8 minutes.

4. Fill the crêpes with the raspberries and roll up. Butter an ovenproof dish, sprinkle with sugar, and place the crêpes in the dish.

5. Preheat the oven to 350ºF. Beat together the eggs and sugar. Stir in the milk and pour the sauce over the crêpes. Sprinkle with macaroons and drizzle the crêpes with the melted butter. Bake for 10 minutes.

CHERRY PUDDING
Kerscheplotzer

INGREDIENTS (Serves 4)

4 soft white rolls

1 1/2 cups lukewarm milk

4 tablespoons unsalted butter

5 tablespoons sugar

3 eggs, separated

1 1/2 pounds (about 6 cups) sweet cherries, pitted

Grated zest of 1 lemon

3 tablespoons chopped almonds

TO SERVE

2 tablespoons sugar

1 teaspoon ground cinnamon

METHOD

1. Preheat the oven to 400ºF. Slice the rolls thinly and pour the milk over the slices.

2. Beat together the butter, sugar, and egg yolks until creamy. Mix with the softened bread rolls. Wash the cherries, drain them, and add them to the bread mixture with the lemon zest and almonds.

3. Butter an ovenproof dish. In a small bowl, beat the egg whites until stiff and fold into the bread mixture. Turn the mixture into the buttered dish. Bake for about 45 minutes in the oven. As soon as the pudding comes out of the oven, sprinkle it with the sugar and ground cinnamon. Serve the pudding immediately.

CIDER CUSTARD WITH CARAMELIZED APPLE RINGS

Viez-Creme auf karamelisierten Apfelringen

INGREDIENTS (Serves 4)

FOR THE CUSTARD

2 eggs, separated
5 tablespoons sugar
3 cups heavy cream
*1¹/₂ tablespoons vanilla-
   flavored sugar*
*5 leaves of gelatin or
   1 package powdered
   unflavored gelatin*
*2 sweet apples, peeled and
   chopped*
Pinch of ground cloves
¹/₂ cup hard cider

FOR THE CARAMELIZED APPLES

2 tablespoons sliced almonds
2 tablespoons brown sugar
²/₃ cup very dry hard cider
*1¹/₂ tablespoons apple
   schnapps*
*2 ripe but firm apples,
   cut into rings*
*4 fresh lemon balm sprigs
   (optional)*

METHOD

1. To make the custard, beat the egg yolks with half the sugar until foaming. Place 2 cups of the cream, the remaining sugar, and vanilla sugar in a saucepan and bring to boiling point.

2. Remove the saucepan from the heat and stir the egg yolk mixture into the cream, using a balloon whisk. Return the saucepan to the heat and whisk the custard until it thickens. The custard should not be allowed to boil.

3. Soften the gelatin in cold water, then stir it into the warm custard. Remove the pan from the heat.

4. In a blender or food processor, process the apples to a smooth purée. Stir the puréed apple, ground cloves, and cider into the custard and leave to cool. Whip the remaining cream until stiff. Before the custard sets, carefully fold in the cream and fill individual molds with the mixture. Leave the molds in the refrigerator to set.

5. Toast the sliced almonds in a frying pan and then sprinkle the sugar on top and leave them to caramelize a little.

6. Stir in the cider and then the schnapps. Add the apple rings to the pan and fry them briefly until soft.

7. Arrange the caramelized apple rings and sliced almonds in a pool of caramel sauce on dessert plates. Turn the custards out of the molds and arrange on top of the apple slices and caramel sauce. Garnish with the sprigs of lemon balm.

POTATO STRUDEL WITH APPLES

Kartoffelstrudel mit Äpfeln (photo below)

INGREDIENTS (Serves 4)

$^3/_4$ *pound potatoes (choose a variety that is firm when cooked)*
2 cups all-purpose flour
2 tablespoons baking powder
2 cups sugar
$^1/_2$ *cup unsalted butter*
$1^1/_2$ *tablespoons vanilla-flavored sugar*
2 eggs
$1^1/_2$ *pounds apples*
$^1/_2$ *cup raisins*
1 teaspoon ground cinnamon
Melted unsalted butter

METHOD

1. The day before, cook the potatoes in their skins in salted water. Peel immediately and leave to cool.
2. Next day, grate the potatoes and mix them with the flour and baking powder. Preheat the oven to 400°F. Add $1^1/_2$ cups of the sugar, the butter, vanilla sugar, and eggs to the potato mixture. Mix quickly to form a smooth dough. If it is a bit sticky, add a little more flour.
3. Roll out the potato dough to form a rectangle 12 by 16 inches in size. Peel the apples, chop finely, and mix them with the raisins, remaining sugar, and cinnamon.
4. Spread the apple mixture over the dough. Roll up the dough from a long side to form a sausage shape. Melt a little butter and brush it on to the roulade. Bake the roulade in the oven for about 30 minutes until golden brown. Serve with custard sauce.

SWEETENED POTATO CAKES WITH RASPBERRY COULIS

Süßer Debbekoche auf Himbeermark

INGREDIENTS (Serves 4)

TO MAKE THE RASPBERRY COULIS
$3^1/_2$ *cups fresh or frozen raspberries*
$^1/_4$ *cup red wine*
6 tablespoons sugar
$1^1/_2$ *tablespoons raspberry liqueur*

FOR THE CAKES
1 pound potatoes, boiled in their skins
$1^1/_2$ *tablespoons vanilla-flavored sugar*
Grated zest of 1 lemon
6 tablespoons sugar
Pinch of salt
1 egg, beaten
2 tablespoons breadcrumbs

TO SERVE
Whipped cream

METHOD

1. Preheat the oven to 475°F. Wash the raspberries and soak them in the red wine until they are soft. Then push them through a fine sieve. Add the sugar to the purée and stir until dissolved. Flavor the raspberry coulis with the liqueur.
2. Peel the potatoes, grate finely, and mix them with the vanilla sugar, lemon zest, sugar, salt and egg.
3. Butter four ramekins and coat with the breadcrumbs. Fill the ramekins with the potato mixture, put them in the oven, and bake them for about 30 minutes.
4. Remove the cakes from the oven and leave to cool for 5 minutes. Turn out of the ramekins and arrange on plates in a pool of raspberry coulis. Decorate with whipped cream.

OSTERTAL POTATO WAFFLES

Ostertaler
Kartoffel-Eier-Waffeln
(photo right)

INGREDIENTS
(Makes 8 waffles)

$5^1/_2$ pounds potatoes
2 leeks, halved lengthwise and
    finely sliced
5 eggs, beaten
5 to 6 tablespoons flour
1 cake (0.6 ounce) fresh com-
    pressed yeast or 1 envelope
    active dry yeast
Salt and pepper to taste

METHOD

1. Peel and grate the potatoes;
squeeze dry in a cloth. Add
the leeks with the eggs and
flour. Season.
2. Dissolve the yeast in a little
lukewarm water and stir into
the potato mixture. Heat a
waffle iron and brush it with
oil. Place some potato batter
on the iron and cook the
waffle until golden brown.
Continue until all the potato
mixture is used up. Serve
the waffles warm.

DRUNKEN SISTERS

Versoffene Schwestern

INGREDIENTS (Serves 4)

1 cup all-purpose flour
$^1/_2$ cup milk
1 egg
4 tablespoons unsalted butter
1 quart Riesling
1 cinnamon stick
3 cloves

METHOD

1. Beat together the flour,
milk, and egg to form a batter.
Leave to rest for an hour.
2. Melt the butter in a frying
pan. Make 2 to 3 crêpes with
the batter. Cut them into strips.
3. Heat the wine in a saucepan, with the spices. Do not
boil. Remove the cinnamon
stick and add the crêpe strips
to the wine.

PALATINE PLUM DUMPLINGS

Pfälzer Zwetschgenknödel

INGREDIENTS (Serves 4)

2 pounds potatoes (choose a variety that stays firm when cooked)
2¹/₂ cups all-purpose flour
2 small eggs, beaten
Pinch of salt
Pinch of grated nutmeg
1 pound tart plums (damsons)
4 tablespoons butter
Sugar cubes
6 to 8 tablespoons breadcrumbs
Sugar and ground cinnamon

METHOD

1. If possible, cook the potatoes in their skins a day in advance. Next day, peel them and press them through a potato ricer. Knead the potato with the flour, eggs, salt, and nutmeg to form a smooth dough.

2. Shape the dough into a sausage about 3 inches in diameter. Cut the dough into thick slices.

3. Remove the pits from the plums and place a cube of sugar in the middle of each plum. Mold the slices of potato dough around the plums, to form dumplings.

4. Bring plenty of salted water to a boil. Reduce the heat and cook the dumplings in the water in batches for 10 to 15 minutes or until done. The water should not boil.

5. Melt the butter in a frying pan and fry the breadcrumbs in it. Drain the plum dumplings and toss them in the buttered breadcrumbs. Dredge the dumplings with sugar and ground cinnamon and serve immediately.

WINE TO SUIT EVERY TASTE

HANNELORE KOHL:
I want a wine to accompany roast beef. What do you think of Pinot Gris?

ALFONS SCHUHBECK:
Always a good choice. Thankfully, the idea that you should drink what *you* like prevails. The rule that you should only drink "red wine with red meat, white wine with white meat and fish" really doesn't apply any more, because it simply restricts personal preference too much.

HANNELORE KOHL:
The first thing Noah is supposed to have done after the Flood is to plant a vineyard. We don't have this problem nowadays because well-stocked liquor stores do all the work for us. But who can still afford to stock a wine cellar?

ALFONS SCHUHBECK:
You have to be really inventive. I even know some people who store the wine in their bedrooms under the bed. But no matter where, it must be stored in a cool, dark place.

HANNELORE KOHL:
What is particularly important when storing wine?

ALFONS SCHUHBECK:
Wine easily absorbs smells through the cork, so you should at all costs avoid storing onions or cans of paint in the cellar next to your wine. Variations in temperature spoil wine. When storing wine, it is also important for the bottles to be stored lying down, so the corks don't dry out. Other-

This is a Pinot Gris from the southern Wine Route. When it comes to grape variety, production area, and vintage, personal preference is the deciding factor.

wise, the wine oxidizes and loses its freshness.

HANNELORE KOHL:
Which wines would you recommend as part of a personal wine cellar?

ALFONS SCHUHBECK:
There's no point in buying "trendy" wines. Instead you should take the time to try different wines and find those that you personally like best. It's a good idea to have "quaffing" wines in the house for everyday use. Then you could have a dry or medium white and a red wine to serve with meals and perhaps a couple of vintage wines for special occasions. Rather than having a colorful array of two or three bottles of this or that wine, it is much better to build up a little stock of the wines you really like. Then you'll be well equipped if a pleasant evening with guests lingers on.

BY HELMUT KOHL

I'm a real bookworm, so naturally I'm drawn to Frankfurt am Main and its book fair. The city has so much to offer. It has been a focal point in history and is today one of the most important banking and commercial centers in the world.

The German Emperors were elected and crowned here. It also brings to mind men like Meyer Amschel Rothschild who, more than 200 years ago, rose from desperate poverty to become a symbol of Jewish emancipation and to found one of the biggest international merchant banks.

▶

Circular St Paul's cathedral is a reminder of our country's liberal and democratic traditions. It stands surrounded by bold skyscrapers, which have earned Frankfurt the name "Mainhattan." This close proximity between the traditional and modern is one of the things that first strikes the millions of visitors to Germany. "Typically German" think tourists or businessmen from Asia, Latin America, and the U.S.A. when they arrive at Frankfurt airport and then make a little sortie into the surrounding area, to the picturesque Bergstrasse, the terraced vineyards in the Rheingau, or the thickly wooded Spessart and Odenwald, where my wife and I enjoy walking.

American soldiers who have been stationed in Hesse have become familiar with, and grown to love the region's customs and have taken them back home with them. It's not just pure chance that the United States is the biggest importer of Frankfurt sausages.

Throughout the world, sausages are just as much a symbol of German hospitality as pork chops with cabbage or for dessert fans Frankfurt ring cake.

Hesse cooks swear that no less than nine herbs belong in the famous green sauce. Popular with beef and traditionally eaten with new potatoes on Good Friday, this was one of Johann Wolfgang von Goethe's favorite dishes.

Another Hessian specialty proves how business activity can influence eating habits. The housekeeper to the banker and councillor, Moritz von Bethmann, is supposed to have served *Bethmännncher* for the first time as a treat with coffee around 1840. This delicacy, coming from a highly regarded Frankfurt family, was soon widely copied and today *Bethmännncher*, little marzipan pyramids with half an almond on each side, are still a part of traditional German Christmas baking alongside *Aachener Printen* and Nürnberg *Lebkuchen*.

Attended by wine experts and enthusiasts from around the world, wine auctions take place from April to June in Rüdesheim, Johannisberg, Eltville, Geisenheim, and at the Eberbach monastery. One quite popular wine is *Ebbelwoi,* the famous apple wine poured from a stone jug. In Hesse it is drunk with *Handkäs mit Musik,* a strongly flavored cheese in a vinegar and oil dressing.

A walk along the River Fulda in Melsungen. The picturesque village is on a popular German vacation route.

HERB AND LIVER PÂTÉ WITH PORK TENDERLOIN

Kräuter-Leber-Pastete mit Schweinefilet

INGREDIENTS (Serves 6–8)

FOR THE PASTRY

2¹/₂ cups all-purpose flour
1 egg
10 tablespoons unsalted butter
3 to 5 tablespoons water
Pinch of salt

FOR THE FILLING

1 stale roll, crumbled
¹/₂ cup lukewarm cream
1 pound ground pork
²/₃ cup chopped cooked ham
¹/₂ pound pork liver
1 egg
Bunch of fresh parsley
Salt and pepper to taste
1¹/₂ tablespoons kirsch
Fresh thyme sprig
1 pork tenderloin roast, weighing
    about 14 ounces
1 egg yolk, beaten

FOR THE SAUCE

1 pound mixed berries, e.g., black
    currants, raspberries, and
    blackberries
3 tablespoons red currant jelly
2 tablespoons medium-hot mustard
Salt and pepper to taste

METHOD

1. To make the pastry, work together the dough ingredients and refrigerate.
2. Preheat the oven to 350°F. Pour the cream over the bread. Squeeze liquid out of the bread and process, with the pork, ham, liver, and egg, to a very smooth paste. During processing, add a few parsley leaves, a little salt, pepper, the kirsch, and a few thyme leaves. Mix thoroughly.
3. Butter a loaf pan, about 11 by 4 inches. Roll out two-thirds of the dough and use to line the pan. Prick all over. Spread half the filling over the bottom. Season the tenderloin, put it in the center of the pan, and cover with the remaining meat mixture. Press down and smooth the top. Cover with the remaining dough. Cut two small holes in the top crust. Use the remaining dough to decorate the terrine. Brush with beaten egg yolk. Bake for about 70 minutes or until thoroughly cooked. Leave to cool in the oven and then unmold.
4. To make the sauce, push one-third of the berries through a sieve. Mix the purée with the red currant jelly and mustard and stir in the remaining berries. Season the sauce with salt and pepper.

STUFFED BAKED POTATOES
Gefüllte Ofenkartoffeln

INGREDIENTS (Serves 4)

4 large baking potatoes
1 onion
1/4 pound prosciutto
1 tablespoon clarified butter
1/2 cup heavy cream
2 eggs, separated
Salt and pepper to taste
4 tablespoons unsalted butter
2 tablespoons chopped fresh chives

METHOD

1. Preheat the oven to 475°F. Wash the potatoes and wrap individually in foil. Bake the potatoes in the oven for about 45 minutes. Peel the onion and dice; do the same with the prosciutto. Heat the clarified butter in a frying pan, fry the onion and prosciutto in it, and then add the cream to the pan and bring it to a boil. Remove the pan from the heat and stir in the egg yolks. In a small bowl, beat the egg whites until stiff, fold them into the onion and ham mixture and season it with salt and pepper.

2. Reduce the oven temperature to 350°F. Remove the potatoes from the foil, cut off a lid, and hollow out the potatoes. Mash the scooped-out potato and heat it up in a saucepan with the butter, stirring all the time. Season to taste with salt and pepper. Fold the chopped chives into the potato mixture. Gradually fold the cream mixture into the mashed potato, then use it to stuff the potato shells. Return them to the oven and bake them until well risen and golden brown.

CALVES' LIVER PÂTÉ WITH PORK TENDERLOIN
Rinderleberterrine mit Schweinefilet (photo above)

INGREDIENTS (Serves 6–8)

2 cups milk
1 1/2 pounds calves' liver
Clarified butter
Pork tenderloin roast, weighing about 1 pound
3/4 pound fresh pork side (belly)
3 onions
3 tablespoons anchovy paste
Salt, dried thyme, and black pepper to taste
1/3 cup port wine
2/3 cup cream
Bay leaves, cocktail cherries, and fresh thyme

METHOD

1. Pour the milk into a bowl. Chop the calves' liver into 1-inch chunks and soak in the milk for an hour.

2. Preheat the oven to 350°F. On the stovetop heat some clarified butter in a frying pan and fry the tenderloin on all sides to seal. Remove the tenderloin from the pan and leave to cool. Chop the pork side into chunks. Drain the calves' liver. Peel the onions. Finely grind or process the calves' liver, pork side, and onions. Add the anchovy paste, salt, thyme, and black pepper to the meat mixture.

3. Mix the meat mixture with the port and cream. Season to taste. The mixture should be quite highly seasoned, so add more salt and pepper if necessary. Spread one-third of the liver mixture over the bottom of a loaf pan or rectangular baking dish, place the tenderloin on top, and cover the pork with the remaining liver mixture. Smooth off the surface.

4. Cover the pan or dish with foil and set it in a bain-marie (a roasting pan half-filled with boiling water). Cook in the oven for about 1 hour. When the pâté is cooked, turn off the oven, open the oven door slightly, and leave the pâté to cool in the oven.

5. Remove the pâté from the oven, unmold onto a serving dish and garnish with the bay leaves, cherries, and thyme. Serve with fresh, crusty bread or walnut bread.

BRISKET WITH HERB SAUCE

Ochsenbrust mit Kräutersauce (photo below)

INGREDIENTS (Serves 4)

1 quart water
1¹/₂ pounds ox or beef brisket
1 onion, peeled
2 bay leaves
2 juniper berries (optional)
2 cloves
Salt to taste

FOR THE SAUCE
Bunch of mixed fresh herbs,
*   e.g., sorrel, watercress, chervil,*
*   dill, and parsley*
²/₃ cup plain yogurt
1 cup sour cream
¹/₄ cup mayonnaise
2 eggs, hard-boiled and chopped
Salt and pepper to taste

METHOD

1. Bring the water to a rolling boil. Place the meat, onion, bay leaves, juniper berries, cloves, and some salt in the water. Cook for about 1¹/₂ hours over low heat.
2. To make the sauce, mix together the chopped herbs, yogurt, sour cream, mayonnaise, and chopped eggs. Season to taste with salt and pepper. The sauce should be well seasoned.
3. Serve the meat, hot or cold, thinly sliced, with the sauce.

STEAK SALAD

Salat mit Rinderfiletspitzen

INGREDIENTS (Serves 4)

1 small head radicchio
1 cup corn salad (mâche)
2 cups sliced mixed mushrooms,
*   e.g., button, crimini, and*
*   meadow*
1 small red onion
1¹/₂ tablespoons unsalted butter
¹/₂ pound boneless sirloin or
*   tenderloin steak*
Salt and pepper to taste

FOR THE DRESSING
2 to 3 tablespoons vinegar
¹/₂ teaspoon sugar
6 tablespoons vegetable oil
Salt and pepper to taste

METHOD

1. Trim the radicchio and corn salad, wash, and drain thoroughly. Tear the radicchio into pieces. Peel and slice the onion.
2. Melt the butter and fry the steak in it for 4 to 6 minutes on each side. Season the steak and cut into strips.
3. Mix together the ingredients for the dressing, toss the salad leaves and vegetables in the dressing, and top with the strips of steak.

CREAMY POTATO SOUP

Sämige Kartoffelsuppe

INGREDIENTS (Serves 4)

1/4 pound slab bacon
5 onions
1 leek
1/2 fennel bulb
2 carrots
1 pound potatoes
1 tablespoon drippings
1 quart beef stock
1 bay leaf
4 juniper berries
Salt and pepper to taste
Pinch of sugar
2 slices white bread
1 tablespoon unsalted butter
1/2 cup cream

METHOD

1. Dice the bacon. Peel and dice three onions, peel and slice the other two in rings. Trim the leek and fennel and peel the carrot; dice them. Peel and slice the potatoes.
2. Melt the drippings in a saucepan, fry the bacon in the drippings to render the fat, then add the diced vegetables and diced onion (reserving the sliced onion), and fry briefly. Add the potatoes to the pan and add the stock. Add the bay leaf and the juniper berries to the pan. Season the soup with salt, pepper, and sugar. Cover and cook for about 30 minutes.
3. Meanwhile, dice the white bread and toast it in a nonstick pan. Melt the butter in a frying pan and fry the onion rings until caramelized.
4. Stir the soup thoroughly with a balloon whisk, add the cream, and mix it quickly. Then pour into a warmed soup tureen and scatter the onion rings and croûtons on top. Serve with sausages (*Frankfurter Würtschen, Rindsbratwurst, Fleischwurst*) or smoked ham.

FRANKFURT GREEN SAUCE

Frankfurter Grüne Sauce (photo right)

INGREDIENTS (Serves 4)

2 eggs, hard-boiled
3 tablespoons vegetable oil
2/3 cup plain yogurt
2/3 cup sour cream
1 bunch of fresh herbs, e.g., borage, watercress, chervil, chives, sorrel, and parsley
1 garlic clove
Juice of 1/2 lemon
1 teaspoon German mustard
Salt and pepper to taste
Pinch of sugar
1 pickled gherkin
1 small onion

METHOD

1. Shell the eggs, cut in half, remove the yolks, mash the yolks until smooth and mix to a smooth paste with the oil. Add the yogurt and sour cream. Wash the herbs and chop them. Peel the garlic, crush it, and mix with the sauce. Season to taste with lemon juice, mustard, salt, pepper, and sugar.
2. Mince the egg whites and pickled gherkin, peel and grate the onion, and mix all three ingredients with the sauce. The sauce goes well with hard-boiled eggs.

BEET SALAD

Rote Rüben

INGREDIENTS (Serves 4)

1 pound beets
2 onions
1 teaspoon finely grated horseradish
4 to 6 tablespoons vinegar
Salt and sugar to taste
1/2 teaspoon caraway seeds

METHOD

1. Leave the roots and green tops on the beets, so that they don't lose too much color during cooking. Scrub the beets carefully with a brush under running water. Bring a pan of salted water to a boil, add the beets to the pan, and cook for about 1 to 1 1/2 hours or until tender.
2. Drain off the cooking water and refresh the beets with cold water. This makes it easier to remove the skin. Peel and slice the warm beets. Peel and slice the onions and mix with the sliced beets and horseradish. Mix together the vinegar, a little water, salt, sugar, and caraway, and pour over the beet salad. Place the beet salad in a jar or bowl, cover, and leave to marinate for 2 to 3 days. The beet salad goes well with boiled beef, sausages, or meatballs.

HANNELORE KOHL

"*U*se potatoes with a high starch content for the potato soup, ensuring it has a nice, creamy consistency."

BEEF AND ONION STEW

Rindfleisch-Zwiebel-Topf (photo below)

INGREDIENTS (Serves 4)

1 pound beef chuck or blade
   steak
1/4 pound slab bacon
2 pounds onions
2 tablespoons clarified butter
1 teaspoon caraway seeds
1/2 teaspoon paprika
2 cups meat stock
2 cups white wine
1 pound potatoes
1/4 pound processed cheese
   spread

METHOD

1. Cut the beef into large
cubes and the bacon into
small cubes. Peel and slice
the onions.
2. Heat the clarified butter
in a flameproof casserole.
First, seal the bacon in it
and then the beef. Add the
onions to the pot, season
the contents with caraway
and paprika, and cook
together briefly. Add the
wine and stock to the pan,
cover and braise the meat
for 50 minutes.
2. Peel and dice the potatoes, add to the stew and
cook for 30 to 40 minutes
or until cooked. Finally,
melt the cheese spread in
the stew.

BRAISED PORK BACK RIBS

Geschmortes Schweinekarree

INGREDIENTS (Serves 4)

3 1/2 pounds pork loin back ribs
1 carrot
1 leek, white only
1/2 celery stalk
1 onion, spiked with 2 cloves
3 garlic cloves, crushed
1 tablespoon pork drippings
Salt to taste

METHOD

1. Chop the carrot, leek, and
celery into small pieces and
place in a large pot with the
meat. Add the onion and
crushed garlic. Pour in enough
water to come 1 inch above
the pork. Salt the water, bring
to a boil, and skim. Simmer
the meat over low heat for
about 45 minutes. Remove the
pork; drain the vegetables
and reserve.
2. Preheat the oven to 475°F.
Melt the pork drippings in a
roasting pan. Place the pork
in the pan, baste with the hot
drippings, and brown in the
oven for a few minutes. Serve
with the boiled vegetables.

LAMB CHOPS WITH FINES HERBES

Lammkoteletts mit feinen Kräutern

INGREDIENTS (Serves 4)

8 lamb loin chops, weighing about 3 ounces each
Salt and white pepper to taste
1 small garlic clove
1/2 cup unsalted butter
1/2 cup white wine
Bunch of fresh parsley, chopped
1/2 teaspoon chopped fresh chervil
1/2 teaspoon minced fresh basil
Grated zest and juice of 1 lemon
1/2 cup hot meat stock
2 tomatoes, peeled
Fresh tarragon sprig

METHOD

1. Season the chops with salt and pepper.
2. Crush the garlic and soften it in a frying pan, with half of the butter. Fry the chops in the garlic butter over medium heat for about 5 minutes on each side. Remove from the pan and keep warm.
3. Deglaze the meat residues with the white wine. Bring to a boil and add the chopped herbs, lemon juice, and zest. Then add the meat stock and reduce for 10 minutes. Whisk pieces of the remaining butter into the sauce. Pour the sauce over the chops. Serve the chops garnished with peeled tomatoes and the sprig of fresh tarragon.

LAMB CHOPS WITH MINT SAUCE

Lammkoteletts mit Minzsauce

INGREDIENTS (Serves 4)

FOR THE SAUCE
2 cups fresh mint leaves
1/4 cup sugar
1 cup water
Juice of 1 lemon

8 lamb rib chops, each weighing 3 ounces
Clarified butter
Salt and freshly ground green peppercorns to taste

METHOD

1. To make the sauce, coarsely chop the mint leaves. Bring the sugar and water to a boil. Pour the syrup over the mint leaves and leave to infuse for an hour. Drain off the syrup, return it to the pan, mix with the lemon juice and reduce it a little.
2. Heat some clarified butter in a frying pan and fry the cutlets on both sides. Season with salt and pepper. Pour the sauce over the cutlets. Serve with sautéed potatoes.

HANNELORE KOHL

"*Fresh herbs often lend the finishing touch to many dishes. If you have a small herb garden, even in a window box, it will ensure you have a steady supply of fresh herbs all year round.*"

VEAL BRAISED IN CIDER

Kalbsbraten in Apfelwein (photo above)

INGREDIENTS (Serves 4)

2 pounds boneless veal breast or
*   shoulder roast*
Salt and pepper to taste
1 large apple
1 carrot
¹/₄ fennel bulb
2 onions
1 garlic clove
2 tablespoons unsalted butter
2 cups hard cider
1¹/₂ tablespoons apple schnapps
1 tablespoon dried, rubbed
*   marjoram*
¹/₄ cup cream
Worcestershire sauce to taste

METHOD

1. Rub the veal with the salt and pepper. Peel, halve, and core the apple. Peel the carrot, onion, and garlic and trim the fennel; chop them coarsely.
2. Melt the butter in a flame-proof casserole and seal the meat in it on all sides. Pour the cider and apple schnapps into the pot, add the vegetables and the dried marjoram, cover, and braise over a low heat for about 2 hours.
3. Remove the meat from the casserole and keep it warm. Pass the meat juices through a sieve, enrich it with cream, and season to taste with salt, pepper, and Worcestershire sauce. Serve with boiled potatoes and braised celeriac (celery root).

MARINATED BRAISED BEEF

Marinierter Rinderschmorbraten

INGREDIENTS (Serves 4)

3 pounds beef sirloin tip roast
Salt and pepper to taste
Clarified butter
1 tablespoon wholegrain mustard
¹/₂ bunch of fresh savory,
*   chopped*
¹/₂ bunch of fresh thyme
¹/₂ pound sliced bacon
6 to 8 large fresh or preserved
*   grapevine leaves*
1 cup dry white wine
2 cups seedless grapes

METHOD

1. Rub the beef with salt and pepper. Heat some clarified butter in a frying pan and seal the meat in it until well browned on all sides. Mix together the mustard and savory and brush on the meat. Cover the meat with the thyme and bacon slices. Rinse the grapevine leaves and lay them on a flat surface, overlapping them. Place the meat in the middle of the leaves and fold the leaves in over the beef.
2. Preheat the oven to 350°F. Tie up the meat with kitchen string, place in a lidded roasting pan, and add the wine to the pan. Cover the pan and braise in the oven, allowing 15 minutes for each ¹/₂ inch thickness of meat. Twenty minutes before the end of the cooking, add the grapes to the pan.
3. Remove the grapevine leaves from around the beef. Arrange the beef on a serving platter with the grapes and moisten with the meat juices.

Brisket of Beef with Chive Sauce

Rinderbrust in Schnittlauchsauce (photo above)

INGREDIENTS (Serves 4)

1¹/₂ pounds beef brisket roast
3 cloves
1 bay leaf
1¹/₂ tablespoons peppercorns
*Bunch of fresh vegetables and
   herbs, e.g., carrots, celery,
   leeks, and parsley*

FOR THE SAUCE
¹/₄ cup mayonnaise
²/₃ cup plain yogurt
Juice of 1 lemon
*Salt, white pepper, and celery
   salt to taste*
1 small onion
1 egg, hard-boiled
2 bunches of fresh chives
¹/₂ cup watercress
2 pickled gherkins, sliced

METHOD

1. Bring a pot of salted water
to a rolling boil, add the beef,
cloves, bay leaf, and peppercorns to the pot, cover, and
cook for 1¹/₂ hours. Wash and
trim the vegetables, add them
to the pot, and cook with the
meat for 30 minutes longer.
Keep the meat covered and
leave it to cool in the liquid.
2. To make the sauce, mix the
mayonnaise, yogurt, and
lemon juice. Season with salt,
pepper, and celery salt. The
sauce should be piquant. Peel
and mince the onion and
hard-boiled egg. Mince the
herbs and add everything to
the sauce.
3. Slice the cold meat and
arrange on a platter. Pour a
little sauce over the sliced
meat and serve the rest separately. Garnish the platter
with pickled gherkins. Serve
with bread.

Beef with Mustard and Cheese

Rinder-Senfbraten

INGREDIENTS (Serves 4)

*¹/₂ pound Emmenthal cheese (or
   other hard, mild cheese like
   Edam or Gouda)*
*1³/₄ pounds boneless beef round
   rump roast*
2 tablespoons clarified butter
2 carrots, peeled and sliced
1 slice of black bread, crumbled
6 peppercorns
Salt to taste
*3 tablespoons medium-hot
   mustard*
1 cup meat stock
1 cup sour cream

METHOD

1. Preheat the oven to 350⁰F.
Cut the cheese into sticks
and spike the meat all over
with them.
2. Heat the clarified butter
in a flameproof casserole
and briefly fry the sliced
carrots, half the breadcrumbs,
and the peppercorns in the
butter. Season the beef with
salt and spread it thickly
with the mustard. Put it in
the casserole and pour in the
meat stock. Cover the pot
and braise the meat in the
oven for 2 hours, basting it
occasionally.
3. At the end of cooking time,
remove the meat and keep it
warm. Enrich the gravy with
the sour cream and the
remaining breadcrumbs.
Serve with boiled potatoes
and savoy cabbage.

HESSIAN FARMER'S BREAKFAST

Hessisches Bauernfrühstück (photo right)

INGREDIENTS (Serves 4)

2 pounds potatoes
4 tablespoons unsalted butter
3 tablespoons minced onion
1 cup cream
1 teaspoon lemon juice
Salt and pepper to taste
Bunch of fresh chervil or
*   parsley, chopped*
1/2 pound sliced ham

METHOD

1. Boil the potatoes, then peel and slice them. Melt the butter in a frying pan and fry the onion in it until translucent. Add the potatoes and fry until golden brown all over.
2. Pour the cream over the potatoes and sprinkle with lemon juice. Season with salt and pepper. Sprinkle the herbs on top, roll up the slices of ham and place them on top of the potatoes. Serve straight from the pan.

SHOULDER OF PORK WITH APPLES

Gebratene Schweineschulter (photo above)

INGREDIENTS (Serves 4)

3 pounds pork shoulder roast,
*   with rind*
2 tablespoons unsalted butter,
*   at room temperature*
2 garlic cloves, crushed
2 teaspoons medium-hot mustard
Salt and pepper to taste
1/2 bunch of fresh lemon balm,
*   chopped (optional)*
1/2 cup stock
1 1/2 cups hard cider
1 1/2 pounds small round potatoes
1/2 pound small onions
1 1/2 pounds apples
1/2 cup heavy cream, whipped

METHOD

1. Score the pork rind in a diamond pattern. Mix together the butter, garlic, mustard, salt, pepper, and lemon balm and brush on to the pork, but not the rind. Heat some of the stock, place the meat in a flameproof casserole, pour a little boiling stock over it, and cook over medium heat until the liquid has evaporated. Deglaze the pot with a little cider. Cover the casserole and continue cooking.
2. Peel the potatoes and after an hour add them to the pot with the remaining liquid. Peel the onions and add to the pot after another 20 minutes. Peel, core, and quarter the apples and add them to the meat 20 minutes later. Braise everything for 10 minutes longer, and remove the meat from the pan and slice it.
3. Surround the meat with the potatoes, onions, and apples. Purée a couple of the cooked apple quarters and use them to thicken the gravy. Enrich the gravy with the whipped cream.

MARINATED LAMB STEAKS

Marinierte Lammschnitzel

INGREDIENTS (Serves 4)

1/3 cup vegetable oil
1 garlic clove, minced
2 tablespoons soy sauce
Clarified butter
4 lamb steaks, weighing about 5
*   ounces each*
1 yellow bell pepper
2 beef tomatoes
3 shallots
1 tablespoon chopped mixed
*   fresh herbs, e.g., thyme, basil,*
*   and tarragon*
1 1/2 tablespoons white wine
Salt, pepper, and paprika to taste

METHOD

1. In a medium bowl, mix together the oil, garlic, soy sauce, and ground pepper. Put the lamb steaks in the bowl and marinate for 3 hours.
2. Remove the meat from the marinade and drain well. Heat some clarified butter in a frying pan and fry the lamb for 5 to 6 minutes on each side.
3. Wash the bell pepper, cut in half, remove seeds, and slice the flesh. Blanch the tomatoes, peel, seed, and cut into strips. Peel and quarter the shallots.
4. Remove the meat from the frying pan and keep it warm. Fry the vegetables and the chopped herbs in the meat juices, until cooked but still crisp, stirring all the time. Add the wine to the pan and reduce the liquid a little. Season with salt, pepper and paprika.
5. Serve the lamb steaks with the vegetables.

SHOULDER OF PORK IN CIDER

Schweinekeule in Apfelwein

INGREDIENTS (Serves 4)

*3¹/₂ pounds smoked pork
    shoulder roast*
1 quart meat stock
2 quarts hard cider
3 bay leaves
3 juniper berries (optional)
Peppercorns
*Bunch of vegetables and herbs,
    e.g., carrots, leeks, celery,
    fresh parsley and fresh thyme,
    chopped*
4 tablespoons unsalted butter
5 tablespoons sugar
4 apples
1 cup heavy cream
Pepper, salt, and sugar to taste

METHOD

1. Put the pork roast in a pot and cover with the meat stock and cider. If necessary, add some water to make sure the meat is covered. Add the bay leaves, juniper berries, peppercorns, and chopped vegetables and herbs to the pot. Bring quickly to a boil, cover, and simmer for 2 hours over low heat. Melt the butter in a saucepan over low heat, add the sugar to the pan, and mix them together.

2. Preheat the broiler. Remove the pork roast from the pot, reserving the stock, and brush with the sugar and butter mixture. Place the pork under the broiler and brown for about 5 minutes.

3. To make the sauce, peel, halve, core, and chop the apples. Bring 2 cups of the strained stock to a boil with a little sugar and cook the chopped apple in it until soft. Add the cream to the apple, bring everything to a boil, and then press the sauce through a sieve. Season the sauce to taste with pepper, salt, and sugar. Serve with spicy creamed cabbage and potatoes.

BONED, ROLLED LOIN OF VEAL WITH VEGETABLES

Gerollter Kalbsnierenbraten mit Gemüse (photo above)

INGREDIENTS (Serves 4)

*4¹/₂ pounds veal loin roast with
    kidney, rolled and tied*
Salt and pepper to taste
*¹/₂ pound veal bones, chopped
    small*
1 carrot, peeled and chopped
1 onion, peeled and chopped
2 tomatoes, peeled and chopped
Bunch of fresh parsley
6 sage leaves
Fresh tarragon sprig
2 cloves
¹/₄ cup clarified butter
¹/₂ cup dry white wine
2 tablespoons crème fraîche

METHOD

1. Preheat the oven to 400°F. Rub the veal generously with the salt and pepper. Place the veal bones in a roasting pan and set the roast on top. Arrange the vegetables and herbs around the roast.

2. Heat the clarified butter and pour it over the veal. Cover with parchment paper and then with a lid and roast for 1³/₄ hours. Occasionally baste with water.

3. Remove the lid and parchment paper. Roast for a further 10 minutes to brown the meat. Take the meat out of the roasting pan and keep it warm. Remove the bones from the pan and deglaze with ¹/₂ cup of hot water. Add the wine to the pan, mix thoroughly, and strain the gravy. Thicken the gravy with the crème fraîche and reduce it a little.

PORK ON A BED OF LEEKS

Schweinehals auf Lauch

INGREDIENTS (Serves 4)

1³/4 pounds boneless pork roast
Salt and pepper to taste
3 to 4 garlic cloves
4 medium leeks
2 tablespoons olive oil
1¹/2 tablespoons unsalted butter
¹/2 cup dry white wine
2 tablespoons chopped fresh
  parsley

METHOD

1. Preheat the oven to 350°F. Wash the pork, pat dry, and rub it with the salt and pepper. Peel the garlic and slice into thin slivers. Pierce the meat all over with a sharp knife and insert the slivers of garlic.

2. Cut off the leek roots and dark green tops. Cut the leeks in half lengthwise and wash thoroughly to remove any grit from between the leaves.

3. On the stovetop heat the oil and butter in a large flameproof casserole and quickly seal the meat in it on all sides. Remove the meat from the pot. Fry the leeks in the meat juices.

4. Place the meat on top of the leeks and pour the wine into the pot. Braise in the oven for 1 hour 20 minutes with the lid on.

5. Remove the meat from the casserole and leave to rest for a little while. Arrange the leeks on a warmed serving dish. If necessary, reduce the juices a little.

6. Slice the meat and arrange the slices on the bed of leeks. Sprinkle chopped parsley over the meat slices and pour the meat juices on top.

Braised Beef in Red Wine

Rinderschmorbraten in Rotwein

INGREDIENTS (Serves 4)

3 cups rich red wine, e.g., Pinot Noir or Rioja
6 peppercorns, crushed
1 bay leaf
Fresh thyme sprig
2 fresh rosemary sprigs
Piece of orange zest
2 pounds beef bottom round roast
Salt and pepper to taste
1/4 cup vegetable oil
2 tablespoons balsamic vinegar
Bunch of vegetables and herbs, e.g., carrots, leeks, celery, and fresh parsley
1 onion
2 tomatoes
1 veal bone
2 tablespoons heavy cream
1 1/2 tablespoons Armagnac

METHOD

1. In a bowl, mix together the red wine, peppercorns, bay leaf, sprigs of thyme and rosemary, and the orange zest to make a marinade. Place the meat in it, cover the bowl, and leave the meat to marinate for at least 2 days.
2. On the day you want to cook the meat, preheat the oven to 325°F. Take the meat out of the marinade, pat it dry, and tie it up with kitchen string if necessary. Rub it with salt and pepper.
3. Heat the oil in a flameproof casserole large enough to take the meat and seal the meat quickly on all sides.
4. Deglaze the pot with the vinegar and allow the juices to reduce a little. Peel or trim and chop the vegetables; peel and quarter the onion; peel and seed the tomatoes and add them all to the pan with the veal bone. Strain the marinade into the casserole. Bring the liquid to a boil, cover the pot, and place it in the oven.
5. Braise the meat for about 3 hours, occasionally turning it and basting it with the liquid.
6. Remove the meat from the pot and leave to rest for a little while. Remove the bone. Press the cooking liquid through a sieve into a small saucepan. Stir in the cream and Armagnac and cook briefly to combine all the flavors.
7. Slice the meat. Serve with tagliatelle or potato cakes and the sauce.

Corned Beef with Horseradish Sauce

Rinderbrust mit Meerrettichsauce (photo right)

INGREDIENTS (Serves 6)

1 quart beef stock
Vegetables and herbs for soup, e.g., carrots, leeks, celery, and fresh parsley
2 pounds corned beef brisket
Piece of fresh horseradish root
1 teaspoon lemon juice
2/3 cup golden raisins
4 tablespoons unsalted butter
2 tablespoons flour
1/2 cup milk
1 teaspoon sugar
2 pounds potatoes
Salt to taste

METHOD

1. Place the stock in a saucepan. Wash and chop the vegetables and herbs, add them to the pan of stock, and bring them to a boil. Add the beef to the pan, cover, and simmer for 1 1/2 to 2 hours over low heat or until cooked. If the water evaporates, fill up to same level. Remove the beef and keep it warm; strain and reserve the stock.
2. Peel the piece of horseradish, grate it, and drizzle with the lemon juice. Place the horseradish in a small saucepan with the golden raisins. Add 2 cups of the meat stock, bring to a boil, and reduce to a simmer.
3. Melt the butter in a separate saucepan until foaming, stir in the flour, and stirring the sauce all the time, gradually add the remaining stock to make a smooth sauce. Add the horseradish and raisin mixture and the milk and season with the sugar and salt to taste.
4. Peel, quarter, and steam the potatoes until cooked. Then place them in a dish and pour on as much meat stock as they will soak up.
5. Slice the meat thinly. Arrange the slices on top of the steamed potatoes. Serve with the horseradish sauce.

HANNELORE KOHL

"*For a really good juicy pot roast the piece of meat should not be too small. The minimum weight is about 2 pounds.*"

HANNELORE KOHL

"*If you don't have any fresh horseradish, use 1 to 2 tablespoons of horseradish from a jar.*"

OXTAIL STEW
Ochsenschwanzragout

INGREDIENTS (Serves 4)

3 tablespoons clarified butter
3¹/₂ pounds oxtail (ask your butcher to cut it into 2-inch pieces)
Vegetables and herbs for soup, e.g., carrot, leek, celery, and fresh parsley
1 Spanish onion, weighing about ³/₄ pound
2 cups red wine
2 teaspoons beef extract
1 tablespoon tomato paste
1 tablespoon crème fraîche
Salt and pepper to taste
Bunch of fresh thyme, chopped

METHOD

1. Heat the clarified butter in a large pot. Quickly seal the pieces of oxtail in the hot butter. Wash and chop the vegetables and herbs for soup. Peel and dice the onion. Add all the vegetables to the pot and fry with the meat. Add the red wine and beef extract to the pot and cook for about 2 hours.
2. Stir the tomato paste and crème fraîche into the stew and season it to taste with salt, pepper, and thyme. Serve the oxtail stew with *Spätzle* or noodles.

CHEESE AND ONIONS WITH VINAIGRETTE DRESSING
Mänzer Handkäs mit Musik

INGREDIENTS (Serves 4)

4 small ripe Harz cheeses or other strong-flavored hard cheese
1 large onion
2 tablespoons cider vinegar
3 tablespoons vegetable oil
Caraway seeds
Pepper to taste

METHOD

1. Thickly slice the cheese. Peel the onion, slice very thinly, and arrange on top of the cheese slices.
2. Beat together the vinegar and oil and add the caraway seeds and pepper. Pour the dressing over the cheese and allow it to infuse briefly. Serve with whole wheat bread and cider.

HANNELORE KOHL

"Cheese made from sour curd, such as Harz or Mainz cheese, is very low in calories. Handkäs mit Musik *is a tasty snack if you're trying to lose weight.*"

FRANKFURT RING CAKE

Frankfurter Kranz

INGREDIENTS (Serves 12)

FOR THE BATTER
1/2 cup unsalted butter
4 eggs, separated
1/2 cup plus 2 tablespoons sugar
Grated zest of 1 lemon
1 1/4 cups all-purpose flour
3/4 cup cornstarch
1 tablespoon baking powder

FOR THE VANILLA CREAM
1 package (1 1/2 ounces) vanilla
*   pudding mix*
2 cups milk
1/2 cup sugar

1 cup unsalted butter
3/4 cup confectioners' sugar
2 tablespoons rum
Crisp cookies, crushed
12 candied cherries

METHOD

1. Preheat the oven to 400°F.
Beat together the butter, egg
yolks, and sugar until
foaming. Mix together the
lemon zest, flour, cornstarch,
and baking powder. Add to
the egg mixture and beat
until smooth. In a separate

bowl, beat the egg whites
until stiff and then fold them
in the batter.
2. Butter a ring mold, fill the
mold with the batter, and
bake for 30 minutes. Turn the
cake onto a cake rack and
leave it to cool.
3. To make the vanilla cream,
prepare the vanilla pudding
with the milk and sugar as
directed on the package. While
cooling, stir frequently to prevent a skin from forming. In a
medium bowl, beat together

the butter and confectioners'
sugar until creamy. Beat the
pudding into the mixture a
spoonful at a time and add
the rum.
4. Cut through the cake in
3 layers, and fill with vanilla
cream. Cover the reassembled
cake with vanilla cream,
and coat evenly with cookie
crumbs. Decorate with piped
vanilla cream and candied
cherries.

CHERRY PUDDING FROM THE HESSE BERGSTRASSE

Kirschenmichel von der hessischen Bergstraße
(photo above)

INGREDIENTS (Serves 4)

1/2 cup unsalted butter, at room
*   temperature*
5 rolls
1 1/2 cups hot milk
1/2 cup plus 2 tablespoons sugar
4 eggs, separated
1/2 teaspoon ground cinnamon
Grated zest of 1 lemon
3 1/2 cups pitted sweet cherries
*   from a can or jar*
1 1/2 tablespoons kirsch
3/4 cup almonds, finely chopped
Pinch of salt

METHOD

1. Preheat the oven to 350°F. Melt 2 tablespoons of the butter in a frying pan. Thinly slice the rolls and fry the slices in the butter until golden brown. Pour the milk over the fried bread and leave it to soak in. Beat together the remaining softened butter, sugar, egg yolks, ground cinnamon, and lemon zest until fluffy. Gradually add the softened bread.
2. In a medium bowl, beat the egg whites with a pinch of salt until stiff. Gradually fold into the bread mixture with the cherries and kirsch.
3. Butter an ovenproof dish, sprinkle the chopped almonds over the bottom and sides, and fill the dish with the cherry mixture. Bake for about 1 hour or until golden brown.

RÜDESHEIM APPLE DESSERT

Rüdesheimer Apfelauflauf (photo right)

INGREDIENTS (Serves 4)

1 quart milk
Pinch of salt
1/2 cup sugar
1 1/2 tablespoons vanilla-flavored
*   sugar*
2/3 cup semolina flour
2 pounds apples
1 cup white wine
Juice of 1 lemon
1/3 cup golden raisins
4 eggs, separated
1/4 cup cream
1/2 teaspoon ground cinnamon
*   mixed with 1/4 cup sugar*

METHOD

1. Bring the milk to a boil with the salt, 1/4 cup sugar, and the vanilla sugar. Stir in the semolina flour and leave to thicken on low heat. When all the liquid has been absorbed, remove from the heat and leave to cool. When cool, put it in the refrigerator.
2. Preheat the oven to 350°F. Peel, quarter, core, and slice the apples. Mix the sliced apples with the wine, lemon juice, 1/4 cup sugar, and golden raisins.
3. Butter an ovenproof dish. Beat the egg whites until stiff and fold them into the cold semolina with the cream, egg yolks, and liquid from the apples. Turn into the buttered dish. Arrange the apples on top and bake it for about 40 minutes or until golden brown. Take the flan out of the oven and sprinkle it with the cinnamon sugar.

RHEINGAU WINE APPLES

Rheingauer Weinäpfel

INGREDIENTS (Serves 4)

3 eggs, separated
1 heaped tablespoon cornstarch
1/2 cup sugar
2 cups milk
1/2 vanilla bean
4 large apples
2 tablespoons golden raisins
1/2 cup chopped walnuts or
*   hazelnuts*
1/2 teaspoon brown sugar
2 teaspoons unsalted butter
2 cups Rheingau Riesling

METHOD

1. Mix together the egg yolks, cornstarch, sugar, and 4 tablespoons of milk to form a smooth paste. Heat the remaining milk in a saucepan with the seeds from the vanilla bean. Add the egg mixture to the hot milk and, stirring constantly, bring it to a boil. Leave the custard to cool. When cool, put it in the refrigerator.
2. Preheat the oven to 350°F. Peel the apples and core them using an apple corer. Place the apples in an ovenproof dish. Mix together the golden raisins, chopped nuts, brown sugar, and butter and use to stuff the apples. Pour the wine over the apples. Bake the apples in the oven until the fruit is soft. Serve the baked apples with the strained vanilla custard sauce.

169

HESSE POTATO CAKE

Hessische Kartoffeltorte

INGREDIENTS (Serves 8)

1 pound potatoes
9 eggs, separated
1 1/4 cups sugar
7/8 cup lemon juice
Grated zest of 1 1/2 lemons
1/3 cup chopped almonds
*1 heaped tablespoon semolina
  flour*
*1 to 2 tablespoons breadcrumbs
  or ground almonds*
Sifted confectioners' sugar

METHOD

1. Preheat the oven to 350°F. Peel the potatoes and boil them in unsalted water until half cooked. Allow to cool and then grate them finely.

2. Beat the egg whites with half of the sugar until stiff. In a separate bowl beat the egg yolks with the remaining sugar until fluffy. Stir the lemon juice, lemon zest, almonds, and semolina flour into the egg yolk mixture and, finally, lightly fold in the egg whites and grated potatoes.

3. Butter a 9-inch springform pan and coat the bottom and sides with the breadcrumbs or ground almonds. Pour the batter into the pan, level off the surface, and bake in the oven on the bottom shelf for about 1 1/2 hours.

4. Unmold the cake onto a cake rack and leave it to cool. Cut a template out of parchment paper, or use a doily, and lay it on top of the cake. Dust the cake with confectioners' sugar and carefully remove the template or doily to leave a pattern.

SAUSAGES—EVERYONE'S FAVORITE

HANNELORE KOHL:
As I was doing some research, I discovered that the German word for sausage, *Wurst,* is one of the oldest words in the German language. It stems from the Indo-Germanic word *Uers* and Old High German *werram,* and means "To turn, to muddle, or mix up."

ALFONS SCHUHBECK:
I didn't know that. But I do know that Germany is a sausage-lover's paradise. We make over 1,500 varieties, and no other country can compare with us. Many of these sausages are closely associated with regional traditions. Take Frankfurt *Würstchen,* for example . . .

HANNELORE KOHL:
. . . or *Nürnberg Rostbratwurst* (grilled sausage), *Rügenwald Mettwurst* (ham sausage), *Thuringian Leberwurst* (liver sausage), *Munich Weißwurst* (white sausage). Speaking of *Weißwurst,* I have to admit that sometimes they burst when I cook them. Do you know a trick to prevent this?

ALFONS SCHUHBECK:
The water shouldn't boil, but of course that's easy to say. All you need is for the telephone to ring at just the wrong moment, or the postman to come to the door! The best way to do it is to bring the water to a boil in a saucepan, remove the pan from the heat, put the sausages in the water, and leave them to cook for ten to fifteen minutes.

Westphalian Mettwurst *(ham sausage) can also be enjoyed in smaller quantities. Every German region has its own specialty sausages.*

HANNELORE KOHL:
And what advice can you give me about frying sausages?

ALFONS SCHUHBECK:
Before you fry sausages, soak them in hot water for a couple of minutes, so they swell and then prick them with a fork. Fry them on a medium heat. This way the sausage shouldn't burst or spurt hot fat as soon as you stick a fork into it.

HANNELORE KOHL:
Statisticians have discovered that in Germany each person eats about 60 pounds of sausage each year and that 88 percent of all German households serve cold cooked meats and sausage for supper.

ALFONS SCHUHBECK:
This is because Germany produces sausages to suit every taste, even for the calorie-conscious. We also consider boiled ham, corned beef, and

head cheese to be part of the sausage family, as well as meatloaf.

Also our quality regulations are particularly strict with regard to sausages. We accord great importance to the ingredients. The main ingredient is always top-quality meat, which means very little fat, tissue, or tendons. Sausage manufacturers regularly undergo tough inspections in order to comply with these quality and purity regulations.

FROM THE FRANCONIAN MOUNTAINS TO THE ALPS

By HELMUT KOHL

I feel linked to the Franconians, quite simply because my father came from Lower Franconia. I'm not sure whether I can also call myself a Bavarian, because in 1930 my birthplace in the Palatinate was still part of Bavaria.

Franconia offers incredible variety in the smallest of spaces; folk costumes, traditions, dialect, and cuisine frequently differ between one place and the next.

The many small towns shelter hidden treasures, alongside well-known sights such as Bamberg Cathedral or the old Imperial city of Nürnberg. It was home to the artist Albrecht Dürer and the sculptor Veit Stoß, who worked for twenty years in Cracow—the former capital city of Poland—and decorated its churches.

▶

A Franconian author once wrote, "The four winds meet in Franconia." He was justified as this has always been a cosmopolitan region.

Like the cuisine of Upper Bavaria, Franconian fare is regarded as substantial and hearty. One has only to think of Nürnberg *Bratwürste,* or *Blaue Zipfel* as they are called when poached in water and vinegar, of cabbage roulade, roast pork with crisp crackling and just about every kind of dumpling. And yet, there is more—German cuisine can offer nothing more delicious than a plate of asparagus from the so-called garlic country around Nürnberg or a trout from a clear stream in the Franconian mountains. Moreover, a genuine Franconian wine, from a *Bocksbeutel,* a wide, rounded bottle peculiar to the region, is proof that the finer things in life are indeed served south of the River Main.

I learned all about Franconia's hearty fare as a 15-year-old boy during agricultural training in Lower Franconia, where I was responsible among other things for the dairy herd on a farm. I kept the "herd book" in which all the newborn animals were recorded and helped to deliver a calf more than once. It was hard work, but I was happy. I enjoyed working in the barns and fields, looking after the animals, and, above all, there was plenty to eat. For a growing lad who was always hungry that was certainly not a foregone conclusion in 1945!

Leaving Franconia and moving to Munich and Upper Bavaria, the food that springs first to mind is *Weißwurst* or "veal sausages." Traditionally, these should be eaten before the church clock chimes midday. This edict is not taken too seriously, of course, although care is still taken to use only the best veal and a very specific mixture of herbs and spices.

This southern part of Germany is rightly considered a vacationer's paradise. Hike up a Bavarian mountain, and you will never forget the supper that follows: cured ham and a smoked sausage called *Räucherwurst,* hearty country bread, and cheese spread, known as *Obatzda* here. We should also remember that the Free State of Bavaria is one of the most important places for state-of-the-art technological development in the whole of the Federal Republic.

Nevertheless, that almost exclusively southern idyll, the *Biergärten* (beer garden), where families gather en masse in fine weather, is part of the Bavarian way of life. Many customers bring picnic baskets stuffed to over-flowing which always amazes newcomers to Bavaria. Can you really take your supper with you to the beer gardens and only buy the beer?! By the way, the Bavarians did not discover beer. It is depicted on murals in Ancient Egyptian tombs, but we do have to thank them for the German Beer Purity Law of 1516, according to which beer can only be made from malted barley, hops, and water. This uncompromising attitude to perfection has without doubt contributed to German beers' renown throughout the world, and is why we fought so hard during the European Community debates on foodstuffs to bring about the equivalent of *Appellation contrôlée,* or protected designation, for German beer.

A Munich tourist attraction—the food market.

LIVER DUMPLING SOUP
Leberknödelsuppe

INGREDIENTS (Serves 4)

1/2 cup milk
4 rolls
1 small onion
Bunch of fresh parsley
1 tablespoon unsalted butter
1/2 pound calves' liver, puréed
Salt, pepper, and dried
*   marjoram to taste*
2 eggs, beaten
1 quart meat stock

METHOD

1. Heat the milk in a saucepan. Thinly slice the rolls and place in a bowl. Pour the hot milk over the bread and leave to soak for 30 minutes.

2. Peel and mince the onion. Wash and chop the parsley. Melt the butter in a frying pan and fry the onion and half of the chopped parsley in the butter until the onion is soft. Squeeze out the bread. Add the fried onion, parsley, and softened bread to the puréed liver. Season with salt, pepper, and dried marjoram. Add the eggs to the mixture and knead until well combined.

3. Dampen your hands, break off portions of the liver mixture and shape them into dumplings. Heat the meat stock in a saucepan, add the dumplings to the stock, and cook them for 20 to 25 minutes or until cooked. Sprinkle the remaining chopped parsley over the soup before serving.

ALLGÄU CHEESE SOUP

Allgäuer Kässüpple (photo above)

INGREDIENTS (Serves 4)

4 tablespoons unsalted butter

6 tablespoons flour

1 quart meat stock

*1/2 pound Allgäu Emmenthal
    cheese, grated (2 cups)*

1 egg yolk

2 tablespoons cream

Pepper to taste

1 onion

2 teaspoons clarified butter

Croutons for serving

METHOD

1. Melt the butter in a frying
pan and cook the flour in it to
form a roux. Add the stock a
little at a time, stirring until
smooth. Bring to a boil and
simmer for 15 minutes.

2. Off the heat, gradually add
the cheese. Bring it briefly to
a boil again and remove from
the heat.

3. Beat together the egg yolk
and cream, thicken the soup
with it, and season the soup
with pepper.

4. Peel and slice the onion.
Heat the clarified butter in
a frying pan and fry the onion
in the butter until golden
brown. Garnish the soup with
croutons and fried onion.

NOTE

Allgäu Emmenthal is a
Bavarian version of Swiss
Emmenthal cheese; the
latter can be substituted,
if necessary.

CHICKEN DUMPLING SOUP

Hennenknödelsuppe

INGREDIENTS (Serves 4)

4 stale rolls

1 cup hot milk

1 tablespoon minced onion

2 eggs

*1/2 pound boneless chicken
    breast, minced*

*Salt, pepper, and grated nutmeg
    to taste*

Bunch of fresh parsley, chopped

2 quarts chicken stock

METHOD

1. Dice the rolls, place them
in a bowl, pour the hot milk
over the bread, and leave to
soak for 15 minutes.

2. Mix together the onion,
eggs, and minced chicken
breast. Squeeze out the bread,
add to the chicken mixture,
and knead until well com-
bined. Season the mixture
with salt, pepper, and nutmeg
and add the chopped parsley
to it.

3. Bring the chicken stock to
a boil. Shape the chicken
mixture into little dumplings
and cook them in the gently
simmering stock.

POTATO PANCAKE WITH SAUERKRAUT FILLING

Kartoffelfleck mit Sauerkrautfülle

INGREDIENTS (Serves 4)

FOR THE POTATO DOUGH

2 pounds potatoes

2 teaspoons salt

2 to 3 eggs, beaten

Grated nutmeg

1³/₄ cups all-purpose flour

1¹/₄ cups clarified butter

FOR THE FILLING

¹/₄ cup pork drippings

1¹/₂ pounds (about 3 cups) fresh
*   sauerkraut (from a jar)*

2 medium onions

¹/₂ pound slab bacon

1 garlic clove, minced

2 teaspoons caraway seeds

2 teaspoons juniper berries

3 bay leaves

1 teaspoon pepper

3 teaspoons salt

1 cup white wine or beef stock

METHOD

1. Boil the potatoes, peel them, and push them through a potato ricer. Leave them to cool. Mix the salt and nutmeg with the eggs, add the flour to the egg mixture, and then add the potatoes and knead quickly to form a dough.

2. Heat the clarified butter in a frying pan. Roll out the potato dough on a floured surface to ¹/₄-inch thickness and cut out squares 4¹/₂ by 4¹/₂ inches. Fry the potato squares in the hot butter on both sides until golden brown. Remove them from the pan and leave to drain on paper towels and keep warm.

3. Melt the pork drippings in a lidded casserole. Briefly rinse the sauerkraut. Peel and dice the onions. Dice the bacon and put it in the casserole with the onions. Fry them both until the onions are translucent. Add the sauerkraut to the pot, followed by the garlic, caraway, juniper berries, bay leaves, pepper, and salt. Mix them all together and then add the wine or stock. Cover the pot and braise the sauerkraut for 20 to 45 minutes, depending on how well cooked you like your sauerkraut. If you want to thicken the sauerkraut, peel and grate a raw potato and add it to the pot shortly before the end of cooking time. Check and adjust the seasoning.

4. Divide the sauerkraut among the potato pancakes, roll them up and serve them immediately.

POT ROAST PORK WITH PORCINI

Steinpilz-Schweinebraten

INGREDIENTS (Serves 4)

1/2 ounce dried porcini (cèpes)
1/2 cup warm water
3 tablespoons clarified butter
2 pounds pork shoulder butt roast
Salt and pepper to taste
1 cup dry white wine
1/2 cup crème fraîche

METHOD

1. Preheat the oven to 350°F. Wash the porcini well and soak them in the warm water. Heat the clarified butter in a flameproof casserole. Season the pork with salt and pepper and seal it on all sides in the hot butter. Remove the meat from the pot and keep it warm.

2. Deglaze the meat residue with the wine and add the porcini and the strained soaking liquid to the pot. Return the meat to the casserole. Cover and braise in the oven for about 1 1/4 hours. Add a little wine or water to the pot as necessary. Season the pot roast and gravy to taste and enrich the gravy with the crème fraîche.

BEEF TERRINE

Tafelspitzsülze (photo left)

INGREDIENTS (Serves 6)

2 onions
1 small piece of parsley root or parsnip
1 carrot
1 small cucumber, weighing about 3 to 4 ounces
1 fennel bulb
1 celery stalk
2 tomatoes
1 garlic clove
2 pounds boneless beef round rump roast
2 tablespoons chopped fresh chervil
1 teaspoon dried lovage
1 teaspoon dried marjoram
2 bay leaves
1 tablespoon white peppercorns
2 tablespoons salt
Salt, pepper, sugar, and vinegar to taste
12 leaves of gelatin or 3 packages powdered unflavored gelatin
3 cups diced carrots
2 1/2 cups diced zucchini
Leaves from a bunch of fresh chervil
1 red onion, diced

METHOD

1. A day in advance, peel and dice the onions, parsley root or parsnip, carrot, and cucumber; trim and dice the fennel and celery. Quarter and slice the tomatoes; peel and slice the garlic. Place the prepared vegetables, meat, chervil, lovage, marjoram, bay leaves, and peppercorns in a bowl. Cover them with 1 1/2 quarts of water, cover the bowl, put it in the refrigerator, and leave to marinate for about 24 hours.

2. Take the meat out of the marinade, transfer the marinade to a large saucepan, add 1 quart of water to the marinade and bring it to a boil. Add the salt to the marinade. Put the beef in the boiling marinade and simmer for about 3 hours over low heat. Skim the surface occasionally.

3. Remove the meat from the pan, strain the marinade, return it to the saucepan, and reduce it to 1 quart. Season generously with salt, pepper, sugar, and vinegar. Soften the gelatin in a little warm water, then dissolve it leaf by leaf in the hot liquid.

4. Slice the meat and blanch the diced carrots and zucchini. Layer the slices of meat, diced vegetables, and chervil leaves in a loaf pan or mold, with enough marinade to cover each layer. Leave it to set a little before adding the next layer. Garnish the terrine with the diced red onion and remaining chervil leaves and fill the mold with the remaining marinade. Refrigerate the terrine for several hours before serving.

NOTE

Parsley root, also called Hamburg parsley, is the variety *Petroselinum crispum* 'Tuberosum.'

HANNELORE KOHL

"Try this pork pot roast in the fall with fresh cèpes. It also tastes really wonderful with a mixture of wild mushrooms."

HANNELORE KOHL

"The terrine looks very appetizing if layered in individual molds and turned out just before serving."

GLAZED HAM

Braten mit Kruste

INGREDIENTS (Serves 4)

2 pounds partially cooked ham
Cloves
3 tablespoons rum
3 tablespoons brown sugar
1/2 teaspoon ground ginger
1/4 teaspoon white pepper
1/2 teaspoon salt
3 tablespoons clarified butter
Bunch of vegetables and herbs
  for soup, e.g., carrots, leeks,
  celery, and fresh parsley
1 pound onions
Salt and pepper to taste

METHOD

1. Preheat the oven to 400°F. Score the fat on the ham in a diamond pattern. Spike with a clove in each diamond. Heat the rum in a saucepan until lukewarm, dissolve the brown sugar in it, and stir in the ginger, pepper, and salt. Rub the sides of the ham with the rum mixture.

2. Heat the butter in a roasting pan. Place the meat in the pan, fat-side up. Wash, peel, and chop the soup vegetables and herbs. Add these to the pan with the peeled and coarsely chopped onions. Bake the ham on the lowest shelf for about 1¼ hours. After 20 minutes, brush the ham several times with the remaining rum mixture until it has all been used up.

3. Remove the meat from the pan. Deglaze the roasting pan with a little hot water. Press the braised vegetables and onions through a sieve and add the purée to the gravy. Season the gravy to taste and reheat it. Slice the meat and pour the gravy over it. Serve with the gravy, Brussels sprouts, and boiled potatoes.

PORK IN BEER

Bierfleisch (photo above)

INGREDIENTS (Serves 4)

1¼ pounds boneless pork
  (sirloin)
Salt and pepper to taste
1/2 teaspoon dried marjoram
1/2 teaspoon dried thyme
1/2 teaspoon dried rosemary
2 onions
2 tablespoons pork drippings
1 tablespoon caraway seeds
2 cups lager-style beer
2 slices of black bread

METHOD

1. Cut the pork into 1-inch cubes. Season it with salt and pepper and toss with the marjoram, thyme, and rosemary. Leave it for 30 minutes.

2. Peel and quarter the onions. Melt the pork drippings in a flameproof lidded casserole dish and fry the onions in the drippings until brown. Add the cubes of pork and fry briefly until sealed. Add the caraway and 1 cup of the beer to the dish, cover, and cook over medium heat for 30 minutes.

3. Shortly before the pork is cooked, crumble the black bread and add it to the pot. Flavor the casserole with the remaining beer. Serve the pork with caraway potatoes.

BAVARIAN SAUERKRAUT DUMPLINGS

Bayerische Sauerkrautklöße

INGREDIENTS (Serves 4)

1 package potato dumpling mix
²/₃ cup sauerkraut
1 tablespoon pork drippings
1 cup diced bacon
1 onion, minced
1 garlic clove, crushed
¹/₂ cup dry white wine
1 teaspoon hot mustard
1 juniper berry (optional)
1 allspice berry
2 cloves
Salt and pepper to taste

METHOD

1. Prepare the dumpling mixture according to the package directions. Rinse the sauerkraut, drain, and mince it.
2. Melt the pork drippings in a frying pan. Fry the bacon in the pork drippings. Add the onion and garlic to the pan. Add the sauerkraut and fry it briefly. Deglaze with the white wine. Add the mustard, juniper berry, allspice berry, cloves, salt, and pepper to the cabbage and cook it for about 25 minutes. Remove the juniper and allspice berries and the cloves.
3. Dampen your hands and make 8 dumplings from the potato mixture. Put a spoonful of the sauerkraut mixture in the center of each dumpling.
4. Bring a pan of salted water to a boil, add the dumplings, and simmer them gently for 20 minutes.

BRAISED BRISKET OF BEEF

Geschmorte Rinderbrust

INGREDIENTS (Serves 4)

3 tablespoons clarified butter
3¹/₂ pounds beef brisket
1 cup sliced carrots
2¹/₂ cups diced bulb fennel
*1 piece of parsley root or
    parsnip, sliced*
3 cups beer
Bunch of fresh parsley
*Salt, pepper, and grated nutmeg
    to taste*

METHOD

1. Heat the clarified butter in a flameproof casserole. Fry the beef on all sides to seal it over high heat. Add the carrots, fennel, and parsley root or parsnip to the pot and fry them. Deglaze the pot with the beer, cover it, and simmer the meat for 1¹/₂ hours on low heat until tender.
2. Remove the meat from the pot and keep it warm. Press the braised vegetables and gravy through a sieve to purée. Season the gravy with salt, pepper, and nutmeg and reheat it. Chop the parsley and add it to the gravy.

NOTE

Parsley root, also called Hamburg parsley, is the variety *Petroselinum crispum* 'Tuberosum.'

VEAL ROULADEN

Kalbsvögerl (photo below)

INGREDIENTS (Serves 4)

3/4 ounce dried morel mushrooms
2 cups milk
1 1/2 to 2 ounces veal bone
  marrow, finely chopped
2 small onions, diced
1 garlic clove, minced
3 tablespoons sour cream
1/2 teaspoon fresh or dried thyme
Grated zest and juice of 1/2 lemon
Salt and pepper to taste
4 large veal cutlets
1/4 cup clarified butter
1/2 cup beef stock
Pinch of gravy thickener or
  cornstarch
1/2 cup heavy cream

METHOD

1. Wash the dried morels and soak them for 30 minutes in 2 cups each of water and milk. Then drain them and slice finely. Melt the chopped marrow in a frying pan, add the onions and garlic and fry them for 4 minutes. Then add the morels and fry for 5 minutes longer, stirring all the time. Stir in the sour cream and season with the thyme and lemon zest. Reduce the sauce for about 15 minutes. Season it with salt and pepper, then leave it to cool, and refrigerate it.

2. Flatten the veal cutlets with a rolling pin or meat pounder. Spread the cold mushroom mixture over the cutlets, roll them up to make rouladen, and tie them up with kitchen string. Heat the clarified butter in a heavy, flameproof casserole dish and quickly seal the rouladen all over in it. Deglaze the casserole with the meat stock and braise the rouladen for 15 minutes.

3. Remove the veal rouladen from the pot and keep them warm. Add the gravy thickener and cream to the juices, bring it to a boil, and season it with salt, lemon juice, and pepper. Serve the veal rouladen with mashed potato or rice and green beans.

STUFFED BREAST OF VEAL

Gefüllte Kalbsbrust

INGREDIENTS (Serves 6–8)

4 1/2 pounds veal breast
2 teaspoons salt
1 teaspoon white pepper
2 teaspoons paprika

FOR THE STUFFING
5 rolls, crusts grated off
2 1/3 coarsely ground almonds
2/3 cup coarsely chopped
  pistachios
6 tablespoons minced fresh
  parsley
Grated zest of 2 lemons
2 pinches of grated nutmeg
1 teaspoon salt
2 pinches of pepper
6 eggs, separated
5 ounces calves' liver, diced

TO BRAISE
1/2 pound slab bacon, diced
1/2 cup unsalted butter
1 cup dry white wine or water

METHOD

1. Ask your butcher to prepare the breast of veal for stuffing. Preheat the oven to 350ºF. Season the veal inside and out with salt and pepper.

2. Soften the rolls in cold water, squeeze them out, and beat them until smooth. Add the almonds, pistachios, and parsley to the bread and season it with the lemon zest, nutmeg, salt, and pepper. Stir in the egg yolks and diced liver. In a separate bowl, beat the egg whites until stiff and fold them into the bread mixture.

3. Place the stuffing in the prepared cavity in the veal, but don't fill it too full, because the stuffing needs room to expand. Sew up the cavity with kitchen string and rub the breast of veal with paprika.

4. Fry the bacon in a roasting pan to render the fat. Fry the veal in the bacon fat on all sides until sealed. Add small pieces of butter to the pan and then cook the veal in the oven for about 2 hours, basting frequently with the pan juices and the wine or water.

5. Remove the stuffed veal from the oven, remove the kitchen string, and slice the meat. Pour the meat juices over the sliced meat. Serve with noodles and a green leaf salad.

BOILED BEEF WITH HORSERADISH SAUCE

Tafelspitz mit Meerrettichsauce

INGREDIENTS (Serves 4)

2 quarts water
1 teaspoon salt
1³/₄ pounds beef brisket
3 carrots
1 leek
1¹/₄ cups diced celery
1 piece parsley root or parsnip
1 onion

FOR THE HORSERADISH SAUCE
2 tablespoons unsalted butter
3 tablespoons flour
1 cup hot meat stock
3 tablespoons heavy cream
¹/₂ small horseradish root, grated
¹/₂ apple, grated
Salt to taste

METHOD

1. Bring the water to a boil in a large saucepan with the salt. Place the meat in the water and simmer it for 2 hours on low heat. Dice the carrots, leek, parsley root, and onion. Add to the pan with the celery about 30 minutes before the end of cooking time.
2. Melt the butter in a saucepan, add the flour, stir it to make a roux, and then add the stock, stirring all the time. Season the sauce with salt, add the cream, and allow the sauce to reduce a little. Finally, add the grated horseradish and apple. Slice the meat and arrange on a platter, surrounded by the boiled vegetables. Pour a little cooking liquid over the sliced meat. Serve with the horseradish sauce and parsley potatoes.

NOTE

Parsley root, also called Hamburg parsley, is the variety *Petroselinum crispum* 'Tuberosum.'

LARDED POT ROAST BEEF

Gespickter Rinderbraten

INGREDIENTS (Serves 4)

¹/₄ pound slab bacon, cut in thin strips
2 pounds beef bottom round pot roast
Salt and pepper to taste
Pinch each of ground cloves and herbes de Provence
1 tablespoon cream
¹/₄ cup clarified butter
2 cups stock
2 cups sliced leeks
2 cups diced celeriac (celery root)
1 large onion
¹/₄ pound button mushrooms, washed
3 tablespoons sour cream
1 teaspoon cornstarch

METHOD

1. Preheat the oven to 400°F. Thread the strips of bacon through the meat at evenly spaced intervals with a larding needle. Season the meat with salt and pepper. Mix the ground cloves and *herbes de Provence* with the cream and rub the mixture all over the meat.
2. Heat the clarified butter in a flameproof casserole and fry the beef in it to seal it.
3. Put the lid on the casserole and roast the beef in the oven for about 2 hours, basting it occasionally with the meat juices.
4. Meanwhile, trim and wash the vegetables. Slice the leek, peel and dice the celeriac and onion. After 1¹/₄ hours of cooking, arrange the vegetables around the beef, replace the lid, and continue cooking it. Fifteen minutes before the end of cooking, add the mushrooms.
5. Remove the meat and vegetables from the pot and keep them warm. Strain the gravy, return it to the pot, and allow it to reduce a little. Mix together the sour cream and cornstarch and use to thicken the gravy.

HANNELORE KOHL

"Freshly grated horseradish is extremely hot, so add it to the sauce a little at a time and then taste the sauce before adding more."

FRESH PORK HOCKS WITH CELERIAC SALAD

Schweinshaxen mit Selleriesalat

INGREDIENTS (Serves 4)

1 quart meat stock
2 large fresh pork hocks
Salt and pepper to taste
Bunch of vegetables and herbs
*   for soup, e.g., leeks, celery,*
*   fresh parsley, and thyme*
1 onion
1 head of celeriac (celery root)
4 carrots
2 tablespoons vegetable oil
2 tablespoons vinegar

METHOD

1. Bring the meat stock to a boil and parboil the pork hocks in it for 15 minutes. Then remove the hocks from the stock, score the rind, and rub the meat with salt and pepper.

2. Preheat the oven to 425°F. Wash, peel, and chop the soup vegetables and herbs and put them in a roasting pan with the meat. Roast the meat for about 45 minutes, until golden brown. Baste the meat occasionally with the stock.

3. Peel the onion, celeriac, and carrots, quarter the onion and celeriac, and cook in the remaining meat stock with the carrots until tender.

4. Remove the vegetables from the stock with a slotted spoon and slice them. Mix together the oil, vinegar, a little stock, salt, and pepper and marinate the vegetables in this dressing.

5. Cut the pork hocks in half, pour the meat juices over them, and serve with the vegetable salad. The meat and vegetables can be accompanied by bread dumplings.

POACHED SHOULDER OF VEAL

Gekochte Kalbshaxe (photo above)

INGREDIENTS (Serves 4)

1¹/₂ quarts meat stock
About 3 pounds boneless veal
*   shoulder roast, bones reserved*
1 fennel bulb, sliced
¹/₄ head savoy cabbage
1 pound small potatoes, peeled
¹/₂ pound carrots, cut in
*   matchsticks*
1 leek, sliced
1 head kohlrabi, peeled and
*   sliced, cut in batons*
3 tablespoons chopped fresh
*   chervil*
Pinch of ground coriander
Salt and pepper to taste

METHOD

1. Bring the meat stock to a
boil in a large casserole. Place
the veal bones in the stock
and simmer over very low
heat for 2 hours. Strain the
stock and season with pepper,
coriander, and a little salt,
if necessary.
2. Pour the stock back into the
pan, add the veal roast, and
simmer for 1 hour. Add the
vegetables to the veal. Cook
gently for 30 minutes longer.
3. When the veal is tender,
remove it from the stock and
slice it. Remove the vegetables
from the stock with a slotted
spoon and arrange them on a
platter with the veal.

STUFFED BREAST OF LAMB

Gefüllte Lammbrust

INGREDIENTS (Serves 4)

2 pounds boneless breast
*   of lamb*
Salt and pepper to taste
¹/₂ pound pork liver
Bunch of fresh parsley
1 onion
1 egg
3 tablespoons breadcrumbs
2 tablespoons clarified butter
2 cups meat stock
¹/₂ cup heavy cream

METHOD

1. Preheat the oven to 425ºF.
Season the inside of the
breast of lamb with salt and
pepper. Dice the liver. Wash,
dry, and chop the parsley.
Peel and mince the onion.
Mix the liver, parsley, and
onion with the egg and
breadcrumbs and spread it
over the lamb. Roll up the
lamb and tie it up with
kitchen string.

2. On the stovetop heat the
clarified butter in a roasting
pan and seal the breast of
lamb all over. Deglaze the
pan with a little meat stock.
Roast the meat for about
1¹/₂ hours in the oven. Remove
the meat from the pan and
keep it warm.
3. Add the remaining meat
stock and stir to mix with the
meat residue. Strain the gravy
and enrich it with the cream.
Allow it to reduce a little and
season the gravy to taste with
salt and pepper. Serve with
broccoli garnished with diced
tomato, and potatoes.

LEBERKÄSE IN BEER BATTER
Leberkäse in Bierteig (photo below)

INGREDIENTS (Serves 4)

1 cup all-purpose flour
1 egg
1/2 cup beer
Pinch of salt
Bunch of fresh chives
1 small onion, diced
1/4 cup clarified butter
4 slices Leberkäse (smooth pork
   sausage), each weighing about
   4 ounces
1 red bell pepper
2 beef tomatoes
1 cup watercress

METHOD

1. Beat together the flour, egg, beer, and salt, to form a thick batter. Mince the chives and stir into the batter with the diced onion. Leave the batter to rest for 10 minutes.
2. Heat the butter in a large frying pan. Dip the slices of *Leberkäse* in the batter and fry them in the hot butter for about 4 minutes on each side.
3. Halve, core, seed, and slice the bell pepper. Cut the tomatoes into wedges. Cut the cress and arrange a bed of it on each of 4 plates. Arrange the *Leberkäse* on top. Garnish with the bell pepper and tomatoes.

NÜRNBERG BLADE ROAST
Nürnberger Schäufele

INGREDIENTS (Serves 4)

2 to 3 1/2 pounds pork shoulder
   blade roast
Salt and pepper to taste
1 teaspoon dried marjoram
2 tablespoons clarified butter
2 onions
2 carrots
1/2 leek
2 cups meat stock

METHOD

1. Preheat the oven to 400°F. Rub the meat with the salt, pepper, and marjoram. On the stovetop heat the clarified butter in a roasting pan and seal the meat all over in it. Then place the meat in the oven and roast for 5 minutes.
2. Meanwhile, peel the onions and carrots and wash the leek. Cut each onion into eight pieces, cut the carrots into matchsticks, and slice the leek into 3/4-inch chunks.
3. Remove the meat from the roasting pan and sweat the vegetables in the meat fat. Replace the meat on top of the vegetables and pour the meat stock into the pan.
4. Return the meat to the oven and roast for about 2 hours until cooked, basting with the meat juices occasionally. Serve with potato dumplings and a green salad.

AUGSBURG SPINACH ROULADEN

Augsburger Spinatröllchen

INGREDIENTS (Serves 4)

16 large spinach leaves
1 roll, softened in milk
1 pound ground beef
1 egg, beaten
1/2 onion, minced
2 fresh parsley sprigs, minced
Salt, pepper, and grated nutmeg
    to taste
6 tablespoons unsalted butter
1 cup meat stock

METHOD

1. Blanch the spinach leaves in boiling water, remove them from the pan, and refresh them in cold water. Then spread them out on a chopping board or work surface and pat them dry.
2. Squeeze out the roll. Mix together the roll, ground beef, egg, onion, and parsley. Season the meat mixture with salt, pepper, and nutmeg.
3. Place two spinach leaves on top of each other, spread about one-eighth of the meat mixture evenly over the spinach, and roll up the leaves. Repeat with the remaining leaves. Melt the butter in a wide shallow pan. Fry the spinach rouladen briefly in the butter, add the meat stock, cover and braise the spinach rouladen for about 20 minutes without turning them.

PICHELSTEINER STEW

Pichelsteiner Eintopf

INGREDIENTS (Serves 4)

2 ounces beef bone marrow
5 ounces each boneless beef,
    pork, lamb, and veal, for stew
2 onions
4 carrots
1/2 fennel bulb
1 1/4 pounds potatoes
1 leek
3 to 4 cups chopped white
    cabbage
3/4 pound green beans
Bunch of fresh parsley
Salt and pepper to taste
1 1/3 cups frozen peas
2 cups meat stock

METHOD

1. Slice the marrow and chop the other meats in 1-inch cubes. Peel the onions, carrots, fennel, and potatoes; wash the leek, trim the string beans. Chop the prepared vegetables and chop the parsley.
2. Line a casserole with the marrow slices. Layer the cubes of meat, all the vegetables except the peas, and the parsley alternately in the pot, seasoning each layer with salt and pepper. Add the stock to the casserole and cook over low heat for about 2 hours. Twenty minutes before the end of cooking, add the peas to the stew.

TURKEY THIGHS

Truthahn-Oberkeule

INGREDIENTS (Serves 4)

1³/₄ pounds turkey thigh portions
Salt, pepper, curry powder, and
*   paprika to taste*
1 cup hot milk or cream
4 stale rolls
1 tablespoon minced onion
1 tablespoon minced ham
¹/₂ teaspoon dried marjoram
1 tablespoon chopped fresh
*   parsley*
1 egg, beaten
2 teaspoons clarified butter
¹/₂ pound fresh cèpes or porcini
1 small onion
1¹/₂ tablespoons unsalted butter
2 tablespoons sour cream
1 tablespoon chopped mixed
*   fresh herbs*

METHOD

1. Ask your butcher to bone
the thighs and cut a pocket in
them. Season the meat with
salt, pepper, curry powder
and paprika.
2. Pour the milk or cream
over the rolls and leave them
to soak for 15 minutes. Add
the onion, ham, marjoram,
parsley, and egg to the bread
and work it to form a smooth
paste.
3. Stuff the prepared turkey
thighs with the mixture; sew
up with kitchen string.
4. Preheat the oven to 350°F.
On the stovetop heat the
clarified butter in a roasting
pan. Fry the turkey thighs all
over in the butter to seal
them, then add a little water
to the pan, and transfer it to
the oven. Roast for 40 minutes, basting occasionally
with the meat juices.
5. Remove the turkey thighs
from the pan and keep them
warm. Wash and slice the
mushrooms. Peel and dice
the onion and fry it with the
mushrooms in melted butter.
Season the onion and mushrooms with salt and stir in the
sour cream and herbs. Slice
the turkey thighs and serve
with the cream sauce. Accompany with steamed baby
carrots and broccoli.

POACHED SAUSAGES

Blaue Zipfel

INGREDIENTS (Serves 4)

1 cup vinegar
3 large onions, peeled and sliced
1¹/₄ cups Franconian wine
2 whole cloves
2 bay leaves
10 peppercorns
10 juniper berries
8 mustard seeds
Pinch of salt
Pinch of sugar
1 cup diced carrots and fennel
18 small Nürnberg Bratwürstchen

METHOD

1. Bring the vinegar and
2 quarts of water to a boil in
a wide saucepan. Add the
onions to the pan and cook
until soft.
2. Add the wine, spices, and
flavorings, and diced vegetables to the pan. Leave for
15 minutes for the flavors to
combine.
3. Add the sausages to the pan
and cook over low heat. The
liquid should not boil. The
sausages are cooked when
they feel firm. Serve with the
stock accompanied by fresh
crusty bread and butter.

HANNELORE KOHL

"The true flavor of this Franconian specialty depends
upon the quality of the sausages."

SLICED BEEF WITH VEGETABLES

Ochsenfleisch mit Gemüse

INGREDIENTS (Serves 4)

1 1/4 pounds ox or beef flank steak

FOR THE MARINADE

1/2 cup meat stock

2 tablespoons each brandy and
    lemon juice

2 tablespoons vegetable oil

1 small garlic clove

Salt and white pepper to taste

TO COOK

2 leeks

4 medium carrots

1/2 pound fresh mushrooms

4 tablespoons unsalted butter

2 cups hot meat stock

1 teaspoon beef extract

1 teaspoon each dried tarragon
    and lemon balm (optional)

METHOD

1. Wrap the beef in foil, place in the freezer, and leave to chill for 20 minutes.
2. To make the marinade, mix together all the ingredients in a large shallow bowl. Cut the beef in paper-thin slices, across the grain. Place the meat in the marinade, cover the bowl with plastic wrap, and leave to marinate for 1 hour. Turn the meat slices once.
3. In the meantime, wash the leeks, carrots, and mushrooms. Thinly slice the leeks, cut the carrots into thin matchsticks, and slice the mushrooms.
4. Drain the meat well. Reserve the marinade. Melt the butter in a large frying pan and fry the meat slices on both sides. Add the vegetables in batches and fry with the meat, turning constantly. Mix together the marinade, stock, and meat extract and add it to the meat. Add the tarragon and lemon balm. Cover the pan and leave everything to braise for 15 to 20 minutes. Season to taste. The dish should be well seasoned. Serve with mashed potatoes.

STUFFED POTATO CAKES

Gefüllte Kartoffelkuchen

INGREDIENTS (Serves 4)

2 pounds potatoes

1 egg

2 egg yolks

Salt, pepper, and grated nutmeg
    to taste

Cornstarch

2 onions

2 tomatoes

5 ounces slab bacon

1 pound ground pork

1/2 pound ground beef

1 tablespoon chopped fresh
    parsley

METHOD

1. Boil the potatoes, peel them, and push through a potato ricer immediately. Add the whole egg and egg yolks to the potatoes while still hot. Season the mixture with salt, pepper, and nutmeg. Add enough cornstarch to form a firm dough. Shape the dough into a 1 1/2-inch thick roll, cover it, and leave it to rest for 30 minutes.
2. Peel and dice the onions; peel, seed, and chop the tomatoes. Dice the bacon and fry half of it in a frying pan to render the fat. Add the ground pork and beef, the onions, and tomatoes. Simmer until all the liquid evaporates. Remove the frying pan from the heat, pour off excess fat, and leave to cool.
3. Cut off 3/4-inch thick slices from the roll of dough. Flatten the slices, place some of the stuffing on top of half of them and cover with another slice of dough. Press the edges of the dough together firmly to seal them.
4. Fry the remaining diced bacon in a frying pan, to render the fat. Fry the potato cakes in the bacon fat until they are golden brown on both sides.
5. Preheat the oven to 350°F. Overlap the fried potato cakes in an ovenproof dish and cook in the oven for a further 10 minutes. Serve with a green salad.

HANNELORE KOHL

"In spring and summer, you can flavor the sliced beef with fresh tarragon and lemon balm. The leaves should not be cooked with the meat but added to the sauce right at the end."

Belly of Pork with Apple Stuffing

Schweinebauch mit Apfelfüllung (photo above)

INGREDIENTS (Serves 4)

$3^1/_2$ pounds fresh side pork (belly)

Salt and pepper to taste

2 rolls

1 cup apple juice

3 tablespoons unsalted butter, melted

3 tablespoons sugar

Pinch of salt

2 eggs, beaten

$1^1/_4$ pounds apples

Juice of $^1/_2$ lemon

2 heaped tablespoons breadcrumbs

$^1/_4$ cup hot clarified butter

2 cups meat stock

3 tablespoons heavy cream

Pinch of sugar

METHOD

1. Preheat the oven to 400°F. Cut a pocket in the meat and score the rind. Rub the pork with salt and pepper, inside and out.

2. Soak the rolls in the apple juice. Add the butter, sugar, salt, and eggs to the bread. Peel, core, and coarsely grate all but one apple and mix with the bread mixture, together with the lemon juice and breadcrumbs. Stuff the cavity with the filling, sew up the opening with kitchen string, and place the pork in a roasting pan. Pour the clarified butter over the pork and roast for $1^1/_4$ hours, basting it with the stock occasionally.

3. Quarter the reserved apple and arrange around the meat in the pan about 20 minutes before the end of the cooking time.

4. When done, remove the pork and apple from the roasting pan and keep warm. Stir in the cream, reduce a little, and season it to taste with sugar, salt, and pepper.

Shoulder of Pork in Milk

Schweinerolle in Milch

INGREDIENTS (Serves 4)

2 pounds boneless pork shoulder roast, untied

Salt and pepper to taste

1 garlic clove, minced

8 coriander seeds, crushed

3 tablespoons clarified butter

$1^1/_2$ quarts milk

$^1/_2$ teaspoon fennel seeds, crushed

1 teaspoon dried marjoram

1 bay leaf

METHOD

1. Season the meat with salt and pepper and rub it with garlic and coriander seeds on the inside. Roll up the meat and tie it with kitchen string. Heat the clarified butter in a heavy flameproof casserole and seal the pork in it on all sides.

2. Bring the milk to a boil in a saucepan and add it to the casserole. The meat should almost be covered by the milk. Simmer the meat for about an hour, turning it occasionally. Then add the fennel, marjoram, and bay leaf.

3. After about 40 minutes, remove the meat from the pot and keep it warm. Reduce the gravy by half, stirring all the time, then strain it. Slice the meat and arrange it on a plate. Thicken the gravy, if you like. Pour the gravy over the sliced meat. Serve with dumplings and a fresh crisp salad.

Bavarian Supper

Bayerische Brotzeit

INGREDIENTS (Serves 4)

FOR THE SAUSAGE SALAD

$^1/_2$ *pound* Fleischwurst *or*
  Schinkenwurst *(meat or ham
  sausage)*

2 to 3 small onions

$^1/_2$ *pound tomatoes*

$^1/_3$ *cup vegetable oil*

1 tablespoon mustard

$^1/_4$ *cup white wine vinegar*

$^1/_4$ *cup mineral water*

Pepper to taste

FOR THE CABBAGE SALAD

1$^1/_2$ pounds head of cabbage

$^1/_4$ *pound slab bacon*

$^1/_4$ *cup vinegar*

Sugar

2 tablespoons minced onion

Salt to taste

METHOD

1. To make the sausage salad, cut the sausage into strips, peel and slice the onions, wash and chop the tomatoes.
2. Mix together the oil, mustard, vinegar, mineral water, and pepper.
3. To make the cabbage salad, cut the head of cabbage into quarters and remove the stem. Bring a pan of salted water to a boil, cut the cabbage into ribbons, and blanch in the water for 5 minutes. Leave the cabbage to drain, collecting the cooking liquid, and keep the cabbage warm.
4. Dice the bacon and fry it in a frying pan to render the fat. Mix together the vinegar, $^1/_2$ cup cabbage cooking water, sugar, and the onion and pour it over the warm cabbage. Pour the dressing over the salad. Then scatter the fried bacon over the top of the cabbage. Season the salad to taste and serve it hot or cold.

"Blue and White" Radish Salad

Rettichsalat "Blau-Weiß"

INGREDIENTS (Serves 4)

2 large white radishes (daikon)

2 red apples

$^1/_2$ *cucumber*

2 thick slices of Leberkäse
  (smooth pork sausage)

Bunch of fresh dill, minced

$^1/_2$ *cup cream*

1 cup plain yogurt

Salt, pepper, and sugar to taste

Juice of 1 lemon

METHOD

1. Wash the radishes and slice thinly using a mandoline. Salt the slices and leave them for about 10 minutes.
2. Wash, halve, core, and thinly slice the apples. Remove seeds from the cucumber and slice thinly.
3. Cut the *Leberkäse* into strips. Drain the radishes, mix with the sliced apple, cucumber, and *Leberkäse* and sprinkle with the dill. Mix together the cream, yogurt, salt, pepper, sugar, and lemon juice and pour the dressing over the salad.

HANNELORE KOHL

"**W**henever I'm in Bavaria, I look forward to the fine veal sausages and crisp pretzels."

CHEESE SPREAD

Obatzda

INGREDIENTS

$^{1}/_{2}$ pound fully ripe German
    Camembert
1 tablespoon unsalted butter
$^{1}/_{2}$ cup cream cheese
1 onion, minced
Salt, pepper, paprika, and
    caraway seeds to taste
$^{1}/_{4}$ cup beer
4 slices rye bread
Bunch of fresh chives,
    chopped
Bunch of red radishes
1 white radish (daikon)

METHOD

1. Mash the Camembert with a fork. Mix it with the butter, cream cheese, and minced onion. Season it with salt, pepper, paprika, and caraway seeds and then stir in the beer. **2.** Leave the cheese for an hour for the flavors to combine. Then spread it on rye bread and serve sprinkled with chopped chives accompanied by red radishes and daikon peeled and cut in spirals.

PLUM DUMPLINGS

Pflaumenknödel

INGREDIENTS (Serves 4)

³/₄ pound potatoes
1 cup all-purpose flour
1¹/₂ tablespoons unsalted butter
Pinch of salt
1 egg
1³/₄ pounds small plums
Sugar cubes
Beurre noisette (browned
    butter)
Ground cinnamon and sugar

METHOD

1. Boil the potatoes, peel them, and push them through a potato ricer immediately. Leave the potato to cool. Add the flour, butter, salt, and egg to the potato and, working quickly with your hands, knead to form a smooth dough. Leave the dough to rest for 10 minutes.
2. Remove the pits from the plums and put a sugar cube in the middle of each plum.

3. Shape the potato dough into a roll, cut off little portions, place a plum on each portion of dough and wrap the plum in the dough. Shape the dough into dumplings. Bring a pan of water to a boil, reduce the heat until the water is simmering gently, and put the dumplings in the water.
4. As soon as the dumplings float to the surface of the water, they are cooked. Remove them from the pan with a slotted spoon. Pour *beurre noisette* over the dumplings and sprinkle them with cinnamon and sugar.

NOTE

To make *beurre noisette*, heat unsalted butter in a small pan until it has a good brown color. Be careful not to allow it to burn.

BAVARIAN CREAM

Bayerische Creme

INGREDIENTS (Serves 4)

2 cups milk
Pinch of salt
1 vanilla bean
10 leaves of gelatin or 2¹/₂ pack-
    ages (2 tablespoons) powdered
    unflavored gelatin
4 egg yolks
¹/₂ cup sugar
2 cups heavy cream
³/₄ pound fresh or frozen mixed
    berries

METHOD

1. Put the milk and salt in a pan. Split the vanilla bean, scrape the seeds into the milk, and add the pod. Bring to a boil and remove it from the heat. Soften the gelatin in a little warm water.
2. Beat the egg yolks and sugar in a bowl over a saucepan of hot water until pale and creamy. Remove the vanilla bean from the milk and gradually add the milk to the egg mixture, stirring until the custard thickens. Dissolve the gelatin well in the warm custard. Place the custard in a bowl of cold water and continue to stir it until it has cooled and has a creamy consistency.
3. Whip the cream until stiff and fold it into the custard before it sets. Pour the dessert into a bowl or individual molds and leave in the refrigerator overnight to set. Unmold and decorate with the berries.

BUTTER DUMPLINGS WITH PRUNES, APPLES, AND PEARS

Butternockerln mit Pflaumen, Äpfeln und Birnen

INGREDIENTS (Serves 6)

FOR THE FRUIT
2/3 cup pitted prunes
1 cup dried apples
1 cup dried pears
3 cloves
1 stick of cinnamon
1 quart water
6 tablespoons sugar

FOR THE DUMPLINGS
4 cups all-purpose flour
1 teaspoon baking powder
3/4 cup sugar
1 1/2 tablespoons vanilla-flavored
   sugar
Grated zest of 1/2 lemon
3 eggs
3 tablespoons plum brandy
10 tablespoons ice-cold unsalted
   butter, cubed
Clarified butter
3 tablespoons confectioners'
   sugar
1/2 teaspoon ground cinnamon

METHOD

1. Soak the dried fruit with the spices in the water overnight. Next day, bring the fruit mixture and sugar to a boil and then leave to cool. Remove the spices from the syrup.

2. Sift the flour and baking powder into a bowl and mix quickly with the sugar, vanilla sugar, lemon zest, eggs, plum brandy, and cubes of ice-cold butter to make a dough. Heat some clarified butter in a frying pan. Using 2 tablespoons, break off portions of dough and fry them in the hot butter until golden brown. Immediately dredge the dumplings generously with the confectioners' sugar and cinnamon. Serve the dumplings with the dried fruit compôte.

SYLVANER PIES

Fränkische Silvanerpastetchen

INGREDIENTS (Serves 6)

FOR THE PASTRY
2 cups whole wheat flour
1/2 cup ice-cold unsalted butter, cubed
1 egg
Pinch of salt
1 to 2 tablespoons water

FOR THE FILLING
2 rolls, crusts removed
1 cup dry Sylvaner wine
2/3 cup ground almonds
1 egg and 2 egg yolks
1 ounce beef bone marrow, diced
2 tablespoons grated Gouda cheese
1 small garlic clove, crushed
1/2 teaspoon salt
1 tablespoon chopped fresh flat-leaf parsley
White pepper and grated nutmeg to taste
Coarsely ground white pepper to taste

METHOD

1. Make a pastry dough and refrigerate it for 2 hours.
2. Preheat the oven to 350°F. Soak the rolls in the wine. Mix together the almonds, egg, 1 egg yolk, marrow, cheese, garlic, salt, pepper, nutmeg, and parsley. Squeeze out the rolls and mix in to form a soft paste.
3. Butter six 4-inch tartlet molds that are 3/4 inch deep and line with disks of pastry. Spoon in the filling and cover with the pastry. Press the edges together to seal. Make a hole in each. Brush with the remaining egg yolk and sprinkle with the coarsely ground pepper. Bake for 20 to 25 minutes.

PRINCE REGENT TORTE

Prinzregententorte (photo above)

INGREDIENTS (Serves 16)

FOR THE CAKE MIXTURE
1 1/2 cups (3 sticks) unsalted butter
1 cup plus 6 tablespoons sugar
3 tablespoons vanilla-flavored sugar
4 eggs
2 pinches of baking powder
3 cups all-purpose flour

FOR THE FILLING
7 ounces bittersweet chocolate
2 cups (1 pound) unsalted butter, at room temperature
3 cups confectioners' sugar
6 egg yolks
1/2 cup apricot jam, melted
1/2 pound couverture (fine coating chocolate), melted

METHOD

1. Beat together the butter, all but 1/2 cup of the sugar, and the vanilla sugar until light and fluffy. Separate 2 eggs and add the 2 egg yolks and 2 whole eggs to the butter. Sift together the flour and baking powder and gradually add to the mixture. In a separate bowl, beat the 2 egg whites with the reserved 1/2 cup sugar, and fold into the cake batter.
2. Preheat the oven to 350°F. Line a springform pan with parchment paper. Divide the batter into 7 portions and bake each separately in the springform pan for 8 minutes until golden. Cool on a cake rack.
3. Break the chocolate into pieces and melt it in a bowl over a pan of hot water. Beat the butter until light and fluffy and gradually add the confectioners' sugar, egg yolks, and, finally, the cooled chocolate.
4. Spread the chocolate cream over 6 of the cake layers and put them together. Reserve a little chocolate cream. Spread apricot jam over the seventh layer, place it on top of the other layers and coat the torte with the melted couverture. Once set, decorate with piped rosettes of the remaining chocolate cream.

"Beautiful Table Decorations— All You Need Is a Little Imagination"

When you set the table, don't just settle for china, silverware, and glasses. Often, all you need is a touch here and there and a few props to conjure up a completely different mood. Erhard Priewe from Wiesbaden has for many years been famous for his table and interior decoration skills. His advice is, "Think of the occasion, the reason why you are inviting guests, and the kind of people you are expecting— then just let your imagination take over." Here are a couple of ideas that will inspire you to experiment further.

Friends made during your last vacation are coming over to look at photos? A handful of white sand (available from pet shops in the aquarium supplies section), a couple of mussel shells, and floating candles in a bowl filled with water would make an attractive centerpiece.

For card-playing friends, decorate the table with playing cards; for those in your sewing circle, scatter colorful spools of thread and a tape measure across the table and hold the napkins in place with safety pins. A vegetable casserole is given the right setting when ingredients are also used decoratively, instead of the ubiquitous bunch of flowers. For an Italian evening, various pasta shapes provide a visual clue.

Fans of classical music can be greeted by a menu written on music score paper. In autumn use dried chestnut leaves as place cards and write on them with a gold or silver pen. During Advent,

"The table is only set lavishly on very special occasions. But you can also achieve a great deal with just a few touches." Erhard Priewe demonstrates a master's touch with the art of decoration.

a few nuts and *Lebkuchen* hearts on the table create the right atmosphere. Generally speaking, blooms and twigs from your own garden or some you have collected on a walk, scattered artfully across the table, create a better effect than a carefully arranged bouquet.

Garlands of ribbons around napkins and candles are very effective and can be used time and time again.

There are no limits to what you can do. Once you've tried unconventional table decorations, you will find them increasingly enjoyable and you will become more and more inventive.

FROM THE RIVER NECKAR TO LAKE CONSTANCE

BY HELMUT KOHL

The dukes of Württemberg and the Hohenzollern line with their family scat at Sigmaringen helped to make German history. Württemberg's castles, popular tourist attractions, are still an indication today of how important this area was. Here, history, an elegant way of life, and a refined cuisine have been preserved side by side and are still influential today.

My personal liking for castles, fortresses, and their histories was perhaps awakened by a Christmas present I received as a young child. While for years only useful things such as a sweater, a scarf, or warm trousers lay under the Christmas tree, one year I was given a knight's castle.

For hours on end I could enact exciting battles and for many years afterward I always asked for more pieces to my castle.

▶

When I was old enough for my parents to allow me to go on a bicycle ride and camp out overnight during the summer vacation, I spent a lot of time exploring the area around Dilsberg fortress near Heidelberg. This may have influenced my subsequent decision to study in Heidelberg.

But it is not just counts and castles which are typical of this area. As early as the Reformation, the desire of farmers and city dwellers alike for freedom blossomed here, sometimes quite forcefully. A liberal tradition developed quite early on, providing the inspiration for the Parliament in St Paul's Cathedral in Frankfurt. Also a great proponent of liberalism was born near Heilbronn—Theodor Heuss, the first President of the Federal Republic. The cuisine of Baden is regarded by many as the most refined in Germany. This is partly because the region was constantly subjected to influences from France. Like so many other border states, Baden acted as a hinge between Germany and France.

Although the Swabians are accused of an almost proverbial meanness, their cuisine, which differs greatly from that of Baden, is the cuisine of gourmets. The *Suppenschwaben,* or "soup Swabians," always start their meal with a consommé, served with *Flädle* (thin strips of crêpe), or little liver, semolina, or marrow dumplings. Given the Swabian liking for *Spätzle* (short, thick noodles), it's hardly surprising that German noodle production is traditionally located in Swabia.

Do you know how the Swabians came by their national dish, *Maultaschen* (pasta parcels similar to ravioli)? Supposedly, a crafty Swabian dreamt up these meat-filled ravioli, so the dear Lord would not notice that he was eating meat on Good Friday. Whether this anecdote is true or not, it is not out of character for the cunning Swabians. *Maultaschen* are worth a little sin or two at any time, served with warm potato salad, dressed with stock, and breadcrumbs fried in butter.

The Swabian Allgäu is dominated by the dairy industry, and so the area around Wangen has become a center of German cheese production. Because of the vast range of cheeses which Germany produces, it is regarded throughout the world as a home to cheese. We are proud to have exported 365,000 tons of cheese in 1994, the first time that Germany exported more cheese than we imported from other countries! If you are visiting the Allgäu, visit a cheese factory, to observe firsthand the complicated production process.

East or west of the Black Forest, wine production in these areas is also something worth shouting about, whether it comes from the Kaiserstuhl where it benefits from the favorable climate in the rift valley of the Upper Rhine; on the shores of Lake Constance; or even from Baden's Frankenland in the far north. The most wonderful grapes flourish here yielding rosé wines, wines from the Trollinger grape, and other delights.

Lindau, on the shores of Lake Constance, one of the southernmost locations on our journey. The promenade and the lighthouse are popular places to visit.

SPICY PORK STEW

Schweinepfeffer

INGREDIENTS (Serves 4)

1 fresh Blutwurst *(blood sausage)*
2 cups red wine
1/4 cup red wine vinegar
1 1/2 tablespoons kirsch
1 onion, finely chopped
1 carrot, finely chopped
2 garlic cloves, finely chopped
2 fresh thyme sprigs
1 fresh rosemary sprig
1 clove
1/4 bay leaf
8 peppercorns
*1 3/4 pounds boneless pork
    shoulder*
2 teaspoons unsalted butter
3 shallots, diced
2 tablespoons tomato paste
2 tablespoons clarified butter
1 teaspoon flour
Salt and pepper to taste

METHOD

1. Skin the sausage, mash the filling in a bowl, and mix it with the wine, vinegar, and kirsch. Add the vegetables and half the garlic to the marinade with the herbs and spices. Add the meat, cover with plastic wrap and refrigerate for 2 days.
2. Melt the butter in a frying pan and soften the shallots and remaining garlic. Stir in half the tomato paste, combine briefly, then remove from the heat.
3. Pat dry the meat. Heat the clarified butter in a flameproof casserole and quickly seal the meat in it. Sprinkle the flour over, add the remaining tomato paste, and mix with the fat. Gradually add the softened shallots and the marinade. If necessary, add a little water and simmer for 50 to 60 minutes.
4. Remove the meat. Strain the sauce over the meat. Serve with bread dumplings.

Pork Tenderloin with Lentils

Schweinefilet mit Linsen

INGREDIENTS (Serves 4)

1¼ pounds pork tenderloin roast
1 leek
2 carrots
3 tablespoons unsalted butter
1⅓ cups lentils, cooked
1 cup chicken stock
Salt and pepper to taste
1 pound baby new potatoes
1½ tablespoons clarified butter
½ cup medium dry white wine
½ cup gravy or concentrated
    stock

METHOD

1. Remove the skin and tendons from the pork. Wash the leek thoroughly, peel the carrot, and dice them both.
2. Heat 2 tablespoons of the butter in a frying pan and sweat the vegetables. Add the lentils to the pan, add the chicken stock, and season it with salt and pepper. Leave to simmer gently.

3. Boil the potatoes in their skins. When just tender, drain and cool them. Remove the skins when cool enough to handle.
4. Heat the clarified butter and fry the pork in it for about 20 minutes. Remove it from the frying pan, season it with salt and pepper, wrap the meat in foil, and leave it to rest for a few minutes. Deglaze the meat juices with the white wine and gravy and then boil until reduced by half.
5. Melt the remaining tablespoon butter in a frying pan and sauté the potatoes in the butter until golden brown.
6. Slice the meat, arrange the slices on the lentils, pour the gravy over the sliced meat, and serve with the sautéed new potatoes.

Pork Pie

Schweinepastete mit Feldsalat

INGREDIENTS (Serves 4)

4 slices of cold roast pork
1 pound boneless pork loin
4 apples
1 carrot
1 fennel bulb
¾ pound ground pork
3 tablespoons sugar
Soy sauce
½ teaspoon paprika
Pinch of ground cloves
Salt and pepper to taste
¾ pound frozen puff pastry,
    thawed
1 cup meat stock
1 egg yolk

METHOD

1. Preheat the oven to 425°F. Cut the slices of roast pork and the loin of pork into short, pencil-thick strips. Peel and dice the apples, carrot, and fennel. Bring a pan of water to a boil and blanch the vegetables in it briefly.

2. Mix the ground pork with the sugar, soy sauce, paprika, ground cloves, salt, and pepper and add the diced vegetables and apple.
3. Unroll the pastry and cut out a disk large enough to line the bottom and sides of an 11-inch cake pan. Cut out another disk to make a lid. Spread the meat mixture in the pastry shell and cover it with the smaller pastry disk. Seal the edges together firmly. Pierce the top crust several times.
4. Beat together the egg yolk and stock and glaze the pastry with it. Bake the pie for about 10 minutes. Reduce the oven temperature to 350°F and bake the pie for 40 minutes longer. Serve with corn salad (*mâche*) and sliced tomato.

GAISBURG HOTPOT

Gaisburger Marsch (photo below)

INGREDIENTS (Serves 4)

1 pound bones for soup
1 fennel bulb
2 carrots
1 small parsley root or parsnip
1 leek
1/2 onion
1 pound boneless beef (chuck)
1 bay leaf
2 cloves
Peppercorns
Salt to taste
1 pound potatoes

TO SERVE

2 tablespoons unsalted butter
3 onions, peeled and sliced
Cooked Spätzle

METHOD

1. Place the bones in a saucepan of water and bring it to a boil; skim the stock. Meanwhile, wash the vegetables and add them to the hot stock with the meat, bay leaf, cloves, peppercorns, and salt. Cover the pan and cook the meat and vegetables for about 1½ hours.
2. Wash, peel, and dice the potatoes. Bring a pan of salted water to a boil and cook the potatoes in it for about 20 minutes. After 1½ hours, remove the meat from the stock and cut it into bite-sized pieces. Strain the stock.
3. Melt the butter in a frying pan and fry the onion rings in it until golden. To serve, layer the meat, potatoes, and cooked *Spätzle* in a soup tureen, and pour the hot stock over. Top the dish with the fried onion rings.

WINEMAKER'S ROULADEN

Winzerroulade

INGREDIENTS (Serves 4)

3/4 to 1 pound boneless beef, cut in 8 strips
8 grapevine leaves (from a jar)
2/3 to 1¼ cups red wine
1 bay leaf
8 thin slices bacon
4 to 5 tablespoons clarified butter
1 cup meat stock
1¼ cups pickled cocktail onions
1 to 2 tablespoons tomato paste
Salt, pepper, and German mustard to taste

METHOD

1. Wrap each strip of beef in a grape leaf, place in a shallow dish, pour the red wine over them, add the bay leaf, cover with plastic wrap, and refrigerate overnight.
2. Carefully take the beef slices out of the grape leaves and season with salt and pepper. Reserve the marinade.

Wrap in the leaves again, wrap the bacon slices around the grape leaves. Tie up with kitchen string.
3. Heat the clarified butter in a flameproof casserole and fry the rouladen until crisp. Gradually add the marinade and reduce over medium heat. Remove the bay leaf. Add the meat stock to the pan. Cover and braise the rouladen for about 25 to 30 minutes. Remove the rouladen from the pot. Untie and keep the rouladen warm. Drain the pickled onions. Strain the stock, mix it with the tomato paste and the onions, bring it to a boil. Replace the rouladen and heat them through. Season the sauce to taste with salt, pepper, and mustard. Serve with mashed potato, and celery and grape salad.

BEEF AND PEPPER RAGOÛT

Ochsenragout

INGREDIENTS (Serves 4)

1³/₄ pounds boneless ox or
    beef chuck
3 ounces slab bacon
4 small onions
1 package of frozen soup
    vegetables
¹/₂ ounce dried porcini or cèpes
1 cup canned tomatoes
1 teaspoon tomato paste
1 cup red wine
1 cup hot meat stock
3 red bell peppers
3 green bell peppers
1 small can of whole mushrooms
Pinch of sugar
3 tablespoons crème fraîche
Salt and white pepper to taste
Brandy to taste

METHOD

1. Cut the meat into 1-inch cubes. Dice the bacon. Peel and chop the onions. Fry the diced bacon in a flameproof casserole to render the fat. Add the meat, onions, frozen vegetables, and dried mushrooms to the pot. Fry all the ingredients together for 10 minutes.
2. Chop the tomatoes, drain them well, reserving the juice. Add them to the casserole together with the tomato paste, salt, and pepper. Cook for 10 minutes. Deglaze the casserole with the red wine, stock, and tomato juice.
3. Quarter the bell peppers, remove seeds, and cut them into strips. Drain the canned mushrooms. Add the peppers and mushrooms to the meat. Put the lid on the casserole and cook the ragoût for 10 minutes longer.
4. Season the ragoût to taste with salt, pepper, sugar, and brandy and enrich it with the crème fraîche. Serve with buttered noodles and a green salad.

BADEN CORNED BEEF

Badische Rinderbrust (photo right)

INGREDIENTS

2 pounds corned beef brisket
3 to 5 bay leaves
Juniper or allspice berries
1 leek
3 large carrots
1 small fennel bulb with
    green tips
Bunch of fresh flat-leaf parsley,
    chopped
Salt to taste

METHOD

1. In a saucepan, bring 1¹/₂ quarts of water to a boil. Place the corned beef, the bay leaves, and juniper or allspice berries in the pan. Simmer gently for 60 to 80 minutes, depending on the thickness of the meat.
2. Meanwhile, wash, peel, and coarsely chop the vegetables. Add them to the beef and cook it for a further 20 minutes.
3. Remove the meat and vegetables from the pan. Slice the meat and arrange it on a platter with the vegetables. If necessary, salt the stock. Stir in the chopped parsley and serve it with the meat. Accompany the beef with fresh crusty bread and parsley potatoes.

HANNELORE KOHL

"**B**eef tastes best when delicately marbled with fat. Don't use as much fat when roasting such cuts."

BEEF IN A CREAMY SAUCE

Rahmgeschnetzeltes (photo above)

INGREDIENTS (Serves 4)

1 pound boneless beef sirloin or tenderloin
1 garlic clove
1 tablespoon clarified butter
Salt and pepper to taste
2 to 3 tomatoes, skinned and diced finely
1 onion, peeled and diced finely
2 pickled gherkins, diced finely
²/₃ cup crème fraîche
1 teaspoon tomato paste
1 teaspoon German mustard
1 cup cream

METHOD

1. First, preheat the oven to a low setting. Thinly slice the beef and cut it into strips.
2. Peel and halve the garlic clove. Rub a sauté pan with the cut garlic and heat the clarified butter in the pan. Seal the strips of meat in the butter, season them with salt and pepper, remove them from the pan, and keep them warm in the oven. Fry the diced onion in the meat juices until translucent. Add the diced tomato and gherkin and fry them briefly with the onions. Add the crème fraîche, tomato paste, mustard, and cream to the pan and stir well. Season to taste. Return the meat strips to the pan and serve immediately with tagliatelle.

SWABIAN PLATTER

Schwäbischer Teller

INGREDIENTS (Serves 4)

¹/₄ cup clarified butter
¹/₂ pound boneless sirloin steak
¹/₂ pound boneless veal loin
¹/₂ pound pork tenderloin
Salt and pepper to taste
1 onion, minced
¹/₂ teaspoon paprika
1 cup heavy cream
3 tablespoons sour cream
Bunch of fresh chives, chopped

METHOD

1. Heat the clarified butter in a sauté pan. Slice the meats and fry them for 3 minutes on each side in the butter. Season them with salt and pepper, remove them from the pan, and keep them warm.
2. Soften the onion in the meat juices. Add the paprika and a little salt and deglaze the pan with the cream. Reduce the sauce until thick and creamy and stir in the sour cream. Garnish the sauce with chopped chives and pour it over the sliced meats. Serve with a mixed salad and *Spätzle*.

Beef and Mushroom Goulash

Rinder-Pilzgulasch

INGREDIENTS (Serves 4)

2 pounds boneless beef (chuck)
1½ tablespoons clarified butter
1 pound onions
Flour
3 cups meat stock
Salt and pepper to taste
Bunch of fresh thyme, chopped
1½ pounds mixed, fresh
  mushrooms, e.g., crimini,
  oyster mushrooms,
  chanterelles
1 cup cream
2 bunches of fresh chives,
  chopped

METHOD

1. Cut the meat into large cubes. Heat the clarified butter in a casserole dish and quickly seal the meat in it. Peel and slice the onions, add them to the meat, and soften them also. Sprinkle a little flour over the meat and onions, stir in well, and then add the stock. Season the meat with salt, pepper, and thyme and cook it over a low heat for 1¼ hours.

2. Wash and slice the mushrooms. Ten minutes before the end of cooking time, add the sliced mushrooms and the cream to the casserole. Serve, sprinkled with chopped chives.

Pot Roast Beef with Chestnuts

Braten mit Maronen

INGREDIENTS (Serves 4)

1¾ pounds boneless beef round
  rump roast
1 teaspoon dried thyme
Salt and pepper to taste
¼ cup clarified butter
¾ pound onions, peeled and
  diced
1 cup red wine
1 cup meat stock
½ pound chestnuts
½ pound carrots, peeled and
  sliced
2 tablespoons crème fraîche
1 tablespoon red currant jelly

METHOD

1. Rub the meat with thyme, pepper, and salt. On the stovetop heat the clarified butter in a flameproof casserole and seal the beef in it. Add the onions to the pot and fry them with the beef. Deglaze the pot with the red wine and stock. Braise the meat for about 1½ hours.

2. Preheat the oven to 475°F. Score a cross in the top of the chestnuts and roast them in the oven for 15 minutes. When cool enough to handle, remove the shells. Peel and slice the carrots. Add the carrots and chestnuts to the meat and continue cooking it for 30 minutes longer. Remove the meat from the pot. Add the crème fraîche and red currant jelly. Slice the meat, arrange it on a platter, and serve it with the gravy and potato croquettes.

LARDED POT ROAST

Gespickter Ochsenbraten

INGREDIENTS (Serves 4)

TO COOK THE MEAT

3 ounces slab bacon
1¹/₂ pounds beef sirloin tip roast
Salt and white pepper to taste
3 tablespoons pork drippings
3 onions
1¹/₂ cups hot meat stock

FOR THE GRAVY

¹/₂ pound cucumber
Bunch of fresh dill
1 tablespoon medium-hot
    mustard
1 cup crème fraîche
Juice of ¹/₂ lemon

METHOD

1. Slice the bacon into ¹/₂ inch thick strips. Cover it with plastic wrap and place it in the freezer for 20 minutes. Thread the strips of bacon through a larding needle and draw them through the meat in the direction of the grain. Rub the meat with salt and pepper.
2. Melt the pork dripping in a flameproof casserole. Seal the meat all over in it for 10 minutes. Peel and coarsely chop the onions and add them to the meat. Add a little hot meat stock to the pot, cover, and braise the meat for 2 hours.
3. During cooking, turn the meat several times. Uncover the pot and cook the meat for another 25 to 30 minutes, turning it occasionally. Then remove the meat and keep it warm.
4. Deglaze the meat residue with the remaining stock and boil it for 10 minutes, stirring all the time, to reduce it.
5. Wash and finely dice the cucumber. Chop the dill and add both to the gravy. Mix together the mustard and crème fraîche and add them to the gravy. Season with lemon juice, salt, and pepper. Slice the meat, arrange it on a warmed platter, and pour a little gravy over the top. Serve the remaining gravy separately. Serve with boiled potatoes or bread dumplings and a mixed salad, if desired.

SWABIAN POT ROAST IN BEER

Schwäbischer Rinderbraten

INGREDIENTS (Serves 4)

3¹/₂ pounds beef chuck
    pot roast
1 pound carrots
8 parsley roots or parsnips
1 Spanish onion
3 cloves
2 cups dark beer
¹/₄ cup clarified butter
1 cup meat stock
Salt and white pepper to taste
Pinch of sugar
6 tablespoons sour cream

METHOD

1. Rub the beef all over with pepper and place it in a bowl. Wash and peel the vegetables. Chop the carrots and parsley root or parsnips into bite-size pieces and dice the onion. Add the vegetables to the beef with the cloves and beer. Cover the bowl with plastic wrap and leave the meat to marinate for 2 days, turning it daily.
2. Preheat the oven to 425°F. Heat the clarified butter in a saucepan. Remove the meat from the marinade, pat it dry, place it in a casserole and pour the hot butter over the meat. Season the meat with salt, put the lid on the pan, and cook the meat for 1 hour in the oven.
3. Strain the marinade. Then add the vegetables from the marinade and some of the marinade itself to the meat. Cook the meat for 1 hour longer.
4. Remove the meat and vegetables from the pot and keep them warm. Add the remaining marinade and the stock to the gravy to make 2 cups. Season the gravy to taste with salt, pepper, and the sugar. Allow the gravy to reduce a little. Finally, stir the sour cream into the gravy and do not let the gravy boil any more. Slice the meat, pour the gravy over it, and serve it with the vegetables. Accompany with tagliatelle.

NOTE

Parsley root, also known as Hamburg parsley, is the variety *Petroselinum crispum* 'Tuberosum.'

VEAL MEDALLIONS

Kalbsmedaillons

INGREDIENTS (Serves 4)

1 pound green asparagus
1¹/₂ pounds white asparagus
1 teaspoon sugar
Juice of ¹/₂ lemon
8 veal medallions, each
weighing about 3 ounces
Salt and pepper to taste
1¹/₂ tablespoons clarified
butter
¹/₂ cup dry white wine
¹/₂ cup meat stock
¹/₂ cup heavy cream
1¹/₂ tablespoons unsalted
butter

METHOD

1. Peel the bottom of the green asparagus stalks; peel the whole white asparagus stalks. Bring a pan of water to a boil with salt, sugar, and lemon juice. Cook the white asparagus in it for 15 minutes and the green asparagus for 10 minutes.

2. Season the veal medallions with salt and pepper. Heat the clarified butter in a frying pan and fry the veal for about 3 minutes on each side. Take the veal out of the pan and keep it warm.

3. Deglaze the meat juices with the white wine, add the stock to the pan, and allow the gravy to reduce a little. Add the cream to the gravy and reduce it a little more. Season the gravy to taste with salt and pepper.

4. Melt the butter in a saucepan and toss the cooked asparagus in it. Arrange the asparagus on warmed plates with the veal medallions. Serve with the gravy and a potato gratin.

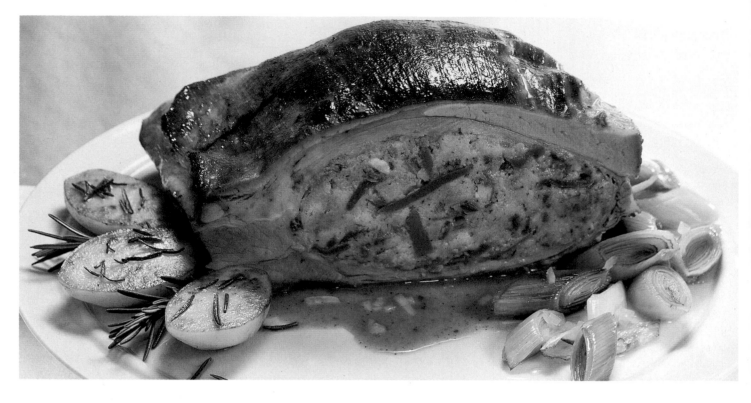

BADEN-STYLE STUFFED VEAL

Gefüllte Kalbsbrust badische Art (photo above)

INGREDIENTS (Serves 4)

1 ounce dried porcini (cèpes)
1/2 cup milk
41/2 pounds breast of veal
Salt and pepper to taste
1 pound carrots
1/4 fennel bulb
2 onions
1/4 pound fresh mushrooms
1/2 bunch of fresh parsley
8 to 10 cups white bread cut
  in cubes
4 tablespoons unsalted butter
3 eggs
Pinch of grated nutmeg
1/4 cup clarified butter
2 cups meat stock
Fresh thyme sprig
Fresh marjoram sprig

METHOD

1. Soak the dried mushrooms in the milk for 3 hours. Cut a flap in the veal and season it inside and out. Peel and coarsely dice the carrots, the fennel, and onions. Quarter the fresh mushrooms and chop the parsley. Put the bread in a bowl. Add the milk and dried mushrooms. Meanwhile, melt 11/2 tablespoons of the butter, add half of the carrots, the fresh mushrooms, and parsley. Fry for 3 to 4 minutes; leave to cool. Add the eggs to the bread mixture and season with nutmeg, salt, and pepper. Add the fried vegetable mixture. Stuff the cavity in the veal and sew up with kitchen string.
2. Preheat the oven to 400⁰F. On the stovetop, heat the clarified butter in a roasting pan. Seal the veal all over, add the diced fennel, onions, and remaining carrots, and roast the meat for about 11/2 hours.
3. When the meat is nicely browned, pour the stock into the roasting pan, add the herbs, and cook for another hour, basting occasionally.
4. Keep the meat warm. Sieve the gravy and, if liked, enrich it with the remaining 21/2 tablespoons butter.

VEAL ROULADEN WITH EGG AND SPINACH FILLING

Kalbsvögerl mit Ei-Spinat-Füllung

INGREDIENTS (Serves 4)

4 veal cutlets, each weighing
  about 7 ounces
1 tablespoon German mustard
4 slices boiled ham
1/2 pound spinach
4 eggs, hard-boiled
Salt and pepper to taste
4 tablespoons unsalted butter
11/2 cups veal stock
1 tablespoon tomato paste
4 heaped tablespoons whipped
  cream

METHOD

1. Flatten the veal cutlets with a rolling pin or meat pounder and spread each one with a thin layer of mustard. Cover each slice of veal with a slice of ham.
2. Wash the spinach and blanch it in a very little boiling salted water. Drain the spinach well and divide it among the veal cutlets. Shell the hard-boiled eggs and place an egg on top of each cutlet. Roll up the cutlets to form rouladen. Tie up the rouladen with string or secure them with toothpicks. Season them with salt and pepper.
3. Melt the butter in a flame-proof casserole and fry the rouladen in it until sealed and well browned. Pour the stock into the pot, put the lid on the casserole, and braise the rouladen over low heat for about 1 hour.
4. Remove the rouladen from the casserole. Remove the string or toothpicks. Bring the gravy to a boil and add the tomato paste. Finally stir in the cream. Pour a little gravy over the rouladen and serve the rest separately. Accompany the rouladen with *Spätzle*.

SWABIAN VEAL ROULADEN

Schwäbische Kalbsvögerl

INGREDIENTS (Serves 4)

1 roll, softened in water
1/2 pound ground veal
1 small onion, minced
1 egg, beaten
Salt, pepper, and grated nutmeg
  to taste
2 tablespoons chopped fresh
  parsley
4 veal cutlets, each about
  4 ounces
3 tablespoons clarified butter
Bunch of vegetables and herbs,
  e.g., carrots, leeks, celery, and
  thyme, chopped coarsely
1 bay leaf
1/2 cup white wine
1 cup meat stock
Grated zest of 1/2 lemon
1 1/2 tablespoons unsalted butter
2 1/2 tablespoons flour
1 tablespoon capers, minced
2 anchovy fillets, minced
1/4 cup cream
Lemon juice

METHOD

1. Squeeze the water out of the roll. Combine with the ground veal, onion, egg, salt, pepper, and nutmeg.

2. Season the cutlets and spread the stuffing over them. Roll up and secure with toothpicks or kitchen string.

3. Heat the clarified butter in a flameproof casserole and seal the rouladen all over. Add the vegetables to the pot with the bay leaf. Pour in the wine and stock, add the lemon zest, put the lid on, and braise for 45 minutes on low heat.

4. Take the rouladen out of the pot and keep them warm. Press the gravy through a sieve and bring it to a boil. Mix together the butter and flour and use it to thicken the gravy. Add the capers and anchovies with the cream. Season to taste with salt, pepper, and lemon juice. Reheat the rouladen in the gravy and serve them with *Spätzle*.

HANNELORE KOHL

"**I**f you don't want to thicken the gravy with beurre manié, *simply let it reduce until it is thick and smooth.*"

ONION TART

Zwiebelkuchen

INGREDIENTS (Serves 8–12)

1/2 pound slab bacon
2 tablespoons unsalted butter
2 pounds onions
1 teaspoon caraway seeds
1 pound bread dough (or ready-to-bake biscuits)
4 eggs
1 cup sour cream
Salt, pepper, and grated nutmeg to taste

METHOD

1. Preheat the oven to 400°F. Dice the bacon. Melt the butter in a large frying pan and fry the diced bacon in the pan over moderate heat. Peel and slice the onions, add them to the frying pan, and fry them until translucent. Season the onions to taste with salt, pepper, and caraway seeds.

2. Roll out the bread or biscuit dough on a floured surface, so that it will cover a baking sheet. Butter and flour the baking sheet and place the dough on top of it, drawing up the sides of the dough to form a crust. Spread the onion mixture over the bread base. (You could also use ready-to-bake pizza dough.)

3. Beat together the eggs and sour cream until foaming and season the eggs with salt and nutmeg. Pour the egg mixture over the onions and bake the tart in the oven for 45 to 50 minutes. When cooked, take the tart out of the oven, slice it immediately, and serve it warm. Serve with a dry white wine or wine from a new vintage.

PANFRIED VEAL STEAKS

Pfannabrätle

INGREDIENTS (Serves 10)

4 1/2 pounds boned veal rib roast with tenderloin, rolled and tied
Salt and white pepper to taste
1/4 cup clarified butter
3 cups diced vegetables, e.g., onions, carrots, leeks and fennel
3 tablespoons diced bacon
2 cups white wine
3 cups heavy fresh cream

METHOD

1. Cut the veal into finger-thick steaks and season them with salt and pepper. Heat the clarified butter in a large frying pan and fry the veal steaks on both sides over medium heat until golden brown. Take the meat out of the frying pan and keep it warm.

2. Fry the diced vegetables and bacon in the meat juices until the vegetables are soft. Deglaze the pan with the wine and reduce it by half. Add the cream and reduce the gravy by half again. Press the gravy through a sieve, then reheat it briefly.

3. Remove the string from the veal steaks. Place a pool of gravy on each plate and place a steak in the middle. Serve with noodles topped with breadcrumbs and onion fried in butter as well as a lettuce salad.

BADEN CARROT PURÉE

Badisches Gelbrübenpüree (photo below)

INGREDIENTS (Serves 4)

1 pound carrots
2 onions
2 tablespoons vegetable oil
¹/₂ cup water
1 pound potatoes
1 cup hot milk
2 tablespoons unsalted butter
*Salt, white pepper, and grated
   nutmeg to taste*

METHOD

1. Wash, peel, and slice the carrots. Peel and coarsely chop the onions.
2. Heat the oil in a wide pan. First fry the onions in it and then the carrots until both are translucent. Add the water to the pan, cover it, and simmer the onions and carrots over a low heat.
3. Meanwhile, peel and slice the potatoes and add them to the carrots. Cook the vegetables for another 30 minutes until the potatoes and other vegetables are very soft.
4. Then purée the vegetables in a food processor and gradually add the hot milk and the butter. Season the purée to taste with salt, pepper, and nutmeg. Serve with roast beef or pork or meat loaf.

CUCUMBER WITH SPÄTZLE

Gurkengemüse mit Spätzle

INGREDIENTS (Serves 4)

4 cucumbers
1 large onion
2 tablespoons unsalted butter
²/₃ cup sour cream
1 teaspoon flour
Salt and pepper to taste
Bunch of fresh dill
¹/₂ pound Spätzle
4 Rindsbratwürste *(beef sausages)*

METHOD

1. Peel and slice the cucumbers. Be careful not to slice them too thinly. Peel and dice the onion. Melt the butter in a frying pan, fry the onion, and add the cucumber.
2. Mix the sour cream with the flour and add it to the vegetables. Season with salt and pepper and cook for about 8 minutes.
3. Reserve a few sprigs of dill. Mince the remaining dill and add it to the vegetables.
4. Meanwhile, bring a pan of salted water to a boil and cook the *Spätzle* in it. Make diagonal cuts in the sausages and broil or fry them until crisp. Arrange the cucumber, *Spätzle,* and sausages on plates and garnish with sprigs of dill.

Warm Salad of Calves' Liver

Lauwarme Kalbsleber

INGREDIENTS (Serves 4)

FOR THE CROÛTONS
White bread, cut in small cubes
Unsalted butter

1 head Lollo Rosso or other
  green lettuce
2 heads frisée
2 tablespoons vinegar
3 tablespoons vegetable oil
1 teaspoon German mustard
1/2 cup whipped cream
Salt and pepper to taste
2 tablespoons chopped mixed
  fresh seasonal herbs
1 pound calves' liver
Flour

METHOD

1. To make the croutons, melt the butter in a frying pan and fry the cubes of bread until crisp and golden. Drain them on paper towels and reserve them. Wash the lettuces and dry in a salad spinner.
2. Mix together the vinegar, 1 tablespoon oil, and mustard and stir in the cream. Add the pepper, salt, and chopped herbs.
3. Heat the remaining 1 tablespoon oil in a frying pan. Cut the calves' liver into strips, dust it with flour, and fry quickly in the hot oil. Season the liver with salt and pepper. Arrange the strips of liver on a bed of greens, spoon on the dressing, and garnish it with the croûtons.

Ravioli in Broth

Maultaschen als Suppeneinlage

INGREDIENTS (Serves 4)

1 cup all-purpose flour
1 egg, beaten
1 cup mixed ground meats
1 small onion, minced
2 tablespoons chopped fresh
  parsley or chervil
Salt, pepper, and paprika to taste
1 egg yolk, beaten
1 quart meat stock

METHOD

1. Work the flour, egg, and a pinch of salt together with enough water to form a firm pasta dough. Leave it to rest for 30 minutes. Then roll out the dough as thinly as possible.
2. Mix together the ground meats, onion, herbs, pepper, salt, and paprika.
3. Cut the pasta into small squares, and brush the edges with egg yolk. Divide the meat mixture evenly among the squares, placing it on one half of each pasta square. Fold the pasta over and press the edges of the squares together firmly. Bring the meat stock to a boil in a saucepan and gently cook the ravioli in it.

Patty Shells with Veal

Pastete mit Kalbsfilet

INGREDIENTS (Serves 4)

1 cucumber
Bunch of scallions
2 carrots
2 tablespoons unsalted butter
Pinch of ground saffron
2/3 cup crème fraîche
Salt and pepper to taste
1 pound veal tenderloin or
  boneless loin
1 tablespoon clarified butter
4 baked patty shells (vol-au-vents)

METHOD

1. Wash the cucumber, cut it in half, and scrape out the seeds with a spoon. Finely slice the cucumber and scallions. Peel and dice the carrots. Melt the butter in a saucepan and fry the vegetables in it until soft. Sprinkle the saffron over the vegetables, stir in the crème fraîche, and season to taste with salt and pepper.
2. Finely dice the veal. Heat the clarified butter in a frying pan, and fry the diced veal in it for 3 to 4 minutes. Add the meat to the vegetables and bring quickly to a boil.
3. Fill the patty shells with the meat and vegetable filling and serve them immediately.

Lamb with Tarragon

Lammnüßchen in Estragon

INGREDIENTS (Serves 4)

1 pound lamb rib eye from
  the rack
2 tablespoons clarified butter
1/2 cup red wine
Leaves from a bunch of fresh
  tarragon
1 cup heavy cream
Pepper and salt to taste

METHOD

1. Heat the clarified butter in a frying pan. Cut the lamb into small slices, rub them with pepper, and fry them quickly in the butter for 2 minutes until sealed and well browned. Season them sparingly with salt, remove them from the pan, and keep them warm.
2. Deglaze the meat juices with the red wine and reduce the volume by one-third. Add the tarragon leaves to the sauce, stir in the cream, and reduce the sauce for 5 minutes. Season the sauce to taste with salt and pepper. Pour the sauce over the lamb and serve with green beans or fresh peas and sautéed potatoes.

SWABIAN RAVIOLI

Schwäbische Maultaschen

INGREDIENTS (Serves 4)

3¹/₄ cups all-purpose flour

6 eggs

¹/₂ pound (2 cups) mixed
    ground meat

¹/₂ pound Kalbsbratwurstbrät
    (veal sausage meat)

¹/₂ pound spinach

Bunch of fresh parsley, chopped

Salt, pepper, grated nutmeg,
    dried thyme, and dried
    marjoram to taste

1 egg white

1 quart meat stock

4 onions

2 tablespoons
    clarified butter

METHOD

1. Knead together the flour, 4 eggs, a little salt, and 6 to 8 tablespoons water to make a firm pasta dough. Leave the dough to rest for an hour.

2. Mix together the ground meats and veal sausage meat. Wash the spinach, blanch in boiling salted water, drain, and chop it. Knead together the meat, spinach, parsley, and 2 eggs to make a stuffing, and season it with salt, pepper, nutmeg, thyme, and marjoram.

3. Roll out the dough thinly and cut it into 6 by 6–inch squares. Place as much filling as possible in the center of each square. Brush the edges with egg white and fold in half, sealing firmly. Bring the stock to a boil in a saucepan, and cook the ravioli in the stock for 10 minutes until they float to the surface.

4. Peel and slice the onions. Heat the clarified butter in a frying pan and fry the onions until golden brown. One way to serve the ravioli is to arrange it in soup plates with a little stock and the onion rings.

ONION SOUP

Zwiebelsuppe

INGREDIENTS (Serves 4)

2 tablespoons butter
1 pound onions, sliced
White pepper to taste
1 quart stock
2 tablespoons clarified butter
2 rolls, sliced
1 cup grated medium-aged
  Gouda cheese

METHOD

1. Melt the butter in a medium saucepan and fry the onion rings until translucent. Season with pepper and add the stock. Cover and simmer for 20 to 25 minutes.
2. Preheat the oven to 425°F or preheat the broiler. Melt the clarified butter in a frying pan and fry the slices of bread on both sides.
3. Ladle the soup into large ovenproof bowls. Place a slice of bread on top of each and sprinkle cheese on top. Bake for about 10 minutes or cook under a preheated broiler until the cheese melts and turns golden brown.

STUFFED CABBAGE

Gefülltes Kraut

INGREDIENTS (Serves 10)

2 cups coarsely ground mixed
  game (raw or cooked)
4 onions
2 pounds ground pork
1¹/₂ pounds ground beef
1¹/₄ cups ground slab bacon
2 juniper berries, crushed
2 cups flat-leaf parsley, chopped
4 heaped tablespoons
  breadcrumbs
2 heads white cabbage
20 thin slices of bacon
Salt, white pepper, and black
  pepper to taste

METHOD

1. Preheat the oven to 350°F. Peel and mince the onions. Mix them with the pork, beef, bacon, salt, juniper berries, parsley, and breadcrumbs and some salt and pepper to make a stuffing.
2. Cook the whole heads of cabbage in boiling salted water. Drain the heads of cabbage, separate the leaves, and cut out the thick stems.
3. Spread the meat mixture over the cabbage leaves, layer them together to make a ball, and place it in a shallow pan. Cover the cabbage with the slices of bacon. Add a little water to the pan and cook the cabbage in the oven for 40 minutes or until meat is done.

TREE FROGS (SPINACH PARCELS)

Laubfrösche

INGREDIENTS (Serves 4)

10 large spinach leaves
Milk
1 roll
¹/₂ cup ground roast meat
1 egg, beaten
2 cups ground raw meat
1 teaspoon minced onion
¹/₂ teaspoon minced parsley
2 tablespoons clarified butter
1 cup meat stock
Salt and grated nutmeg to taste

METHOD

1. Bring a saucepan of water to a boil. Blanch the spinach leaves in the boiling water, drain them, and spread them out to dry.
2. Put a little milk in a bowl. Slice the roll, soak the slices of bread in the milk, drain well. Mash with a fork, then mix with the cold roast meat, egg, raw meat, onion, parsley, salt, and nutmeg.
3. Place two spinach leaves on top of each other and spread a tablespoon of the meat mixture over them. Fold the spinach leaves over the meat to make a neat package. Make the remaining parcels in the same way. Heat the clarified butter in a frying pan and, seam down, fry the parcels in the hot butter.
4. Deglaze the pan with the stock and cook the parcels for 20 minutes. Don't turn the parcels over, so they stay green. Serve the parcels with mashed potato.

LENTILS

Linsen

INGREDIENTS (Serves 4)

1¹/₃ cups lentils
1 onion
2 to 3 garlic cloves
1 bay leaf
1¹/₂ tablespoons unsalted butter
2 tablespoons flour
¹/₂ cup red wine
Red wine vinegar, if liked
Salt and pepper to taste
4 Saitenwürste (Frankfurter sausages)
4 slices of smoked meat, each weighing 3 to 4 ounces

METHOD

1. Soak the lentils for several hours.
2. Peel the onion and garlic. Drain the lentils. Put them in a pan with 1 quart of cold water, the onion, garlic, and bay leaf. Bring slowly to a boil and cook gently for 35 to 45 minutes, until soft. (In the meantime, prepare some *Spätzle*.)
3. Meanwhile, in another saucepan, melt the butter and add the flour. Stir it to form a roux and allow it to brown. Remove the onion, garlic, and bay leaf from the lentils and add the lentils and cooking liquid to the roux. Season the lentils with the wine, vinegar, salt, and pepper. The lentils should taste spicy and sour.
4. Heat the sausages and slices of smoked meat through in the lentils. Serve with the *Spätzle*.

SPÄTZLE

Spätzle

INGREDIENTS (Serves 4)

3 cups all-purpose flour
2 eggs
Salt to taste
1 tablespoon vegetable oil or melted unsalted butter

METHOD

1. Mix together the flour, eggs, and a little salt and gradually add up to 1 cup of water (depending on the size of the eggs) to make a smooth, batterlike dough. Beat the dough until it develops bubbles. Then stir in the oil or butter.
2. Bring plenty of salted water to a boil in a large saucepan. Dampen a small wooden chopping board with cold water. Place a small portion of the dough on the chopping board, and shave off narrow strips of dough with a knife, pushing them into the boiling water. Dampen the knife occasionally, so that the dough does not stick to it. (You could also use a S*pätzle* press.) As soon as the S*pätzle* rise to the surface of the water, remove them from the pan with a slotted spoon. The faster you work at this stage, the more texture the S*pätzle* will have.
3. Either rinse the prepared *spätzle* immediately in hot water or immerse them briefly in a saucepan of hot (not boiling) water. Then drain them well and serve them with the lentils in the previous recipe.

SADDLE OF VENISON

Rehrücken

INGREDIENTS (Serves 6)

1/2 cup unsalted butter
*Bunch of vegetables and herbs
   for soup, e.g., carrots, leeks,
   celery, and parsley, finely
   chopped*
1 onion, finely chopped
Salt and pepper to taste
5 to 6 peppercorns
2 cups strong red wine
1 cup heavy cream
*1 saddle of venison (double loin
   roast), weighing about 2 1/2
   pounds, boned and bones
   reserved*
1 pound fennel bulb
*5 heaped tablespoons whipped
   cream*

METHOD

1. Melt 1 1/2 tablespoons butter
in a stockpot and fry the venison bones, vegetables, and
onion. Add salt, pepper, and
peppercorns to the pot and
pour in the wine. Cook the
sauce over medium heat for
about 30 minutes until
reduced by half. Strain, return to the pot, and add the
cream. Reduce by half again.
2. Preheat the oven to 425°F.
Melt 4 tablespoons butter in a
roasting pan. Seal the saddle
of venison all over. Roast the
venison for 20 minutes.
3. Trim and mince the fennel.
Cook in a little salted water
until soft, and the water has
evaporated. Put the fennel
and whipped cream in a food
processor to make a very
smooth sauce. Mix in the
remaining butter.
4. Cook the *Spätzle* in boiling, salted water and drain
them. Take the meat off the
bone, slice it, and arrange
it on warmed plates with
the fennel sauce, *Spätzle*,
and cranberry sauce. Serve
with the reduced stock as
a sauce.

SPÄTZLE OMELETTES

Spätzle im Eiermantel

INGREDIENTS (Serves 4)

FOR THE SPÄTZLE

4 cups all-purpose flour
4 eggs
1 teaspoon salt
2 tablespoons unsalted butter
*3 tablespoons chopped fresh
   parsley*

FOR THE OMELETTES

8 eggs
Salt and grated nutmeg to taste
1/4 cup chopped fresh chives
2 tablespoons unsalted butter

METHOD

1. Place the flour in a bowl
with the eggs and salt and
mix together to make a
smooth batterlike dough.
If the dough is too thick,
add 1 to 2 tablespoons water.
Beat the dough until it
develops bubbles.
2. Bring a large pan of salted
water to a boil. Spread the
dough over a dampened
wooden chopping board,
spreading it more thinly
toward the edge of the board.
Cut off thin strips with a
knife and drop them straight
into the boiling water. (Or
you can use a *Spätzle* press.)
Cook over low heat until the
Spätzle float to the surface.
Remove them from the pan
with a slotted spoon and
place in cold water. Melt the
butter in a saucepan, add
the chopped parsley to it,
and toss the *Spätzle* in the
hot butter and parsley. Keep
them warm.
3. To make the omelettes, beat
the eggs, season them with
salt and nutmeg, and stir in
the chopped chives. Melt the
butter in a frying pan and
cook 4 omelettes. Fill each
omelette with *Spätzle* and
fold the omelette over.

SWEET RAVIOLI
Süße Topfen-Maultaschen

INGREDIENTS (Serves 8)

FOR THE PASTA
1³/₄ cups all-purpose flour
3 eggs
About 4 tablespoons water
Pinch of salt

FOR THE FILLING
¹/₂ cup unsalted butter
. 3 tablespoons sugar
Grated zest and juice of ¹/₂ lemon
2 eggs, separated
2 teaspoons rum
1³/₄ cups Quark or ricotta
2 tablespoons marzipan
¹/₂ cup bread or cookie crumbs

TO SERVE
2 tablespoons unsalted butter
¹/₂ cup breadcrumbs
Confectioners' sugar

METHOD

1. Work the ingredients together to make pasta dough and leave to rest for an hour.
2. To make the filling, beat together the butter, sugar, lemon zest, and juice until light and fluffy. Gradually add the egg yolks, rum, cheese, marzipan, and crumbs. Leave to rest for 30 minutes.
3. Roll the dough out thinly. Cut an even number of 2-inch rounds. Put a spoonful of filling on half the rounds and brush the edges with beaten egg white. Cover with the remaining rounds and press the edges together firmly, to seal them. Bring a large saucepan of water to a boil, add the ravioli, and cook for about 4 minutes.
4. Heat the butter until foaming and cook the crumbs until golden brown, stirring all the time. Scatter over the ravioli. Then dust with confectioners' sugar. Serve the ravioli with stewed plums.

RED CURRANT TORTE

Träublestorte

INGREDIENTS (Serves 12)

3/4 cup unsalted butter
3/4 cup sugar
1 egg
2 1/2 cups all-purpose flour
1/2 teaspoon baking powder
4 cups red currants
5 egg whites
1 3/4 cups confectioners' sugar
1 cup sliced almonds
6 tablespoons cornstarch

METHOD

1. Beat together the butter and sugar until light and fluffy and then add the egg. Mix together the flour and baking powder and mix it quickly into the butter and egg mixture. Refrigerate the dough for 30 minutes.

2. Butter a springform pan, 10 1/2 inches in diameter. Roll out the dough and line the bottom and sides of the springform pan with it. Prick the bottom of the pastry shell all over with a fork.

3. Preheat the oven to 350°F. Wash and drain the red currants. In a medium bowl, beat together the egg whites and confectioners' sugar until stiff. Carefully fold in the almonds. Reserve one-third of the mixture. Fold the cornstarch and red currants into the remaining mixture and spread it in the pastry shell. Spread the remaining meringue on top of the red currant mixture. Bake for about an hour.

HANNELORE KOHL

"This juicy summer torte tastes best with freshly picked red currants, and it should be eaten on the day it is made."

CHERRY CREAM

Kirschcreme

INGREDIENTS (Serves 4–6)

1 1/4 pounds (about 5 cups) sour cherries
1 cup red wine
3 tablespoons plus 1 teaspoon cornstarch
1/2 cup plus 2 tablespoons sugar
2 tablespoons kirsch
1 1/4 cups milk
1 vanilla bean
4 leaves of gelatin or 1 package powdered unflavored gelatin
3 eggs
1 egg yolk
2 1/2 cups heavy cream, whipped
1 ounce semisweet chocolate, grated

METHOD

1. Pit the cherries. Put them in a saucepan with the red wine and bring them to a boil. Mix the 3 tablespoons of cornstarch with 4 tablespoons of water. Add 2 1/2 tablespoons sugar and the mixed corn- starch to the pan. Boil for 1 minute. Stir in the kirsch and leave to cool.

2. To make the custard, put the milk and the remaining sugar in a saucepan, scrape in the seeds from the vanilla bean, and add the bean as well. Bring to a boil and then remove the vanilla bean. Soften the gelatin in water. Beat the whole eggs and egg yolk with the 1 tea- spoon of cornstarch and add this to the hot milk, stirring all the time. Heat the custard almost to boil- ing point, remove the pan from the heat, and stir in the gelatin to dissolve. Re- frigerate the custard. As soon as it starts to set, fold in the whipped cream.

3. Divide the cherry mix- ture among dessert dishes, spoon the custard on top, and decorate it with grated chocolate. Refrigerate for at least 2 to 3 hours.

CHEESE AT ANY TIME

HANNELORE KOHL:
To me, a nice piece of cheese, with a slice of fresh crusty bread or a crusty roll makes a lovely meal without a lot of effort . . .

ALFONS SCHUHBECK:
. . . which never gets boring, because we here in Germany have a huge variety of cheeses that are the envy of many countries.

HANNELORE KOHL:
What's the correct way to store cheese?

ALFONS SCHUHBECK:
The best way is under a traditional cheese dome in a cool, dark larder. Since most homes no longer have a larder, the refrigerator is the next best option. The cheese must be able to breathe.

You should keep it in plastic wrap and take it out of the refrigerator about an hour before you want to eat it, so the full flavor can develop.

HANNELORE KOHL:
Cheese slices or a piece of cheese—opinions differ as to which is best. Anyway, a piece of cheese looks a bit messy after several people have hacked off chunks from it!

ALFONS SCHUHBECK:
Nevertheless, I would still advise you to buy pieces of cheese rather than slices, simply because it stays fresh longer. I cut off unattractive looking sides and use them to make a cheese topping or a cheese sauce. Cheese can be used in countless ways.

"If you're in a hurry, a nice piece of cheese provides a quick snack."

HANNELORE KOHL:
What about wine and cheese? What combination would you recommend?

ALFONS SCHUHBECK:
As a basic rule of thumb, white wine goes well with mild cheeses and cream cheese.

Pungent cheeses and blue cheese go well with a red wine. You should always experiment, but not necessarily when you have guests! Sometimes you might get it wrong, but if you have the courage to try something different, you will often be pleasantly surprised.

INDEX BY REGION

ALPHABETICAL INDEX OF RECIPES

PHOTOGRAPHY CREDITS
IFA-Bilderteam: pages 6
    (top left, center right, bottom
    right), 7 (bottom), 8, 10, 34, 82,
    102, 104, 150, 172, 196
ZEFA: pages 6 (top right, center
    left, bottom left), 7 (top), 32,
    56, 58, 80, 148, 198
The Image Bank: pages 7
    (center), 124
Jürgen Schneck: page 174
MDR/Eckert: page 126
Martin Joppen, Frankfurt:
    page 195
Francis Hoff, Munich: pages 31,
    55, 79, 101, 147, 171, 219
fotostudio backofen, Mannheim;
    page 4
Fritz Reiss, Königswinter:
    page 224
RECIPE PHOTOS
    CMA Centrale Marketing-
    Gesellschaft der Deutschen
    Agrarwirtschaft mbH, Bonn;
    FoodPhotographie Eising,
    Munich (page 127); Stockfood,
    Munich (page 16); "Fleisch—
    Die neue große Schule," Verlag
    Zabert Sandmann (page 163)
JACKET FRONT COVER
    IFA-Bilderteam (background
    image); CMA (center)
JACKET BACK COVER
    CMA
JACKET BACK COVER FLAP
    Michael Ebner, Bonn
ENDPAPER IMAGE
    Look/Max Galli